NES English to Speakers of Other Languages (ESOL)

Teacher Certification Exam Guide
Sharon A. Wynne, M.S

XAMonline, INC.
Boston

Copyright © 2017 XAMonline, Inc.
All rights reserved. No part of the material protected by this copyright notice may be reproduced or utilized in any form or by any means, electronic or mechanical, including photocopying, recording or by any information storage and retrievable system, without written permission from the copyright holder.

To obtain permission(s) to use the material from this work for any purpose including workshops or seminars, please submit a written request to:

XAMonline, Inc.
21 Orient Avenue
Melrose, MA 02176
Toll Free 1-800-509-4128
Email: info@xamonline.com
Web: www.xamonline.com
Fax: 1-617-583-5552

Library of Congress Cataloging-in-Publication Data
Wynne, Sharon A.

NES English to Speakers of Other Languages (ESOL) Teacher Certification/Sharon A. Wynne
ISBN 978-1-60787-614-4

1. English to Speakers of Other Languages (ESOL)   2. Study Guides.
3. NES   4. Teachers' Certification & Licensure   5. Careers

Disclaimer:
The opinions expressed in this publication are solely those of XAMonline and were created independently from the National Education Association, Educational Testing Service, and any State Department of Education, National Evaluation Systems or other testing affiliates.

Between the time of publication and printing, state-specific standards as well as testing formats and website information may produce change that is not included in part or in whole within this product. Sample test questions are developed by XAMonline and reflect similar content to real tests; however, they are not former tests. XAMonline assembles content that aligns with state standards but makes no claims nor guarantees teacher candidates a passing score. Numerical scores are determined by testing companies such as NES or ETS and then are compared with individual state standards. A passing score varies from state to state.

Printed in the United States of America
NES English to Speakers of Other Languages (ESOL)
ISBN: 978-1-60787-614-4

TEACHER CERTIFICATION STUDY GUIDE

TABLE OF CONTENTS

DOMAIN 1 — FOUNDATIONS OF LANGUAGE AND LANGUAGE INSTRUCTION 1

OBJECTIVE 1.0 — LINGUISTIC AND SOCIOLINGUISTIC CONCEPTS AND HOW TO APPLY THEM TO INSTRUCTION 1

- Skill 1.1 Phonology 1
- Skill 1.2 Morphology 3
- Skill 1.3 Syntax and Semantics 5
- Skill 1.4 Oral and written forms of discourse 11
- Skill 1.5 Pragmatics 14
- Skill 1.6 English variations (e.g., registers, dialects) and their relevance to ESOL instruction 14

OBJECTIVE 2 — THEORIES AND PROCESSES OF LANGUAGE ACQUISITION AND LITERACY DEVELOPMENT AS APPLIED IN THE ESOL CLASSROOM 18

- Skill 2.1 Historical and current theories in language acquisition (including bilingualism/multilingualism and the role of L1 in L2 development) 18
- Skill 2.2 Historic and current theories in literacy development (role of L1 literacy in L2 literacy development; concepts and challenges in ESOL teaching) 21
- Skill 2.3 Stages and sequence of language learning; difference between social and academic language; features of ELL proficiency levels 24
- Skill 2.4 Individual, academic and sociopolitical factors that affect English language acquisition and development 28
- Skill 2.5 Cognitive, metacognitive and socio-communicative strategies supporting ELLs 30

DOMAIN 2 — FOUNDATIONS OF ESOL INSTRUCTION 33

OBJECTIVE 3 — ROLE OF CULTURE IN LANGUAGE LEARNING AND ACADEMIC ACHIEVEMENT 33

- Skill 3.1 Content of culture (values/beliefs) and effects of culture differences in classroom and school 33

Skill 3.2	Sociocultural variables that can affect L2 learning (e.g., racism, discrimination, etc.)	35
Skill 3.3	Cultural differences in communication as well as cross-cultural communication	37
Skill 3.4	How to create culturally diverse and inclusive learning environment	39

OBJECTIVE 4 — STANDARDS BASED ESOL INSTRUCTION: APPROACHES AND RESOURCES 41

Skill 4.1	Characteristics, goals and research on ESOL models and program effectiveness; historical and research bases of past and current ESOL models and methodologies	41
Skill 4.2	How to plan standards-based instruction (assessment-driven and differentiated)	45
Skill 4.3	Criteria and methods for selecting, applying and designing resources	49
Skill 4.4	Using resources for standards-based and content-area learning	50
Skill 4.5	Using technology to enhance effective teaching and learning	52

OBJECTIVE 5.0 — CONCEPTS AND ISSUES RELATED TO ASSESSMENT 55

Skill 5.1	Different types of assessment (as well as indicators of their quality)	55
Skill 5.2	Purposes of assessment and how to communicate assessment results to stakeholders	58
Skill 5.3	Importance of regular, aligned assessments and use to inform and refine instruction	60
Skill 5.4	How to interpret standardized assessments results for English language learners	61

OBJECTIVE 6.0 — IMPACT OF NATIONAL LAWS AND POLICIES ON ESOL INSTRUCTION; PROFESSIONAL DEVELOPMENT AND SCHOOL/COMMUNITY PARTNERSHIPS 63

Skill 6.1	Understand legal decisions and legislation on ESOL programs	63
Skill 6.2	Strategies for pursuing professional goals and growth opportunities	65
Skill 6.3	Collaborating with colleagues	66
Skill 6.4	Serving as an ESOL resource in the community	66

Skill 6.5	Understand role of family and community in ELL development	67
DOMAIN 3	**INSTRUCTION AND ASSESSMENT OF ENGLISH LANGUAGE LEARNERS**	**69**
OBJECTIVE 7	**RESEARCH BASED PRACTICES IN ESOL INSTRUCTION**	**69**
Skill 7.1	Creating, organizing and managing a student-centered learning community	69
Skill 7.2	Apply research-based practices that promote English language development (e.g., comprehensible input, regular feedback and integration of skills)	72
Skill 7.3	Strategies for exceptional students	75
Skill 7.4	Vocabulary instruction	78
OBJECTIVE 8	**ORAL AND AURAL LANGUAGE DEVELOPMENT**	**80**
Skill 8.1	Assessment of oral and aural development	80
Skill 8.2	Instruction to promote listening skills	82
Skill 8.3	Instruction to promote speaking skills	83
Skill 8.4	Development of listening skills for academic purposes	85
Skill 8.5	Development of speaking skills for academic purposes	87
OBJECTIVE 9.0	**ASSESS AND PROMOTE LITERACY DEVELOPMENT**	**89**
Skill 9.1	Classroom-based assessment of reading development	89
Skill 9.2	Classroom-based assessment of writing development	92
Skill 9.3	Strategies for promoting beginning reading and writing skills	94
Skill 9.4	Development of reading skills for social and academic purposes	99
Skill 9.5	Development of writing skills for social and academic purposes	101
OBJECTIVE 10	**CONTENT-AREA LEARNING AND ACCESS TO THE CORE CURRICULUM**	**106**
Skill 10.1	Classroom-based assessment of content-area learning and concept development	106

Skill 10.2	Principles, features and applications of content-based and sheltered approaches to content instruction 106
Skill 10.3	Instructional strategies to make academic language and content-area concepts accessible (i.e., authentic uses of language and scaffolding) 111
Skill 10.4	Instructional strategies to develop ELL students' development of learning skills and strategies (e.g., critical thinking skills) to support content-area learning 117

REFERENCES 118

SAMPLE TEST 130

ANSWER KEY 162

RATIONALES 163

TEACHER CERTIFICATION STUDY GUIDE

How to Use This Book

Help! Where do I begin?

Begin at the beginning. Our informal polls show that most people begin studying up to 8 weeks prior to the test date, so start early. Then ask yourself some questions: How much do you really know? Are you coming to the test straight from your teacher education program or are you reviewing subjects you haven't considered in 10 years? Either way, take a diagnostic or assessment test first. Also, spend time on sample tests so that you become accustomed to the way the actual test will appear.

A diagnostic can help you decide how to manage your study time and reveal things about your compendium of knowledge. Although this guide is structured to follow the order of the test, you are not required to study in that order. By finding a time-management and study plan that fits your life, you will be more effective. The results of your diagnostic or self-assessment test can be a guide for how to manage your time and point you towards areas that needs more attention.

You may also want to structure your study time based on the weighting of the different sections of the test and your confidence in your knowledge. For example, Foundations of ESOL Instruction represents 40% of the test score. If you are confident in this area, you may not need to devote as much time here as another section even though it is a major section.

Week	Activity
8 weeks prior to test	Take a diagnostic or pre-assessment test, then build your study plan accordingly to your time availability and areas that need the most work.
7 weeks prior to test	Read the entire study guide. This does not have to be an in-depth reading, but you should take the time to mark sections or areas you know you'd like to return to.
6-3 weeks prior to test	For each of these 4 weeks, choose a content area to study. You don't have to go in the order of the book. It may be that you start with the content that needs the most review. Alternatively, you may want to ease yourself into your plan by starting with the most familiar material.
2 weeks prior to test	Take the sample test, score it, and create a review plan for the final week before the test.
1 week prior to test	Following your plan (which will likely be aligned with the areas that need the most review), go back and study the sections that align with the questions you missed. Then go back and study the sections related to the questions you answered correctly. Create flashcards and drill yourself on any area that you makes you anxious.

TEACHER CERTIFICATION STUDY GUIDE

Other Helpful Study and Testing Tips

What you study is as important as how you study. You can increase your chances of mastering the information by taking some simple, effective steps.

Study Tips

1. You are what you eat. Good eating habits while studying and on the day of the test are very important. Eating well and staying hydrated help you learn and retain information. The better you eat, the better you'll feel as you study and, most importantly, on the day of the exam!

2. The pen is mightier than the sword. Learn to take great notes. A by-product of our modern culture is that we have grown accustomed to getting our information in short doses. We've subconsciously trained ourselves to assimilate information into neat little packages. Messy notes fragment the flow of information. Your notes can be much clearer with proper formatting. The Cornell Method is one such format. Walter Pauk popularized this method in How to Study in College, Ninth Edition. You can benefit from the method without purchasing an additional book by simply looking the method up online. Below is a sample of how The Cornell Method can be adapted for use with this guide.

2 ½"	6"
Cue Column	Note-Taking Column 1. Record: During your reading, use the note-taking column to record important points. 2. Questions: As soon as you finish a section, formulate questions based on the notes in the right-hand column. Writing questions helps to clarify meanings, reveal relationships, establish community, and strengthen memory. Also, the writing of questions sets the stage for exam study later. 3. Recite: Cover the note-taking column with a sheet of paper. Then, looking at the questions or cue words in the question and cue column only, say aloud, in your own words, the answers to the questions, facts, or ideas indicated by the cue words. 4. Reflect: Reflect on the material by asking yourself questions. 5. Review: Spend at least ten minutes every week reviewing all your previous notes. Doing so helps you retain ideas and topics for the exam.
	Summary After reading, use this space to summarize the notes from each page.

*Adapted from *How to Study in College,* Ninth Edition, by Walter Pauk, ©2008 Wadsworth

3. See the forest and the trees. In other words, get the concept before you look at the details. One way to do this is to take notes as you read, paraphrasing or summarizing in your own words. Putting the concept in terms that are comfortable and familiar may increase retention.

4. Question authority. Ask why, why, why. Pull apart written material paragraph by paragraph and don't forget the captions under the illustrations. For example, if a heading reads Stream Erosion put it in the form of a question. (Why do streams erode? Or what is stream erosion?) Then find the answer within the material. If you train your mind to think in this manner you will learn more and prepare yourself for answering test questions.

5. Play mind games. Using your brain for reading or puzzles keeps it flexible. Even with a limited amount of time your brain can take in data (much like a computer) and store it for later use. In ten minutes you can: read two paragraphs (at least), quiz yourself with flashcards, or review notes. Even if you don't fully understand something on the first pass, your mind stores it for recall, which is why frequent reading or review increases chances of retention and comprehension.

6. Place yourself in exile and set the mood. . Set aside a particular place and time to study that best suits your personal needs. If you're a night person, burn the midnight oil. If you're a morning person set yourself up with some coffee and get to it. Make your study time and place as free from distraction as possible and surround yourself with what you need, be it silence or music. Studies have shown that music can aid in concentration, absorption, and retrieval of information. Not all music, though. Research indicates that classical music is most effective.

7. Apply what you are learning to the classroom. It is not enough to memorize the theories, instructional strategies, standards and assessment types in this book. In order to do well on the exam, you will need to understand them well enough to apply them to specific school, classroom and student scenarios. Many of the questions on the NES provide you with a school, classroom or student scenario and ask you to identify the relevant theory, strategy, or assessment practice from a list of possible options. When you study, make sure you spend time applying what you are learning.

8. Get pointed in the right direction. Use arrows to point to important passages or pieces of information. It's easier to read than a page full of yellow highlights. Highlighting can be used sparingly, but add an arrow to the margin to call attention to it.

9. Check your time budget. You should at least review all the content material before your test, but allocate the most time to the areas that need the most refreshing. It sounds obvious, but it's easy to forget. You can use the study rubric above to balance your study budget.

And Another Thing

Question Types

You're probably thinking, enough already, I want to study! Indulge us a little longer while we explain that there is actually more than one type of multiple-choice question. You can thank us later after you realize how well prepared you are for your exam. There are two main types of multiple choice questions; single item and items with stimulus. Single item questions may look like this:

Which of the Following: One way to test your answer choice for this type of question is to replace the phrase "which of the following" with your selection. Use this example: Which of the following words is one of the twelve most frequently used in children's reading texts:

- a. There
- b. This
- c. The
- d. An

Don't look! Test your answer. ____ is one of the twelve most frequently used in children's reading texts. Did you guess C? Then you guessed correctly.

Complete the Statement. The Dolch Basic Sight Words consist of a relatively short list of words that children should be able to:

- a. Sound out
- b. Know the meaning of
- c. Recognize on sight
- d. Use in a sentence

The correct answer is C. In order to check your answer, test out the statement by adding the choices to the end of it.

Stimulus questions may include reading excerpts, infographics, or classroom situations as the stimulus. As ever, read the question carefully. It likely asks for a very specific answer and not broad interpretation of the visual. Here is a simple (though not statistically accurate) example of a graph question:

According to the following graph in how many years did more men take the NES exam than women?

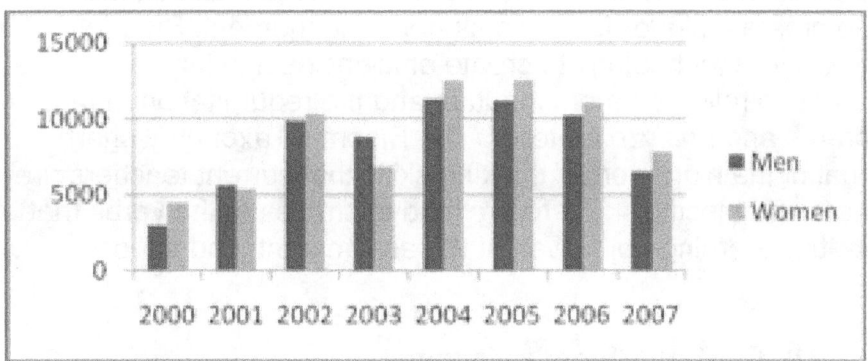

   a. None
   b. One
   c. Two
   d. Three

It may help you to simply circle the two years that answer the question. Once you've made your determination, double-check your work. The correct answer is C.

Make sure that you read all questions carefully to determine whether they ask for a very specific answer or a broad interpretation of the visual.

Negative Questions

Watch out for negative questions. This type of question contains words such as "not," "least," and "except." Each correct answer will be the statement that does not fit the situation described in the question. Such as: Multicultural education is not:

   a. An idea or concept
   b. A "tack-on" to the school curriculum
   c. An educational reform movement
   d. A process

Think to yourself that the statement could be anything but the correct answer. This question form is more open to interpretation than other types, so read carefully and don't forget that you're answering a negative statement.

Current Teaching Trends

Digital pedagogy and the use of 21st century teaching methods have shifted the landscape of teaching to create a bigger focus on student engagement. Student-centered classrooms now utilize technology to create efficiencies and increase digital literacy. Classrooms that once relied on memorization and the regurgitation of facts now push students to *create* and *analyze* material. The Bloom's Taxonomy chart below gives a great visual of the higher order thinking skills that current teachers are implementing in their learning objectives. There are also examples of the verbs that you might use when creating learning objectives at the assignment, course, or program level.

21st Century Bloom's Taxonomy

Lower- order			Higher- order		
Remember	Understand	Apply	Analyze	Evaluate	Create
• Define • Describe • Recall	• Classify • Explain • Summarize	• Determine • Organize • Use	• Deduct • Estimate • Outline	• Argue • Justify • Support	• Construct • Adapt • Modify

Most importantly, you'll notice that each of these verbs will allow teachers to align a specific assessment to assess the mastery of the skill that's being taught. Instead of saying "Students will learn about parts of speech," teachers will insert a measurable verb into the learning objective. The 21st century model uses S.M.A.R.T. (Specific, Measurable, Attainable, Realistic, Time-bound) assessment methods to ensure teachers can track progress and zero in on areas that students need to revisit before they have fully grasped the concept.

When reading the first objective below, you might ask yourself the following questions:

Students will:

1. Learn about parts of speech

How will they learn? How will you assess their learning? What does "learn" mean to different teachers? What does "learn" look like to different learning styles?

In this second example, the 21st century model shows specific ways students will use parts of speech.

Students will be able to:

1. Define parts of speech (lower)
2. Classify parts of speech (lower)
3. Construct a visual representation of each part of speech (higher)

Technology in the 21st Century Classroom

Student-centered classrooms now also rely heavily on technology for content delivery (PowerPoint, LMS) assessment (online quizzes) and collaborative learning (GoogleDrive). Particular to ESL classrooms, teachers can now record themselves speaking using lecture capture software. Students can then watch the video multiple times to ensure they've understood concepts. They have the ability to pause/rewind/replay any sections they are confused about, and they can focus on taking better notes while having the ability to watch the video a second or third time.

Online assessments also give students and teachers a better idea for comprehension level. These quick, often self-grading assessments give teachers more time to spend with students instead of grading. They eliminate human error and give teachers data needed to zero in on concepts that need to be revisited. For example, if 12 of 15 students got number 5 wrong, the teacher will know to discuss this concept in class. Online assessments may include listening, speaking, reading, and/or writing practice. This reinforces the content that was taught in the classroom and gives opportunity for practice at students' leisure. In addition, adaptable learning will help teachers by tracking user data to demonstrate learning gains. This can be completed in pre-posttest form, with conditionals within an assessment, or through small, formative assessments.

SMART Technologies, Inc. is a very popular company that creates software and hardware for educational environments. You may have heard of a "SmartBoard" before. These are promethean boards (interactive whiteboards) and are most commonly gained using grant money. They can be used as a projector for PowerPoints, their speakers can be used for audio practice, and their video options can allow you to "bring" a guest speaker into your classroom using videoconferencing, such as Skype. They record notes made on the whiteboard and record audio from lectures, which can then be saved and sent to students that were absent, or used to review for tests on varying concepts.

Google has created ample opportunity for secondary teachers in creating efficiencies for document sharing, assessment tools, and collaborative learning environments. Their drive feature can allow for easy transfer of assignment instructions, essays, and group projects. Slides can be used to create and post PowerPoints for students to have ongoing access. Forms is a great way to create quizzes, and the data can be sorted and manipulated in a number of ways. They can also be used for self-assessment, peer evaluation, and for pre-post analyses.

As technology continues to evolve, it's critical for teachers to continue to implement tools that make their classrooms more effective and efficient while also preparing students to successfully function in a technology-driven society. Through simple lessons and technology demonstrations, students will have a great start at applying technology skills in the outside world. The classroom is a great starting place for ESL students to learn how to use technology and how to practice their own reading, writing, listening, and speaking.

Testing Tips

1. Get smart, play dumb. Sometimes a question is just a question. No one is out to trick you, so don't assume that the test writer is looking for something other than what was asked. Stick to the question as written and don't overanalyze.

2. Do a double take. Read test questions and answer choices at least twice because it's easy to miss something, to transpose a word or some letters. If you have no idea what the correct answer is, skip it and come back later if there's time. If you're still clueless, it's okay to guess. Remember, you're scored on the number of questions you answer correctly. You're not penalized for wrong answers. The worst case scenario is that you miss a point from a good guess.

3. Turn it on its ear. The syntax of a question can often provide a clue, so make things interesting and turn the question into a statement to see if it changes the meaning or relates better (or worse) to the answer choices.

4. Get out your magnifying glass. Look for hidden clues in the questions because it's difficult to write a multiple-choice question without giving away part of the answer in the options presented. In most questions you can readily eliminate one or two potential answers, increasing your chances of answering correctly to 50/50, which will help if you've skipped a question and gone back to it (see tip #2).

5. Call it intuition. Often your first instinct is correct. If you've been studying the content you've likely absorbed something and have subconsciously retained the knowledge. On questions you're not sure about, trust your instincts because a first impression is usually correct.

6. Become a clock-watcher. You have three hours to answer the questions. Don't get bogged down laboring over a question you're not sure about when there are ten others you could answer more readily. The NES test allows you to skip a question and flag it for review so that you can go back to it. If you finish early, you can go back and check all of your answers carefully.

TEACHER CERTIFICATION STUDY GUIDE

Ready? Ready.

Do the Drill

No matter how prepared you feel it's sometimes a good idea to apply Murphy's Law. So the following tips might seem silly, mundane, or obvious, but we're including them anyway.

1. Remember, there is no food or drink of any kind allowed in the exam room, including gum. You will put all food, drink and any other personal items in a locker before you enter the exam room.

2. You're not too sexy for your test. Wear comfortable clothes. You'll be distracted if your belt is too tight, or if you're too cold or too hot.

3. Lie to yourself. Even if you think you're a prompt person, pretend you're not and leave plenty of time to get to the testing center. Map it out ahead of time and do a dry run if you have to. There's no need to add road rage to your list of anxieties.

4. **No ID, no test. Bring** one piece of current, government-issued, photo identification printed in English with your signature, in the name in which you registered (e.g., driver's license, passport, state ID, etc.) Check the test site before you go to make sure that your ID is acceptable.

5. You can't take it with you. Leave any study aids, dictionaries, notebooks, computers and the like at home.

6. Prepare for the desert. Any time spent on a bathroom break cannot be made up later, so use your judgment on the amount you eat or drink.

7. Quiet, please! Keeping your own time is a good idea, but not with a timepiece that has a loud ticker. If you use a watch, take it off and place it nearby but not so that it distracts you. Also: cell phones are not allowed in the test area.

To the best of our ability, we have compiled the content you need to know in this book and in the accompanying online resources. The rest is up to you. You can use the study and testing tips or you can follow your own methods. Either way, you can be confident that there aren't any missing pieces of information and there shouldn't be any surprises in the content on the test.

If you have questions about test fees, registration, electronic testing, or other content verification issues please visit http://www.nestest.com/Home.aspx.

NES ESOL

TEACHER CERTIFICATION STUDY GUIDE

About the Test

The National Evaluation Series (NES) test for teachers of English to Speakers of Other Languages (ESOL) consists of 150 multiple-choice questions. The national benchmark for the test is 220, with some states setting their own passing scores. You will receive a scaled score immediately after testing, and detailed score reports are issued approximately two weeks later.

The test is computer-based and takes approximately three hours to complete. Testing is by appointment year round at Pearson test centers around the country. Your session will start with a 10-minute tutorial on the computer-based testing system. The tutorial is designed to help you become familiar with navigation between questions and how to keep track of time during the exam. You will also learn how to mark questions for later review. This is useful if there are questions that you are not sure about as you can continue with the test and return to those items later.

On test day, you will need to report to the testing center with identification. You can expect to be photographed and to have a palm vein scan taken. Anything you bring will need to be storied in one of the provided lockers.

The NES exam for ESOL teachers is divided into three primary content domains. The table below shows the different sections and their relative weightings in determining your score.

Content Domain	Percentage of total test score
Foundations of Language and Language Acquisition	20%
Foundations of ESOL Instruction	40%
Instruction and Assessment of English Language Learners	40%

Each domain includes several core competencies. This study guide follows a very similar pattern to assist you in preparing for the test and in identifying areas for which you may need additional study time.

NES ESOL

DOMAIN 1 FOUNDATIONS OF LANGUAGE AND LANGUAGE INSTRUCTION

OBJECTIVE 1.0 LINGUISTIC AND SOCIOLINGUISTIC CONCEPTS AND HOW TO APPLY THEM TO INSTRUCTION

SKILL 1.1 Phonology

The definition of **phonology** can be summarized as "the way in which speech sounds form patterns" (Diaz-Rico, Weed, 1995). Phonology is a subset of the linguistics field, which studies the organization and systems of sound within a particular language. Each language has its own system of sounds or phonology.

Phonology analyzes the sound structure of a given language by:

- Determining which phonemic sounds are present in a language; and
- Explaining how these sounds influence communication.

As children learn to speak, they experiment with the sounds in the language they hear spoken around them. This baby talk gradually becomes organized into patterns that eventually can be identified as words. Eventually, as speech and language development continues, children can join sounds into complex words and words into complex sentences.

Phonemes (the different units of sound such as the sound made by the 'p' in 'pull') are important to learn when studying phonology. These sounds make it possible to distinguish words and their meanings. For some English Language Learners (ELLs), the phonology and phonemes of English may pose several problems. There may be phonemes in English that do not exist in their first or home language. Similarly there may be sounds that are difficult to distinguish (like the 'p' and 'b' in *pin* and *bin*).

Mastering a sound that does not occur in the learner's first language requires ongoing repetition, both of hearing the sound and attempting to say it. The older the learner, the more difficult this becomes, especially if the learner has only spoken one language before reaching puberty. Correct pronunciation may literally require years of practice because initially the learner may not hear the sound correctly. Expecting an ELL to master a foreign pronunciation quickly leads to frustration for the teacher and the learner. Most importantly, it is not the most important goal in an ESOL environment. Communication of increasingly complex ideas is a more important focus of instruction than working towards perfect English pronunciation.

As noted above, a phoneme is the smallest unit of sound that affects meaning (as in the 'p' and 'b' from *pin* and *bin*). The difference in sound between 'p' and 'b' changes the meaning of the word though the sounds are quite similar.

In English, there are approximately 44 speech sounds yet only 26 letters. Letters in English do not consistently make the same sounds (e.g., the 'a' in *back* and *bake*) and, when combined, can make entirely new sounds (e.g., 's' and 'h' vs. 'sh'). For this reason, English is not considered a phonetic language with one-to-one correspondence between letters and sounds. The sounds, when combined, become words.

For students who have difficulty distinguishing between English phonemes when speaking or listening, pronunciation practice can allow them to have fun while they learn to recognize and say sounds. Working with rhyming words that start with different phonemes (e.g., rat, cat, fat, bat) or with alliteration (e.g., ten, ton, tan, and tin) in tongue twisters can be useful ways to build phonemic awareness in students.

Though learning any language presents its own set of unique challenges, the variability of the sounds created by English letters when they are combined in different ways make learning to read and write in English challenging. Unlike Spanish and French and many other languages, in English one symbol can represent many phonemes, and there are multiple pronunciations of vowels and consonants. Phonetic rules are critical to learning to read and write. However, because of the numerous exceptions, the rules themselves do little to assist listening and speaking skills, which makes English a difficult language to master.

When working with ELL students, the wide variation of phonemes represented by a single symbol must often be taught explicitly. If it is difficult for native speakers to learn the English spelling system, then it is a great leap for the ELL. **Graphemes**, the written letter or group of letters that represents a single sound, can be introduced using strategies like phonics in order to help make sense of written English.

Since sound-symbol correspondence in English is difficult, recognition of repeating patterns helps students develop decoding skills. For example, consonant blends such as /ch/, /ph/, and /sh/ are readily recognizable and make the same sound with quite a bit of consistency. Earliest beginners can scan for those language patterns and recognize the sounds they make.

As students develop language skills, they will often begin to recognize **phonographemic differences** between English words. These are a common source of confusion and thus need to be taught explicitly with learning activities designed to enable learners to understand sufficiently the various distinctions. Some areas of focus for the ESOL classroom include:

- Homonyms: Words that have the same spelling but different meanings
- Homographs: Two or more words that have the same spelling (and sometimes pronunciation) but different meanings, e.g., *bow* (like the decoration on a present) and *bow* (like bending your knee or dropping your head out of respect)
- Homophones: Two or more words that have the same pronunciation but different meanings and spellings, e.g., wood/would, cite/sight
- Heteronyms: Two or more words that have the same spelling, but have a different pronunciation and meaning, e.g., Polish/polish

Though these would not be priorities with beginner ELL students, knowledge of these phonographemic differences will become a step in their growing language proficiency. Some useful approaches for instruction in this area would be to identify misspelled words, to recognize multiple meanings of words in sentences, to spell words correctly within a given context, and to match words with their meanings. In addition to phonemes, there are other sound aspects of communication that will challenge beginning English language learners.

Pitch is another element of communication that affects meaning. A string of words can communicate more than one meaning – for example, when posed as a question or statement. For instance, the phrase "I can't go" acts as a statement, if the pitch or intonation falls. However, the same phrase becomes the question "I can't *go*?" if the pitch or intonation rises for the word "go." For ELL students, changes in pitch may be difficult to recognize if they are still building basic vocabulary or learning English syntax.

Similarly **stress** can dramatically change meaning. At the word level, different stresses on a syllable can actually modify the word's meaning. Consider the word "conflict." To pronounce it as a noun, one would stress the first syllable, as in "CONflict." However, to use it as a verb, the second syllable would be stressed, as in "conFLICT.

People from different regions in the United States sometimes pronounce the same word differently, even though both pronunciations have the same meaning. For example, in some parts of the United States the word "insurance" is pronounced by stressing the second syllable, while in other parts of the country the first syllable is stressed. Regional differences in language are often referred to as **dialects**.

At the "sentence" level, stress can also be used to vary the meaning. For example, consider the following questions and how the meaning changes, according to the stressed words:

He did that? (Emphasis is on the person.)
He **did** that? (Emphasis is on the action.)
He did **that**? (Emphasis is on object of the action.)

This type of meaning differentiation is difficult for most ELL students to grasp and requires innovative teaching, such as acting out the three different meanings. Since pitch and stress can change the meaning of a sentence completely, students must learn to recognize these differences in order to develop proficiency in English language speaking and listening skills.

Skill 1.2   Morphology

Morphology refers to the study of how words are formed and to their relationship to other words in the language. For example, analyzing the root, prefix, and suffix of a word and how they come together to give the word its meaning is part of morphology. Using morphology as a tool to analyze word meanings can be an effective way to help ELL students build their vocabulary, both for basic communication and for academic purposes.

A **morpheme** is the smallest unit of a language system that has meaning by itself (e.g., *in* as part of the word *incorporate*). These units are more commonly known as:

the roots, the prefix, and the suffix. They cannot be broken down into any smaller units.

- The root word or base word is the key to understanding a word, because this is where the actual meaning is determined.
- A prefix is a syllable or syllables, which appear in front of the root or base word and can alter the meaning of the root or base word. ('un' in unbelievable)
- A suffix is a letter or letters, which are added to the end of the word and can alter the original tense or meaning of the root or base word. ('ing' in seeing, changes the word to a gerund)

Below is an example of how morphemic analysis can be applied to a word:

- Choose a root or base word, such as "kind."
- Create as many new words as possible, by changing the prefix and suffix.
- New words would include "unkind", "kindness", and "kindly."

Learning common roots, prefixes, and suffixes greatly helps ELLs to build receptive and productive vocabulary. This can make a big difference in how well a student understands written and spoken language. Students who can decode unfamiliar words become less frustrated when reading in English and, as a result, are likely to enjoy reading more. They have greater comprehension and their language skills improve more quickly. Having the

Analyzing words to determine possible meaning (using knowledge of morphemes) should be encouraged. Too often, students become dependent on translation dictionaries, which cause the students not to develop morphemic analysis skills. Practice should include identifying roots, prefixes, and suffixes, as well as using morphemic knowledge to form new words.

English language learners benefit from understanding the structure of words in English and how words may be created and altered. Some underlying principles of the morphology of English are:

- Morphemes may be free and able to stand by themselves (e.g., chair, bag), or they may be bound or derivational, needing to be used with other morphemes to create meaning (e.g., un-real, un-sure).
- Knowledge of the meanings of derivational morphemes such as prefixes and suffixes enables students to decode word meanings and create words in the language through word analysis (e.g., un-happy means not happy).
- Some morphemes in English provide grammatical rather than semantic information to words and sentences (e.g., of, the, and).
- Words can be combined in English to create new compound words (e.g., key + chain = keychain).

ESOL teachers also need to be aware that principles of morphology from the students' native languages may be transferred to either promote or interfere with the second-language learning process. For example, the L1 of many ELL students will share some of the same roots as their English counterparts. In addition, their roots

NES ESOL

and suffixes may be similar or have very clear equivalents. This, combined with **cognates**, is another element that can facilitate vocabulary development, comprehension, and language production.

Recognition of cognates and false cognates is very helpful in decoding and can be directly taught. English and Spanish share many cognates, with the only difference being pronunciation. Fortunately for students, as they develop skills in content areas such as math and science, the incidence of these cognates increases. Some examples of English-Spanish cognates are:

- hotel
- radio
- religion
- eclipse
- editor

Other words are very similar English and Spanish, with just small variations in spelling. Some examples include:

- complicated: complicado
- cause: causa
- minute: minuto
- medicine: medicina
- list: lista
- map: mapa
- pharmacy: farmacia

Some examples of false cognates include:

- asistir: to attend   (looks like assist)
- embarazada: pregnant   (looks like embarrassed)
- librería: bookstore   (looks like library)

Skill 1.3   Syntax and Semantics

Syntax involves the order in which words are arranged to create meaning. Different languages use different patterns for sentence structure. Syntax also refers to the rules for creating correct sentence patterns. English, like many other languages, is a subject-verb-object language, i.e., in most sentences the subject precedes the verb, and the object follows the verb. ELLs whose native language follows a subject-verb-object pattern will find it easier to master English syntax.

The English syntactic system
English classifies eight parts of speech, each with a specific role in sentences. Understanding the parts of speech can be quite difficult for ELLs because the same word can have a different role in different sentences, and a different meaning entirely. Identifying the subject and predicate of the sentence helps to distinguish what role a particular word plays in a sentence. Since English is a subject-verb-

object (S-V-O) language, the placement of a word in a sentence relative to the subject or verb often indicates what part of speech it is.

In these examples, the word show is first a noun, then a verb, and finally an adjective:

- That TV *show* was boring.
- I will *show* you my new dress.
- The band plays *show* tunes at half time.

Parts of speech

There are eight different parts of speech in English. For an ELL student, knowledge of these can sometimes help overcome syntactical errors.

The Eight Parts of Speech	
Noun	A person, place, thing or idea. Common nouns are non-specific, while proper nouns name a particular person, place, thing, or idea, and are capitalized. Nouns may be **countable** or **uncountable**.
Verb	An action or state of being.
Pronoun	A word that takes the place of a noun. A pronoun refers back to the word it replaces—its **antecedent**. There are three types of pronouns: • *Personal pronouns* • *Possessive pronouns* • *Indefinite pronouns*
Adjective	A word that modifies a noun or pronoun. Adjectives answer the questions, *What kind? How many?* and *Which?*
Adverb	A word that modifies a verb, an adjective, or another adverb. Adverbs answer the questions, *How? When? Where? How often?* and *To what extent?*
Preposition	A word that, in a phrase with a noun or pronoun, shows the relationship between a noun or pronoun and another word in a sentence. Prepositions describe or show location, direction, or time. Prepositional phrases can have as few as two words, but can include any number of adjectives.
Interjection	A word that shows surprise or strong feeling. An interjection can stand alone (*Help!*) or be used within a sentence (*Oh no, I forgot my wallet!*)
Conjunction Coordinating or Subordinating	**Coordinating conjunctions** (*and, but, or, nor, so, for, yet*) connect words or phrases that have the same grammatical function in a sentence. *Parallel structure* is desired when using coordinating conjunctions, e.g., *to ride, to sing, and to dance.*

NES ESOL

	Subordinating conjunctions are words used to introduce adverbial clauses. Some of the subordinating conjunctions are: • **For time**: *after, before, when, while, as, as soon as, since, until* • **For cause and effect**: *because, now that, since* • **For contrast**: *although, even though, though* • **For condition**: *if, only if, unless, whether or not, in that case*

Though effective English language instruction does not focus on drilling students on their knowledge of parts of speech, recognizing them and how they are used can help students identify errors in their own language use.

Sentences

A sentence is a group of words that has a subject and predicate, and expresses a complete idea. A subject tells us what or whom the sentence is about and the predicate makes a statement about what the subject is or does.

Example sentence: The snow *falls quietly*	
Subject	The subject, or the topic of a sentence, consists of a noun or a pronoun and all the words that modify it. "The snow" is the subject in the above example. The simple subject is the main part of the subject. *Snow* is the simple subject.
Predicate	The predicate makes a statement or a comment about the subject and it consists of a verb and all the words that modify it; *falls quietly* is the predicate in the above example. The simple predicate is the main part of the predicate and is always the verb; *falls* is the simple predicate.
Compound subject	A subject that consists of two or more nouns or pronouns, e.g., Books and magazines *filled the room*.
Compound predicate	A predicate that contains more than one verb pertaining to the subject, e.g., The boys *walked and talked*.

As noted, English uses a subject-verb-object pattern in standard speech and writing. Many students will come from language background that also use this pattern, but some will speak languages that do not (or that have much greater flexibility in word order); knowledge of the S-V-O pattern will help some students communicate more effectively in English.

Sentence Purposes

Sentences serve different purposes. They can make a statement (declarative); ask a question (interrogative); give a command (imperative); or express a sense of urgency (exclamatory). Understanding the different purposes for sentences can help ELLs understand the relationship between what they write and the ideas they want to express.

Sentence Purpose	
Declarative	A declarative sentence makes a statement: "Anna will feed the dog."
Interrogative	An interrogative sentence asks a question: "Anna, have you fed the dog?"
Imperative	An imperative sentence gives a command: "Anna, please feed the dog."
Exclamatory	An exclamatory sentence expresses a sense of urgency: "Anna, go feed the dog right now!"

Constructing sentences involves combining words in grammatically correct ways to communicate the desired thought. Avoiding fragments and run-ons is a struggle for many students (ELL and native speakers) as they become better writers. For students who struggle with this, understanding of what is necessary to form a complete sentence (a subject and predicate to express a complete idea) is important in improving the clarity of their writing.

ELLs often over-generalize that sentence fragments are short and complete sentences are long. When they truly understand what constitutes a sentence, they will realize that length has nothing to do with whether a sentence is complete or not.

For example:

- "He ran." is a complete sentence.
- "After the very funny story began" is a fragment.

To make these distinctions, learners must know the parts of speech and understand the difference between independent clauses and dependent clauses. Practice identifying independent clauses, dependent clauses, and phrases will help ELLs to write complete sentences.

Sentence Transformations
Sentences can be transformed to add, delete, or permute informational content. Noam Chomsky proposed the concept of transformational grammar beginning in the 1950s. The term refers to the idea that sentences have a surface structure and an underlying structure. The rules that interpret the underlying structures and modify them to create the same surface structure are called transformations.

There are numerous possible transformations in the English language. Some of the most common ones used in ESOL teaching are listed below.

Sentence Transformations: ways in which the sentence adds, deletes, or permutes components	
Yes/No Questions	Sentences may be transformed into yes/no questions. **Auxiliary verb + subject + main verb + rest of sentence:** He lives in Chicago. Does he live in Chicago?
Information Questions	Sentences may be transformed into information questions. **Question word + auxiliary verb + subject + main verb + rest of sentence:** Susan lives near Orlando. Where does Susan live?
Active Voice to Passive Voice (or vice versa)	Sentences may be changed from one voice to another. The Romans built the colosseum. (Active) The colosseum was built by the Romans. (Passive)
Indirect objects	The word "to" (phrase marker) may be deleted. I gave a cookie to him. I gave him a cookie.
Imperatives	The imperative or commands have no expressed subject. You, sit. You, jump. Sit! Jump!
Negatives: Whole Sentence Parts of Sentence	Affirmative sentences may be transformed into negative sentences where the whole sentence is negative. Marion is happy. Marion is not happy. **Parts of sentences may be negative.** Juliana is happy. Juliana is unhappy.

As an ESOL teacher, these transformations are important in understanding just how much ELL students have to learn to become fully proficient in English. Through authentic opportunities for language use within the classroom, students can learn these different ways of expressing increasingly complex ideas.

Verb Tense

The basic English verb tenses are itemized below. Tense refers to any conjugated form expressing time, aspect, or mood. The charts omit the negative and interrogative forms.

Verb Tenses	Simple	Progressive	Perfect	Perfect progressive
Present	I write	I am writing	I have written	I have been writing
Past	I wrote	I was writing	I had written	I had been writing
Future	I will write	I will be writing	I will have written	I will have been writing

This table, of course, omits a number of forms that can be regarded as additional to the basic system:

The intensive present: I do write
The intensive past: I did write
The habitual past: I used to write
The "shall future": I shall write
The "going-to future": I am going to write
The "future in the past": I was going to write
The conditional: I would write
The perfect conditional: I would have written
The subjunctive: if I were writing.

Semantics encompasses the meaning of individual words and combinations of words. Native speakers use their language to function in their daily lives in many different types of situations. Through experience, they know the effects of intonation, connotation, and synonyms. For non-native speakers, this is obviously more complicated and must be learned over time. In an ESOL class, we are trying to teach as quickly as possible what the native speaker already knows. The objectives of beginning ESOL lesson plans should deliberately build a foundation that will enable students to meet more advanced objectives.

Teaching within a specific context (as in vocabulary that is tied to a novel or content unit as opposed to vocabulary taught in isolation) helps students to understand the meaning of words and sentences. When students can remember the context in which they learned words and recall how the words were used, they retain that knowledge and can compare it with different applications of the same words as they are introduced.

Using words in a variety of contexts helps students reach deeper understanding of their meaning. They can then infer new meanings that are introduced in different contexts. For example, the word "conduct" can be taught in the context of conducting a meeting or an investigation. Later the word "conductor" can be used in various contexts that demonstrate some similarity but have distinctly different uses of the word, such as a conductor of electricity, the conductor of a train, the conductor of an orchestra, and so forth.

Second language learners must learn to construct meaning in the language they wish to acquire. This can be a daunting task because of the many ways meaning is created. Voice inflection, variations of meaning, variations of usage, and emphasis are some of the subtle factors that affect meaning. High-level proficiency in a language includes semantic understanding in combination with, contextual understanding, as well as knowledge of pronunciation, grammar, and morphemes.

Skill 1.4   Oral and written forms of discourse

The term **discourse** refers to written and spoken communication. It also deals with specialized forms of communication related to different disciplines or situations. For example, academic discourse or medical discourse involves different vocabulary and different styles of communication than regular daily conversation. Discourse shapes the way language is transmitted and how we organize our thoughts. For ELL students learning the basics of English, distinguishing between the different forms of discourse is an additional but necessary challenge, particularly if they are going to maximize their academic success.

The structure of discourse varies among languages and traditions. For example, in some languages good essay writing does not present the main idea at the beginning of an essay; rather, writing builds up to the main idea, which is presented or implied at the end of the essay. This is completely different than English writing, which typically presents the main idea or thesis at the beginning of an essay and repeats it at the end.

In addition to language and structure, topic or focus affects discourse. The discourse in various disciplines approaches topics differently, such as feminist studies, scientific research, and literary theory. Discourse plays a role in all spoken and written language and affects our word choice, phrasing, and complexity of communication.

Written discourse ranges from the most basic grouping of sentences to the most complicated essays and stories. Regardless of the level, English writing demands certain structure patterns. A typical paragraph begins with a topic sentence which states directly or indirectly the focus of the paragraph, adds supporting ideas and details, and ends with a concluding sentence that relates to the focus and either states the final thought on that topic or provides a transition to the next paragraph when there are more than one. As with spoken discourse, organization, tone, and word choice are critical to transferring thoughts successfully and maintaining interest.

Vocal discourse varies significantly depending on context. People speak in different styles depending on with whom they are speaking to and what the occasion demands. Someone giving a speech at an important ceremony will likely use a far more formal style of discourse than s/he will in conversation after the ceremony. The speaker must make choices about how to organize what he or she says to ensure comprehension and to hold the audience's interest while also striking the appropriate tone for the situation.

Oral discourse analysis is often referred to as conversational analysis. In oral discourse, the emphasis is on the behavior of the participants and social constraints such as politeness and face-saving phenomena. Oral discourse analysis is concerned with who initiates the conversation, turn-taking, how not to interrupt, and who speaks next.

ELLs might initially practice set conversations to learn the patterns of English discourse. Practicing in pairs using a question and answer format gives both participants an opportunity to learn the structures of discourse as well as information about the other person or the other person's culture. Such practice also gives students practice with other language skills and can increase vocabulary. The teacher may provide a set of questions, and learners can alternate asking and answering. Short skits that repeat a limited number of words also provide helpful practice. Allowing students time to converse informally, perhaps using suggested topics continues to reinforce speech patterns.

Polite discourse includes what is called "empty language" or perfunctory speech that has little meaning but is important in social exchanges. Frequently English speakers start a conversation by asking, "How are you?" even though they have no real interest in the other person's health. An appropriate response would be, "Fine," even if the person may not feel well. The exchange is simply a polite means of starting a conversation. Likewise, at the end of a discourse empty language is frequently employed: "See you later," or "Take care."

This type of discourse falls into the category of what Jim Cummins called **Basic Interpersonal Communication Skills** (BICS), skills that learners must acquire to function in social situations. It is generally less demanding than **Cognitive Academic Language Proficiency** (CALP), and allows learners to participate in informal conversations. Teaching polite discourse is important as ELL students who do not acquire it are at a disadvantage in pursuing many types of important opportunities.

Written discourse ranges from the most basic grouping of sentences to the most complicated essays and stories. Regardless of the level, English writing demands certain structure patterns. This ranges from the typical paragraph structure to the structure of a story or essay.

Written discourse is generally analyzed for how the text hangs together. Cohesion is the "surface" characteristics of the semantic relationships between the elements of the text. Coherence is the deeper meaning of the logical elements of the text. Other elements of written discourse include theme, anaphora, topic progression, and grammatical choices at the clausal level.

As language skills increase, paragraphs are combined into stories or essays. Each type of writing has specific components and structures. Story writing requires setting, plot, and character. Initially, following a chronological order is probably easiest for ELLs, but as learners become more skillful, other types of order can be practiced, such as adding descriptions in spatial order or using flashbacks in a story. Teachers frequently rely on the standard three- or five-paragraph essay to teach essay writing because it provides a comprehensible structure for organizing and expanding ideas within a single focus. It mirrors the paragraph structure organizationally in that the first introductory paragraph provides the main idea or focus of the essay, each body paragraph adds and develops a supporting idea and details, and the concluding paragraph provides a summary or other type of conclusion that relates to the main idea or focus stated in the first paragraph.

For English Language Learners, the structure of the 3-5 paragraph essay teaches the basic organizational concept of English essay writing. By offering strictly defined limits, the teacher reduces the number of variables to learn about essay writing.

Starting with a blank page can be overwhelming for ELLs. Working within this structure enables learners to focus on developing each paragraph, which is a challenging enough task when one considers the language skills required. As learners become better able to control their writing and sustain a focus, variations can be introduced and topics expanded.

Different types of written discourse have built-in expectations associated with them. The ESOL teacher must explicitly teach the structural features of important varieties of written discourse.

Academic discourse is one of the most difficult and important for language learners to master. It includes all of the four language skills: listening (e.g., to a lecture), reading (e.g., academic texts), speaking (e.g., formal debates and discussions), and writing (e.g., essays, experimental results, etc.). Academic discourse is important in order for students to succeed in school. Cummins differentiated between two types of language proficiency: basic interpersonal communication skills (BICS) and cognitive academic language proficiency (CALP). According to research, an average student can acquire BICS within two to five years of language learning whereas CALP can take from four to seven years. A lot of factors are involved in the acquisition of CALP, such as age, language proficiency level, literacy in the first language, etc.

Academic discourse includes not only the knowledge of content-area vocabulary, but also the knowledge of various skills and strategies that are essential to successfully complete academic tasks in a mainstream classroom. It includes skills such as inferring, classifying, analyzing, synthesizing, and evaluating. Textbooks used in classrooms require abstract thinking relating to information that is context reduced. As students reach higher grades, they are required to think critically and apply this knowledge to solve problems.

The language and grammatical structures used in academic discourse are complex and challenging for English language learners. Additionally, the passive voice is normally used to present science and other subject-area textbooks and the use of reference, pronouns, modals, etc. is a common feature of academic discourse that might cause problems for ESL learners. All of the language features of academic discourse help to convey the intended meaning of the author; therefore, it is necessary to explicitly teach these language features to students in order for them to become skilled readers and writers.

Furthermore, genre is an important aspect of academic discourse. Each genre employs a style of writing that is unique to itself. The organization of a text structure differs according to the purpose of the author, for example, mystery and romance. Likewise, in academic reading, students come across multiple texts that vary in organization and style according to the purpose of the author, and the audience in question. Students need to understand the different features of multiple texts to become efficient readers. With respect to writing, students need to determine the purpose of their writing, for example, argumentative writing versus story writing.

In short, explicit instruction of these language skills—grammar, vocabulary, and genre—should be provided to students to help them learn academic discourse in order for them to succeed in a school setting.

Skill 1.5   Pragmatics

Pragmatics is the study of how context impacts the meaning of language. Situations often have as much to do with meaning as the words themselves. Without context, even seemingly simple statements become ambiguous. For example, take a look at this conversation:

"How was your trip?"
"Um..the hotel was nice."

For an English language learner, the meaning of this exchange may be unclear without sufficient context. They may not understand that the speaker is also communicating that the trip was not good.

Pragmatic knowledge provides the listener or reader with a set of expectations to understand what they are hearing/reading. In addition, gestures, the appropriate distance between speakers, seating arrangements, nodding and shaking of the head, signs, and touch are all examples of nonverbal pragmatic conventions. These elements are different in different cultures and may be taught.

When communicating with students and community members from different cultures and in different social contexts, pragmatics involving nonverbal cues and body language can be confusing. While they are still learning these nuances of English, ELLs may make mistakes in using or understanding these cues. It is the teacher's responsibility to be sensitive to these different behaviors and acknowledge them when they become obvious in the classroom, and to guide students to adopt behaviors appropriate to their audience, purpose, and setting.

For the ESOL teacher, understanding the role that pragmatics play in comprehension and language use is essential. It is a key area in which the ESOL teacher can support English language learners.

Skill 1.6   English variations (e.g., registers, dialects) and their relevance to ESOL instruction

As noted previously (1.4), we often modify our language use (or discourse) in speaking and in writing to suit different purposes. We write differently for literary essays than we do for short stories, and we speak differently when we make speeches than we do in conversation. This is related to several sociolinguistic concepts. Sociolinguistics is the study of how social conditions influence the use of language. Social factors such as ethnicity, religion, gender, status, age, and education all play a role in how individuals use language.

Choice of language for a particular discourse refers to register. Register varies with many factors including context, age, gender, and culture, level of education, social class, and vocation. British linguist Michael Halliday first defined the broadened term of register as three factors leading to variations in the formality between the participants:

- Field of discourse: A reference to the subject matter being discussed
- Mode of discourse: Speaking or writing, and the choice of format
- Manner of discourse: A reference to the social relations between the participants

American English usage is influenced by the social and regional situation of its users. Linguists have found that speakers adapt their pronunciation, vocabulary, grammar and sentence structure depending on the social situation. For example, the decision to use "-ing" or "-in'" at the end of a present participle depends on the formality of the situation. Speakers talking with their friends will often drop the "g" and use "–in'" to signal that the situation is more informal and relaxed. These variations are also related to factors such as age, gender, education, socioeconomic status, and personality.

We call this type of shift a "change in register," how language is used in a particular setting or for a particular purpose. People change their speech register depending on such sociolinguistic variables as:

- Formality of situation
- Attitude towards topic
- Attitude towards listeners
- Relation of speaker to others

Changing speech registers may be completely subconscious for native speakers. For example, if a university professor takes his/her car in for servicing, the manner and speech s/he uses to communicate with the mechanic differs significantly from the manner and speech s/he uses to deliver a lecture. Likewise, when the mechanic explains the mechanical diagnosis, s/he most likely chooses a simplified vocabulary rather than using completely technical language, or jargon, that the professor wouldn't understand. Using the jargon of a profession or field with which the listener is unfamiliar will likely make communication difficult or awkward.

Social language is different from academic language. The languages are used in different contexts and for different purposes. Their vocabularies are distinct. Structures and grammar may also be distinct. Social language is generally used with peers, in relaxed and informal contexts. Academic language is often used to convey scholarly concepts with concern for accuracy, objectivity, and dispassionate comment.

ESOL teachers should be aware of these sociolinguistic functions of language and compare different social functions of language with their students. Knowing and being able to use appropriate registers allows learners to function more effectively in social and academic situations. Learners must acquire the social, as well as the linguistic, aspects of American English. Sociolinguistic functions of a language are best acquired by using the language in authentic situations.

Sociolinguistic diversity, which is language variations based on regional and social differences, affects teachers' language attitudes and practices. Teachers must respect the validity of any group's or individual's language patterns, while at the same time teaching traditional English. Vernacular versions of English have well-established patterns and rules to support them. Making learners aware of language variations leads to increased interest in language learning and better ability to switch among one or more registers or dialects and Standard English.

Another topic of sociolinguistics is dialect. Dialect usage often differs depending on similar factors to those affecting register. Sociolinguistics tries to understand the relationship between language and social elements. Different dialects, or how language is spoken, are frequently referred to today as varieties of a language. Varieties of a language may be considered separate languages if there is a strong literary, religious, or other tradition.

MAJOR THEORISTS

Fishman
Fishman studied how language evolved and changed over time. His work with Gaelic, Welsh, and Yiddish speakers helped identify the forces in society that may help languages survive. Fishman differed from Ferguson's (1959) original concept of diglossia - a situation in which two varieties of the same language are used under different conditions (usually related to status or situations of formality/informality) within the same community. Diglossia previously applied to languages in which there are very distinct formal and colloquial versions. Fishman, however, believed there could be more than two unrelated languages within a diglossic community. Thus, diglossia ranges from the use of separate dialects to the use of separate languages.

Hymes
Hymes' early work focused on the relationship between language and its social context. His notion of communicative competence was devised (using the SPEAKING acronym below) to study how people talked. Hymes believed that native speakers' competence to speak their language is not sufficient to explain their ability to use grammatically correct forms. He felt that the native speaker also knows when and where to use them, leading to communicative competence.

SPEAKING:
S- setting and scene
P- participants (speaker and audience)
E- ends, purpose, goals
A- act sequence (form and order of event)
K- key (cues that establish the tone, manner or spirit)
I - instrumentalities (forms and styles of speech)
N - norms (social rules)
G- genre (kind of speech act or event)

Dialect variation may occur in the sound system, the grammar, or the lexicon of a language. It may be a gradual change in the pronunciation of a word, or it may be abrupt, as in the case when contact with a new culture occurs. It is beyond anyone's control, but language is constantly changing. In the words of H. L. Mencken, "A living language is like a man suffering incessantly from small hemorrhages, and what it needs above all else is constant transactions of new blood from other tongues. The day the gates go up, that day it begins to die." France is a prime example of a country that has tried to keep its language "pure." In spite of tremendous efforts, the French language has evolved. It has acquired new terms for twentieth- and twenty-first-century technology and experiences. Immigrants who have moved to France have modified it. Living languages are simply not static.

Another element of sociolinguistics is the influence of contemporary culture on language. Factors such as popular culture, slang, advertising, contemporary events, and inventions/technological advances can quickly bring new words into the language. This has particularly influenced English with thousands of new words added as the culture has changed.

Technology can also shape how we use language. Text messaging, for example, has created a kind of shorthand variation of English: CUL8R means "see you later"; BRB means "be right back"; and TTYL means "talk to you later." ESL teachers might be surprised at how adroit their students are with technological language. Students who make English-speaking friends and want to adapt to U.S. culture will quickly learn this new language.

The emergence of work-related language (jargon) is another sociolinguistic change. Though most jargon may not filter out to the general public, some does. To the professionals using it, jargon may be a kind of shorthand that makes long explanations unnecessary. Consider the multitude of terms used to refer to those learning English as an additional language - e.g., ESL students, EFL students, ELL, and LEP - to name a few. Teachers may be referred to as TESOL, ESL, or EFL teachers. The general public would be hard-pressed to understand the distinctions made by professionals using these terms.

Though it is impossible to teach all these variations to English, it is important as an ESOL teacher to be responsive to and aware of the sociolinguistic factors that may pose challenges to student learning.

OBJECTIVE 2 THEORIES AND PROCESSES OF LANGUAGE ACQUISITION AND LITERACY DEVELOPMENT AS APPLIED IN THE ESOL CLASSROOM

Skill 2.1 Historical and current theories in language acquisition (including bilingualism/multilingualism and the role of L1 in L2 development)

Contemporary theories of language acquisition are the results of years of research on many different language learners in many different cultures. These theories have led to a solid basis upon which to base teaching practices and can guide teachers in their interactions with learners of all types. Below are brief summaries of some of the most important theories about the language acquisition process.

SKINNER: BEHAVIOURIST THEORIES (1950s)
Skinner believed that babies/children acquire language through a process of trial and error, and rewards. After a while, children learn how to ask for what they want and how to communicate what they need. Through this system, children learn language the same way they learn everything else. This is referred to as a behaviorist model because its ideas are clearly on the side of nurture as opposed to nature. In Skinner's view language-learning functions as a series of learned habits.

CHOMSKY: THE UNIVERSAL HYPOTHESIS and the LAD (1960s)
Chomsky's language acquisition theories developed as a counter to behaviorist theories and fall squarely on the nature side of the nature vs. nurture binary. Chomsky's Universal Hypothesis theory asserts that children are born with the biologically determined ability to learn language, with a part of their brain that already contains linguistic information, like language rules or structures. The term he used to describe this mechanism is Language Acquisition Device (LAD). He believed that when babies and children hear speech, their Language Acquisition Device is activated and it allows them to interpret what they are hearing. Chomsky based his assumptions on his work in linguistics after studying children in different parts of the world.

His universal grammar theory posits the idea that grammar is a property of every language and therefore, no matter where a child grows up, s/he will innately understand and produce the grammar of his/her language. His evidence for this is that in every culture and language, children rarely get their subjects, verbs or objects in the wrong order and that in every culture, children begin to form language phrases that they have not heard before. By studying the mistakes that children make while they acquire language, Chomsky and other innate language theorists, show that children's language development is more than what is proposed by behaviorist theory (which asserts that children learn language merely by being rewarded for imitating). The largest criticism of innateness, the Universal Hypotheses, universal grammar and the LAD is that just because children are not merely imitating does not mean that they have an innate biological language mechanism that is 'set off' when they hear speech. Other theorists have argued that in fact, language learning could be acquired through interactions with others, in some of the same way that other skills are learned and that the process of language learning is more complex than Chomsky initially laid out.

PIAGET: COGNITIVE CONSTRUCTIVISM (1930s)

Piaget's central interest is children's cognitive development. Piaget believed that neither behaviorist nor innate models could account for the complexity involved in learning. He argued that learning is a process of active discovery and knowledge; language learning is something that is actively constructed as a result of children's innate mechanisms and interactions with the outside world. He articulated 4 stages of cognitive and language development and that in each one, children produce knowledge, create meaning and produce language based upon their experiences. The states are the Sensory-Motor Period (birth to 2 years old), the Preoperational Period (2-7 years old) and two Operational Periods (7-12 years old). He argued that the best learning, including language learning, takes place when students are provided with opportunities to play, to practice, to scaffold and to cognitively process what they are learning. For Piaget, skill and drill techniques (behaviorist models) are not effective methods for real learning and knowledge acquisition.

VYGOTSKY: SOCIAL INTERACTIONIST THEORY (1920s but popular in the 1980s)

Unlike Chomsky and Piaget, Vygotsky's central focus is that language is used for communication and that the environment and culture where language learning is taking place has an impact on how children conceptualize themselves and the world around them. Social interaction plays a major part in cognition. Vygotsky suggests that what Piaget saw as the young child's egocentric speech was actually private speech, the child's way of using words to think about something. HIs zone of proximal development theory (ZPD) became popular as a counter to Piaget's theories and posited that there was a zone between where students could and could not do something. Education would provide learners with experiences within that zone and interactions with teachers and peers could move them from one part of the zone to the other.

PINKER: THE LANGUAGE INSTINCT (1994)

Pinker agrees with Chomsky that humans are born with an innate capacity for language and that the "basic organization of grammar is wired into their brains" through biological evolution. Pinker claims language was created through evolution to solve communication problems among social hunter-gathers. He does not believe that language creates complex thought, as others do but instead believes that complex thought is also an innate ability.

Pinker posits that during critical periods in childhood, specific language learning structures in the brain are activated. When this period is over, Pinker argues, these structures are disassembled allowing the brain to use this energy for other purposes. Pinker believes that language itself is constantly changing and developing as new words are added and people express ideas in new ways.

KRASHEN: THE MONITOR MODEL (1970s and 1980s)

Krashen's Monitor Model consists of 5 main hypotheses:

1. *The Acquisition/Learning Hypothesis*: Distinguishes between "acquisition", a subconscious event resulting from natural communication where emphasis is on communication and "learning" which occurs as the result of conscious study of formal properties of language.

2. *The Natural Order Hypothesis*: Learners follow a more or less invariable path when learning a language and that grammatical structures are acquired in a predictable order.
3. *The Monitor Hypothesis*: Learners use an internal monitor to edit "learned" language production. The three conditions for successful 'monitor' use are: sufficient time, a focus on form and not on meaning, and the need for the user to know the grammar rule – the user must have had instruction on the language form.
4. *The Input Hypothesis*: Acquisition of language takes place when the learner is exposed to comprehensible input a little beyond the learner's current level of competence, or at "i + 1".
5. *The Affective Filter Hypothesis*: The Affective Filter is low in learners with high motivation and self-confidence but high in learners with low motivation and self-confidence. This filter affects the amount of input a learner comes in contact with and how much of that input becomes intake.

CUMMINS: BICS AND CALPS (1980s)

Cummins distinguishes between language used for Basic Interpersonal Communication Skills (BICS) and Cognitive Academic Language Proficiency (CALPS). BICS are the "surface" skills that language students acquire quickly. CALPS are skills needed to perform in an academic setting. Cummins states that children can acquire BICS in approximately 2 years of immersion in the target language and that CALPS requires between 5-7 years to develop.

Complete language proficiency (our goal for ELL students) requires both BICS and CALP - they represent a continuum of language proficiency moving from context-embedded to context-reduced and from cognitively undemanding to cognitively demanding. The base for BICS and CALP is a set of skills that Cummins refers to as a Common Underlying Proficiency (CUP). These are skills, ideas, and concepts that learners can transfer from their first language to their English learning. Similarities and differences between languages can both help learners comprehend and learn aspects of English.

CRITICAL PERIOD HYPOTHESIS

This hypothesis is the cause of much debate among linguistics and language acquisition theorists. The critical period hypothesis posits that a person who learns a second language before reaching puberty will be more proficient than a person who learns after childhood. A person who begins to learn a second language after the onset of puberty will likely find language learning more difficult and depend more on repetition. Evidence for this argument is most notable in studies of 'accent' among second language learners. Some theorists advocate for a change in terminology from 'critical' to 'optimal', which would leave more room for interpretation of second language acquisition data.

BILINGUALISM/MULTILINGUALISM

Language and brain researchers have advocated for bilingual or multilingual education for children. In general, they argue that bilingual/multilingual learners:

- Have higher executive function skills than monolingual learners (paying attention and switching from one task to another);

- Have more empathy than monolingual learners as they have learned to read social cues to pick up on which language to use in what particular space or time;
- Have improved English language reading skills compared to their monolingual peers;
- Have metalinguistic awareness skills that can help with decoding;
- Encourage more comfort with diversity (income, culture, language) for learners; and
- Encourage more support from family and community as home language is valued (dual immersion programs).

There are many studies currently being conducted and results vary. The strongest evidence to support the above assertions has been found with children and older adults. In the meantime, several states have expanded dual-language opportunities for students for many of the reasons above.

Skill 2.2 Historic and current theories in literacy development (role of L1 literacy in L2 literacy development; concepts and challenges in ESOL teaching)

GESELL's MATURATIONIST THEORY (1920s)
The maturationist theory proposes that children will learn to read when they are ready. This readiness is dependent on the acquisition of reading readiness skills and that these skills cannot be pushed or rushed by parents or teachers. He believed that even though social and cultural environments play a role in literacy development, they are more effectively channeled to help children when they are 'mature' enough to learn. He paralleled literacy development and physical development to make his point. Gesell's theories were used to support specific reading instructional strategies until the 1960s (e.g. not teaching reading until children are about 6 years old and invented spelling).

BEHAVIORIST THEORIES (1950s-1970s)
Based on Skinner's theories and still practiced in the 1970s (and today), behaviorist theories of literacy development take the knowledge and skills to be learned and break them down into smaller units and teach them (often without context). This approach often employs "skill and drill" and requires checking students' work regularly to provide them with reinforcement. This is a teacher-centered approach by necessity. The belief at the backbone of this approach is that children will develop literacy skills by repeating words and sentences modeled by adults and working through reading and writing skills sequentially and through isolated practice.

COGNITIVE DEVELOPMENT THEORIES (1930s - present)
Based on Piaget's work, these theories look at the ways that children process the world around them and the stages and strategies for optimal literacy development. This theory is largely used to help ESOL instructors and other teachers to understand children's cognitive development as it applies to the acquiring, development and achievement of literacy skills.

HOLDAWAY'S THEORY OF LITERACY DEVELOPMENT (1980s)

Holdaway's Foundation of Literacy was written as a result of Holdaway's work with Maori and Polynesian children developing literacy skills. He believed that learning to read and write should be a positive experience and that the development of literacy skills begins at home in the form of meaningful experiences like story time or shared reading with parents and other family members. From this, he developed a series of instructional practices based on the oral literacy practices in the home, including the 'shared book experience' instructional strategy. With shared reading of big books, teachers read 'big books' to children and shared the excitement of reading and understanding shared texts they loved. Essential components of successful literacy development process according to Holdaway are: children observe literacy behaviors; children collaborate with others to learn; children practice (alone) so that they can improve; and children perform (with others) these literacy skills in order to share what they have learned. Classroom uses come to big books, shared reading and stages of reading.

STAGES MODEL OF READING DEVELOPMENT (1980s-present)

A well-known practitioner and researcher of the stages model was Chall, who focused on 6 key stages of reading development. Generally, these stages are:

1. Learning the letters of the alphabet and what sounds those letters make
2. Applying Stage 1 to read words and stories
3. Stage 1 and 2 combine to transition children from learning to read to reading to learn
4. Learn new things by reading
5. Learning about more than one viewpoint
6. Learners become selective about what to read, when, how and why

EMERGENT LITERACY THEORY MARIE CLAY (1980s, 2000s - present)

Marie Clay was a psychologist who worked and studied young children's literacy development. Her Emergent Literacy theory identified the steps that children engaged in before the acts of 'reading' and 'writing' formally take place. These steps are developmental and necessary in order to develop literacy skills (e.g., oral language skills, phonological awareness, letter awareness). These pre-literacy foundations are built through listening to stories, touching books and seeing letters, numbers and words. Listening, speaking, reading and writing are all interrelated as Clay defines reading as "...a message-getting, problem-solving activity which increases in power and flexibility the more it is practiced."

Reading Recovery

One of the key findings of Clay's research was that if young children didn't have literacy skills developed enough by Grade 1, then they continued to struggle with literacy as they continued with schooling. She analyzed the specific behaviors involved in reading and writing as well as trying to understand the thought processes of the children who were learning. From her research and theorizing, she created the reading recovery program, which helped struggling young readers, with a specific set of instructional strategies that many schools use to this day.

FAMILY LITERACY (2000s)

Family literacy, as articulated by Morrow and Taylor, identifies how children learn literacy skills before grade 3 and focuses on the roles that the families play in developing and using literacy skills to communicate and to accomplish tasks. Family Literacy sees a connection between this and a child's progress in literacy development in school. One result of Morrow's theorizing and research was the creation and implementation of family literacy programs in schools to help promote the development of literacy skills as a family in the home and to help struggling young readers and writers by working with them and their families together. There are several complications with these strategies as they have been implemented over the years (i.e. Successful programs are the ones that value the families and do not try to evaluate and superimpose general ideas on specific families).

CRITICAL LITERACY (1980s - present)

Critical literacy is generally defined as the literacy skills necessary to deconstruct a text - to not only decode the words on the page and comprehend the meaning of a passage but also to analyze and interpret a text's implied meaning and implications. When learners read critically, they are able to read texts actively, reading between the lines, reading reflectively, noticing language use, tone, evidence, ideas and, when necessary, identify the bias or challenge the power relations the text is framed around. The development of critical literacy skills in schools is something that affects with the role of the teacher, making teaching less direct and more about questioning and asking students to provide evidence to support their thinking. Critical literacy encourages students to read and reflect on all of the pieces that go into creating the text and not just the essence of what a text is trying to communicate. Teaching critical literacy has an impact on instructional strategies, especially for middle and high school classrooms.

The literacy development theories above are not entirely disconnected from each other, especially when it comes to adapting or transforming these theories into instructional practices. Well balanced approaches to literacy development based on what works in the theories above, can help the ESOL teacher make good choices about when, where, and with whom to use a specific approach.

L1 and L2 Influences

Interlanguage is a strategy used by a second language learner to compensate for his/her lack of proficiency while learning a second language. It cannot be classified as first language (L1), nor can it be classified as a second language (L2), rather it could almost be considered a third language (L3), complete with its own grammar and lexicon. Interlanguage is developed by the learner, in relation to the learner's experiences (both positive and negative) with the second language. Larry Selinker introduced the theory of interlanguage in 1972 and asserted that L2 learners create certain learning strategies, to "compensate" in this in-between period, while the learner acquires the language.

Interlanguage Strategies	
Overgeneralization	Overgeneralization occurs when the learner attempts to apply a rule "across-the-board," without regard to irregular exceptions. For example, a learner is over-generalizing when he/she attempts to apply an "ed" to create a past tense for an irregular verb, such as "buyed" or "swimmed."
Simplification	Simplification refers to the L2 learner using resources that require limited vocabulary to aid comprehension and allow the learner to listen, read, and speak in the target language at a very elementary level.
Code-switching	A switch between languages or the combination of elements of different languages within one conversation. This can be a function of limited proficiency (as speakers may not have the skills to express some ideas) or of advanced proficiency (as speakers find one language more useful for expressing certain concepts or ideas than others).
L1 interference or language transfer	L1 interference or language transfer occurs when a learner's primary language influences his/her progress in the secondary language, L2. Interference most commonly affects pronunciation, grammar structures, vocabulary and semantics

Fossilization is a term applied by Selinker to the process in which an L1 learner reaches a plateau and 'accepts' a less-than fluent level of proficiency, which prevents the learner from achieving L2 fluency. Fossilization occurs when non-L1 forms become fixed in the interlanguage of the L2 learner. L2 learners are highly susceptible to this phenomenon during the early stages.

Skill 2.3   Stages and sequence of language learning; difference between social and academic language; features of ELL proficiency levels

Stages and Sequence of Language Acquisition
Language acquisition is a gradual, hierarchical, and cumulative process. This means that learners must go through and master each stage in sequence, much as Piaget theorized for learning in general. In terms of syntax, this means learners must acquire specific grammatical structures, first recognizing the difference between subject and predicate; learning to put subject before predicate; and then learning more complex variations, such as questions, negatives, and clauses. Experts disagree on the exact definition of the phases, but a set of five general stages has generally been agreed upon:

Stage 1 - Pre Production: The learner knows less than 500 receptive words and does not produce speech. The absence of speech does not indicate a lack of learning and teachers should not try to force the learner to speak. Having the learner point, draw, mime or nod can check comprehension. Also known as the Receptive or Silent stage.

Stage 2 - Early Production: The learner knows about 1,000 receptive words and can produce one- or two-word phrases, present-tense verbs and some key phrases and words. The learner can understand and respond to simple questions and yes/no, either/or prompts. Also known as the Private Speech stage.

Stage 3 - Speech Emergence: The learner knows about 3,000 receptive words and can communicate using short phrases and sentences. Long sentences typically have grammatical errors due to attempts by the learner to communicate increasingly sophisticated ideas. Also known as the Lexical Chunks stage.

Stage 4 - Intermediate Fluency: The learner knows about 6,000 receptive words and begins to make complex statements, state opinions, ask for clarification, share thoughts, and speak at greater length. Also known as the Formulaic Speech stage.

Stage 5 - Advanced Language Proficiency: The learner develops a good level of fluency and can make semantic and grammatical generalizations. Also known as the Experimental or Simplified Speech stage.

Learners use different approaches to mastering these skills. Some use more cognitive processing procedures, thinking through what they know to formulate what they want to communicate. Others tend to use psycholinguistic procedures, processing learning through more speaking.

Understanding that students must go through a predictable, sequential series of stages helps teachers to recognize the ELL's progress and respond effectively. Each progressive step requires the learner to use knowledge from the previous step, as well as new knowledge of the language so providing comprehensible input will help students advance their language learning in all of the stages.

Differences Between Social and Academic Language
Social language is the language that students use with their friends and family. As noted previously (Skill 2.1) learners are usually proficient in social language before they have mastered the academic language that is grade-level appropriate in the native speaking classroom.

Academic language not only includes the knowledge of content-area vocabulary but also the knowledge of various skills and strategies that are essential to successfully complete academic tasks in a mainstream classroom. It includes being able to talk about and apply skills such as such as inferring, classifying, analyzing, synthesizing, and evaluating. Texts (print, digital and multimedia) used in a classroom require more abstract thinking as information is increasingly context-reduced. As students reach higher grades, they are required to think critically and apply new knowledge to solve problems and to use language specific to the subject area and to the cognitive and metacognitive skills they are using. .

Academic language can be very challenging for English language learners. With respect to reading and writing, use of complex grammatical structures is frequently found in academic discourse and the passive voice is often used in science and other subject area texts. Similarly, the use of reference, pronouns, modals, etc., is a common feature of academic discourse, which might cause problems for ESL learners. All of these language features of academic discourse help to convey the intended meaning of the author. Therefore, it is necessary to explicitly teach these language features of the text to the students in order for them to become skilled readers and writers.

Many factors are involved in a learner's readiness and predisposition to CALP. Age, language proficiency level, literacy in the first language and many other factors contribute to the learning of CALP in the classroom. Explicit instruction of social, academic and discipline-specific language skills, grammar and vocabulary, should be provided to the students to help them develop basic communication and academic English language skills in order to succeed in a school setting. (See Objectives 8, 9 and 10 for instructional strategies to develop academic language proficiency in reading, writing, listening and speaking).

Features of ELL proficiency levels
Many states as well as educational consortiums (such as WIDA) have identified five English Language Proficiency levels. Some states, like New York, include descriptions of these levels as well as strategies for teaching and evaluating these levels in different content-areas.

Case Study - New York
In New York State, new ELL students take a proficiency test before starting class to determine their level. These levels help determine whether a student will receive English Language learning services and/or when s/he can exit the ELL program.

The five proficiency levels in New York state are: Entering, Emerging, Transitioning, Expanding and Commanding. A student at the Entering level needs substantial support and structure in English language learning because s/he struggles to demonstrate English language proficiency in academic contexts. A student at the Emerging level is still largely dependent on support and structure in her/his learning and is not yet proficient in academic contexts. A student at the Transitioning level is more independent and needs less support but still has not yet become proficient in English in academic contexts. At the Expanding level of proficiency, students are increasingly able to be more independent and are clearly approaching the English Language proficiency level necessary to function well in various academic contexts. Finally, at the Commanding level, a student is proficient in the English Language in various academic contexts and, therefore, is not an ELL.

Additionally, the language proficiency assessment helps guide instruction and helps identify students' English Language Learners' strengths and challenges in receptive and productive skills (reading, listening, speaking, writing).

Case Study 2: WIDA
WIDA describes six levels of language proficiency that outline the linguistic development of a student learning English as a new/additional language. They are:

- Entering
- Beginning
- Developing
- Expanding
- Bridging
- Reaching

This continuum of language development provides detailed descriptions of what students can do at each level and at each grade level within the different domains of language - speaking, listening, reading and writing. Keep in mind that students may be at higher proficiency levels in one domain than in another. For example, a student may demonstrate faster progress in speaking than in reading comprehension. The six language proficiency levels outline the progression of language development in the acquisition of English as an additional language, from 1, Entering the process, to 6, Reaching the end of the continuum.

Examples of skill progression on the WIDA continuum

From Entering	To Reaching
Concrete concepts in English	Understanding of abstract concepts
Comfort using informal language	Facility in using a formal register
Single word responses	Extended conversation or writing
Non-standard language use	Standard use of English
Basic, general vocabulary	Domain specific vocabulary

Students at the Reaching level of English proficiency will be able to function like their native English-speaking peers. Though this does not necessarily mean that they will not have gaps in language (unfamiliar vocabulary, occasional errors in syntax, etc.) students at the reaching level demonstrate a high level of proficiency in English and can function independent of instructional support or scaffolding for language learners.

WIDA has also created detailed examples of continua describing expected performance by students within specific content area. For example, an elementary school age student asked to investigate and collect information about whether and its impact might demonstrate the following skills at each respective level in reading and writing.

- Entering - Name weather conditions using prompts like charts
- Beginning - Restate weather conditions and their effects
- Developing - Describe the effects of weather conditions
- Expanding - Discuss weather conditions and their effects
- Bridging - Explain in detail weather conditions and their effects

The language proficiency levels delineate expected performance and describe what ELLs can do within each language domain of the standards for designated grade level clusters. These are extremely useful tools for the ESOL teacher, but they are too detailed to include all of them here. Teachers are encouraged to refer to the WIDA website to find detailed descriptions that can helpful in assessing student progress, communicating with parents, working with content-area or classroom teachers, and/or designing instruction.

Many schools and states have some version of these 5 - 6 levels of English language proficiency and use them to place, to assess and to teach English language learners effectively.

Skill 2.4 Individual, academic and sociopolitical factors that affect English language acquisition and development

There are many factors that affect English language acquisition, development and proficiency. Some of those factors are socio-cultural (see Objective 3) and some are factors that affect all learners. Understanding the impact these factors can have on ELLs can help ESOL teachers to better assess, support and differentiate with their students.

Individual Factors:

Life Experience: If students have lived in several countries, they may be better able to adapt to their new experience in the United States because they have lived and attended school with people from many cultures. Learners who come to a new school having learned in several different educational systems alongside people who speak a variety of languages may be more open to language learning in a new culture.

Self-esteem and anxiety: Learning a second language puts learners in a vulnerable frame of mind. Anxiety is inherent in second-language learning. Students are required to take risks, such as speaking in front of their peers. Without a native speaker's grasp of the language, second language learners may be unable to express their individuality, which is even more threatening and uncomfortable. Using teaching techniques that reduce stress and emphasize group participation, rather than focusing on individuals getting the right answer can reduce this anxiety.

However, not all anxiety is debilitative. Bailey's (1983) research on "facilitative anxiety" (anxiety that compels an individual to stay on task) demonstrates that some types anxiety can be a positive factor for some learners (closely related to competitiveness).

Motivation: Motivation can be defined as the degree to which learners choices about what goals they want to accomplish and how much effort they will put forth to accomplish the goal.

Researchers Gardner and Lambert (1972) have identified two types of motivation in relation to learning a second language. Neither type stands completely alone:

- Instrumental/Extrinsic Motivation: Acquiring a second language for a specific reason, such as a job, motivated by a 'reward' of sorts
- Integrative motivation: Acquiring a second language to fulfill a wish to communicate within a different culture, motivated by internal reasons to do the activity itself

Research has shown that intrinsic or integrative motivation can be more powerful, which is similar to Krashen's theory on comprehensible input (i+1). The sense that something is just outside your reach but that you can grasp if if you put forth the effort, can be a strong motivator for next steps.

Understanding an ELL's motivation can help ESOL teachers differentiate and reach more learners by choosing techniques, strategies, texts, communication opportunities and consistent feedback to increase instrumental motivation in students. When motivation is increased, students will work harder to achieve proficiency.

Occupational Pathways: Learners' perceptions of occupations, i.e., whether a certain position is of interest or even feasible, affects second language acquisition. If education is not viewed as a realistic pathway to a career and economic security, academic success and L2 proficiency become less of a priority.

Attention span: The process of learning in a new language environment places many demands on the learner. Some students will have a greater capacity to function without tiring or getting bored in this type of environment. Those that can sustain effort and attention over longer periods of time may make faster progress.

Learning Styles: Students have different learning preferences that can affect the way in which they learn and are able to express themselves. Learning styles (e.g. visual, auditory, kinesthetic), cognitive learning styles (e.g., concrete, analytic, communicative, authority-oriented) and multiple intelligences are several examples of types of learners that schools and businesses have created assessments for (e.g., Myers-Briggs). Although current research on learning 'styles' and personalities, as well as on multiple intelligences is showing these factors as mutable rather than immutable and as more connected than originally conceived of, it is still worth it for ESOL teachers to pay them some attention. Understanding the learning preference or style of their students can assist ESOL teachers in working with every student to meet his/her potential and to maximize their language proficiency.

Academic Factors
If English language learners acquired proficiency in their home languages, they are more likely to achieve proficiency in English.

If an English language learner's native language has similar roots to English (e.g., Spanish or French) they may face fewer challenges than someone whose home language is from a different language family altogether (e.g., Japanese).

Even children who have not had prior educational experiences upon which to build their new language skills may have been taught the alphabet or simple mathematics by their parents. In addition, children from oral cultures may have quite sophisticated language structures already in place upon which to base new language learning.

Schemata, or the prior knowledge students have when beginning a new foreign language, is a valuable asset to be exploited in their language learning. A schema is the framework around information that is stored in the brain. As new information is received, schemata are activated to store the new information. The schema theory (Carrell and Eisterhold, 1983) explains how the brain processes knowledge and how this facilitates comprehension and learning. By connecting what is known with what is being learned, understanding is achieved and learning can take place. Using instructional strategies that that Building on prior knowledge can help ESOL teachers reach more learners.

Sociopolitical Factors

Sociopolitical factors that influence second (or plural) language learning can be described as the attitudes that learners have towards the language(s) they are learning. In the case of English language learning, some students may have perceptions that make them want to learn English or make them reluctant learners. Some students' families, home countries or cultures may have negative attitudes towards the English language and/or North American culture and this might make the student want to disassociate with English rather than learn it. ESOL teachers may notice learning gaps in these cases and if they can identify socio-political factors as possible causes, it can help them to reach out and motivate those particular students.

(See Objective 3 for instructional strategies)

Skill 2.5 Cognitive, metacognitive and socio-communicative strategies supporting ELLs

COGNITIVE STRATEGIES

The ESOL teacher can teach students some basic cognitive strategies that will help them achieve proficiency in English language learning as well as in content-area knowledge and skills. The most basic cognitive strategies can best be remembered by using the acronym, PRAC: Practicing, Receiving and sending messages, Analyzing and reasoning, and Creating structure for input and output.

Practicing: When students practice their new language, they are engaged in constant repetition, in making attempts to imitate a native speaker's accent, in concentrating on sounds, and in trying to practice in a realistic setting.

Receiving and sending messages: When learners work on receiving and sending messages, they skim through information to determine "need to know" vs. "nice to know," They use available resources (print and non-print) to interpret messages.

Analyzing and reasoning: When students analyze and reason, they try to apply general rules for understanding the meaning of texts (written, visual, auditory, digital) before working into specifics. They break down unfamiliar expressions into parts in order to analyze them and then put them back together to understand the holistic meaning of the text.

Creating structure for input and output: When students create structure for input and output, they choose appropriate formats for taking meaningful notes; they practice summarizing and paraphrasing long passages; they may use graphic organizers to help them plan writing and speaking performances.

METACOGNITIVE STRATEGIES

Metacognitive skills are skills related to learning how to learn. The ESOL teacher is responsible for helping students become aware of their own individual learning strategies and for encouraging ELLs to constantly improve and add to those strategies. Each student should have his/her own toolbox of metacognitive skills for planning, managing, and evaluating their language-learning process.

Some metacognitive strategies ELLs can use:

Connecting Concepts: Encourage ELLs to review a key concept or principle by linking it to something they already know. This can help learners reflect on, understand and learn big ideas.

Arranging and planning learning: Teach your students how to create optimal learning conditions, i.e., regulate noise, lighting, and temperature; obtain the appropriate books, etc.; and how to set reasonable long and short-term goals for English language learning tasks and skills.

Evaluating and monitoring learning: Help students keep track of progress and challenges. Paying attention to challenges and coming up with strategies to improve can help ELLs make more progress in language proficiency and content-area knowledge. Keeping track of successes helps learners stay motivated, increases self-esteem and can encourage ELLs to set more challenging goals for themselves.

SOCIOAFFECTIVE STRATEGIES

Socioaffective strategies are strategies that relate to how learners feel about their learning environments (including what they are learning).

Affective strategies are those that help the learner control the emotions and attitudes that may hinder progress in learning the second language. There are three sets of strategies that ESOL teachers can teach their students to help reduce the impact of negative attitudes or emotions, which are easy to remember with the acronym LET.

Lowering anxiety: Participating in physical activities, learning relaxation techniques or mindfulness and/or listening to calming music can all help ELLs reduce anxiety around learning English. Mediation and/or mindfulness can help during class, if necessary. Calming music can help when working on assignments and physical activity helps to reduce anxiety in general.

Encouraging yourself: These strategies help support and motivate the learner to stay positive. ESOL teachers can model self-affirmations, and talk to students about taking risks and giving themselves rewards. When students can encourage themselves, they are more likely to do well.

Taking your emotional temperature: These strategies help learners control their emotions by understanding what they are feeling emotionally as well as why they are feeling that way. These strategies include listening to your body's signals, keeping track of feelings and motivations during the second-language-acquisition process, and sharing feelings with classmates or friends.

Social strategies affect how the learner interacts in a social setting, including the classroom setting. The following are three useful strategies to help learners interact socially, which can be remembered with the acronym ACE.

Ask questions: Encourage ELLS to ask for clarification or help and to request that the speaker slow down, repeat, or paraphrase.

Cooperate with others: Provide plenty of opportunities for students to interact with others, to work cooperatively partners or in small groups. Encourage ELLs to seek out social interactions with students who may be outside of their usual social circles.

Empathize with others: Talk to ELLs about how and why they can learn how to relate to others, reminding them that people usually have more things in common than things that set them apart. Encourage empathy by talking to students about the value of connecting with another student by learning about his/her culture and by being aware of and sensitive to his/her thoughts and feelings.

TEACHER CERTIFICATION STUDY GUIDE

DOMAIN 2   **FOUNDATIONS OF ESOL INSTRUCTION**

OBJECTIVE 3   **ROLE OF CULTURE IN LANGUAGE LEARNING AND ACADEMIC ACHIEVEMENT**

Skill 3.1   **Content of culture (values/beliefs) and effects of culture differences in classroom and school**

Culture encompasses the sum of human activity and symbolic structures that have significance and importance for a particular group of people. Culture is manifested in language, customs, history, arts, beliefs, institutions and other representative characteristics, and is a means of understanding the lives and actions of people.

Cultural beliefs can have a strong emotional influence on ELLs and should always be respected. While customs are often adaptable (similar to switching registers when speaking), no effort should be made to change the beliefs or values of an ELL. Presenting new ideas is a part of growth, learning, and understanding. Even though the beliefs and values of different cultures often have seemingly large differences, they should be addressed. In these instances teachers must set a tone of respect for different ideas so that all students feel their culture is valued. This does not mean that presenting new, contrasting points of view should be avoided because new ideas can strengthen original thinking as well as change it. All presentations should be neutral, however, and no effort should be made to alter a learner's thinking. While addressing individual cultural differences, teachers should also teach tolerance of all cultures. This is especially important in a culturally diverse classroom but will serve all students well in their future interactions.

Second language acquisition, according to the findings of Saville-Troike (1986), places the learner in the position of having to learn a second culture. That process can be tremendously positive, or it can be negative. On the positive side, culture constitutes a rich component of language learning. It offers a means of drawing learners into the learning process and greatly expands their understanding of the new culture, as well as their own.

Incorporating the study of the history and various art forms of different cultures is very revealing and offers opportunities to tap into the interests and talents of ELLs. Comparing the history and art of different cultures encourages critical thinking and often reveals commonalities as well as differences, leading to greater understanding among people.

The learning environment and other outside factors can, however, make learning about a new culture and language a negative experience. The attitudes of the larger community can make ELL students feel unwelcome or looked down upon, making a positive, open attitude particularly important in the learning environment. Similarly, the attitudes and behavior of the learner's family are important. If they feel like they are part of the school community, they are more likely to support the school and embrace the second culture. If acculturation is perceived as rejecting the primary culture, however, then the child risks feeling alienated from both cultures.

NES ESOL

There are many different ways that students are affected by the cultural differences in their native culture and home when compared with the culture being acquired through schooling and daily life in a foreign culture.

The following points, adapted from Peregoy and Boyle (2008), illustrate some of the many different ways that culture affects us daily and thus affect students in their participation, learning, and adjustment to a different society and its schools.

- **Family**: Expectations about education, views of responsibilities at home and at school, and views of children's independence can all influence learning.
- **Stage and age**: What behaviors and responsibilities are considered appropriate for children of different ages? How might these conflict with what is taught or encouraged in school?
- **Roles and interpersonal relationships**: Is competition valued? Is working with others valued? Is deference supposed to be shown to certain people? If so, to whom and by whom? Are there different expectations about gender roles?
- **Discipline**: What is discipline? Which behaviors are considered socially acceptable? Who is considered responsible if a child misbehaves? Who has authority over whom? How is behavior traditionally managed?
- **Time and space**: How important are deadlines? How important is speed in completing a task? How much personal space are people accustomed to?
- **Religion**: What restrictions are there on topics discussed in school? Are dietary restrictions to be observed, including fasting? What restrictions are associated with death and the dead?
- **History, traditions, and holidays**: Which events and people are sources of pride for different groups? To what extent does the group in the United States identify with the history and traditions of the country of origin? What holidays and celebrations are considered appropriate for observing in school? Which ones are appropriate for private observance?
- **Age**: Age can impact second language acquisition. For example, culture can sometimes determine what a person does, as well as when they can do it. For example, as noted by Sindell (1988), many middle-class European-Americans tend to expect that children will play and enjoy childhood, rather than take on more adult responsibilities.

As students learn English, they may come up with phrases, words, and language structures that are not 'typical' of Standard English. These language variations are a natural part of language acquisition and a frequent part of the process of acculturation. These language patterns serve a purpose within the community that uses them. New, nonstandard English words can represent a particular group's identity, or function as a means to solidify social relationships. As long as students recognize that a variation should not be used as if it were Standard English, there should be no problem with its use. This is essentially the same as learning to use the right register for communication.

To minimize the potential of negative effects of cultural differences in a language-learning environment, teachers should focus on creating an atmosphere in which difference is respected. Maintaining a respectful classroom environment that can observe differences while encouraging all students to celebrate and value diversity is essential for a positive learning environment.

Skill 3.2 Sociocultural variables that can affect L2 learning (e.g., racism, discrimination, etc.)

There are many external, sociocultural factors that affect language acquisition. Student learning can be impacted (either positively or negatively) by forces inside and outside the school. As teachers, it is essential to be aware of these factors in order to best support students in the language acquisition process and in content-area learning.

If non-native speakers of English experience discrimination because of their accent or cultural status, their attitude toward the value of new language learning may diminish. One way that schools can work towards an environment of respect for linguistic diversity it to encourage activities between native speakers and ELLs. This can be particularly beneficial to both groups if students learning the ELL student's first language work on projects together. When native speakers get a chance to appreciate the ELL students' language skills in their first language, attitudes change and ELLs have an opportunity to shine. This is also one of the main ideas behind the Two-Way Dual Language Bilingual Education Model

(See 4.1 on Dual Language models).

Teachers and schools play a major role in shaping the attitudes towards immigrants and members of language minorities. If bilingualism and multiculturalism are celebrated within the school community, it is far more likely that ELL students will feel that they are supported in their journey towards English language proficiency. Learning English will more likely be seen as a natural and important part of education rather than something imposed upon them.

Similarly, some students feel that they must make a choice between loyalty towards the culture of their L1 and learning English. This is particularly common when the prevailing attitude towards the language/speakers of that language is negative. In this situation, students may feel that learning English is at the expense of their L1; it can become an issue of loyalty towards their cultural group and that of their family. In this situation, language acquisition is difficult.

Acculturation is the process of becoming accustomed to the customs, language, practices, and environment of a new culture. The factors that influence this process include, but are not limited to, the learner's desire and ability to become a part of the dominant culture.

The relationship between acquiring a second language and adopting the new culture is a strong one. Schumann (1978a) has developed a model of acculturation, which asserts, "The degree to which a learner acculturates to the target language group will control the degree to which he acquires the second language." (p. 34).

According to his model, the following social elements impact the acculturation process:

- ELLs and native speakers view each other with mutual respect and have optimistic attitudes about each other.
- ELLS and native speakers both wish for the primary group to successfully assimilate.
- The length of time ELLs intend to remain in the area (e.g. short term visitors or permanent home)

These factors affect the process of acquiring English for the learners. Likewise, the absence of these factors can contribute to students not learning English and remaining outside the dominant culture. In a classroom setting, if there is no mutual respect, positive attitude, or sense of compatibility between the language learners and native speakers, successful second language acquisition for the L1 group is severely hindered. In turn, without a common language, the chances of acceptance and assimilation become significantly reduced.

It is important that the ESOL teacher try to avoid having students feel that learning English comes at the expense of their first language. This can cause negative feelings about school in general and can adversely affect second language acquisition.

Classroom and school activities that promote interactions among ELLs and native speakers encourage language growth and an exchange of cultures. With an increased ability to communicate, commonalities are discovered and friendships form. Sports, music, art, photography, and other school activities that allow ELLs to participate while they learn more language provide excellent opportunities for increasing acculturation.

These sociocultural factors are closely tied to the affective domain in that these outside forces can very easily impact individual students, creating affective barriers to learning.

AFFECTIVE FACTORS

The term affective domain refers to the feelings and emotions in human behavior that affect how a second language is acquired. Self-esteem, motivation, anxiety, and attitude all contribute to the second language acquisition process. Internal and external factors influence the affective domain. ESOL teachers must be aware of each student's personality and must stay especially attuned to the affective factors in their students.

Self-esteem: As noted in 2.4, learning a second language involves risk-taking. While some learners are less inhibited about taking risks, all learners can easily be shut down if their comfort level is surpassed. Using teaching techniques that lower stress and emphasize group participation, rather than focusing on individuals getting the right answer, reduces anxiety and encourages learners to attempt to use the new language.

Motivation: **See 2.4.** Gardner and Lambert's (1972) two types of motivation related to language learning do not stand completely alone. Instructors recognize that motivation can be viewed as either a "trait" or a "state." As a trait, motivation is more permanent, whereas as a state, motivation is considered temporary because it fluctuates, depending on rewards and penalties.

Anxiety: Anxiety is inherent in second-language learning. Students are required to take risks, such as speaking in front of their peers. Without a native's grasp of the language, second language learners are unable to express their individuality, which is even more threatening and uncomfortable. However, not all anxiety is debilitative. Bailey's (1983) research on "facilitative anxiety" (anxiety that compels an individual to stay on task) is a positive factor for some learners, closely related to competitiveness.

Attitudes: Attitude typically evolves from internalized feelings about oneself and one's ability to learn a language. On the other hand, one's attitude about language and the speakers of that language is largely external and is influenced by the surrounding environment of classmates and family.

The affective domain is closely tied to the sociocultural influences mentioned above. Together they can have a powerful negative or positive effect on language acquisition for ELL students. ESOL teachers can work within their classrooms and schools to try to ensure that students learn in the most positive environment possible.

Skill 3.3 Cultural differences in communication as well as cross-cultural communication

See also 3.1.

Communication and language are essential elements of culture. As such, both are shaped by (and shape) cultural beliefs and practices. Some languages, for example, have very clear forms of formal address - different verb conjugations and/or pronouns to be used when addressing someone older, of higher status, or even a stranger. To not use these is to risk being seen as rude. Switching register in languages with these characteristics is a very clear and marked shift.

English, however, does not have such clear forms of addressing someone formally/informally. Changes in register, therefore, have more to do with the manner of speaking - tone, pronunciation, word choice, etc. Part of learning English (or any language) then becomes learning how to change register to show respect in a way different from one's L1.

Cultural customs play an important part in language learning because they can directly affect interpersonal exchanges. What is polite in one culture might be offensive in another. For example, in the U.S., making direct eye contact is considered polite. Some cultures may view eye contact, especially with someone in a position of authority, as aggressive or rude. Teachers who are unaware of this cultural difference could offend an English language learner, or misjudge them and unwittingly cause a barrier to learning. However, teachers who are familiar with this custom can make efforts not to offend the learner and can teach the difference between the two customs so that the ELL can make more informed decisions about behaviors.

In designing learning experiences, the ESOL teacher must be aware of the potential impact of cultural differences on the effectiveness of certain teaching methods. Group work, for example, has tremendous potential to create opportunities for communication and authentic language use both by ELLs and between ELLs and native speakers. This has clear benefits for student language acquisition.

Many cultures promote group loyalty and cooperation over competition and the idea of winning. Some students may be reluctant to participate in activities that they perceive could cause their peers to 'lose' or be embarrassed. Similarly, within groups some students may defer to others because of perceived status. Recognizing these potential effects will help ensure that teachers create the best possible learning situations for a diverse student body.

These types of cultural differences are best addressed through varied instructional strategies in order to provide students with a range of opportunities to use language. Flexible and varied learning situations promote language in multiple contexts, an excellent way for ELL students to use language in different but authentic scenarios. Group work with peers, for example, puts students in the position of using more informal, conversational language while still researching information for a project. Preparing that information for a presentation then encourages the use of more formal academic language to address the class and teacher.

Using varied discussion formats accomplishes an important instructional goal. Pair or small group conversations about a content-area topic have ELL students addressing their peers about their opinions and ideas. Debates or Socratic seminars, meanwhile, require a different level of preparation and speaking style. This range of learning opportunities allows ELL students to learn, through authentic experience, important variations in communication styles in English.

At the same time, teachers must keep in mind that some common discussion activities may be new or awkward for some ELL students. Depending on students' cultural backgrounds, debates may seem confrontational with one side openly disagreeing with the other in order to prove a point. Students can obviously adapt to this type of format, but it may initially be challenging.

Recognizing and respecting these cultural differences does not mean avoiding these types of teaching strategies. Instead, it means supporting students as they adapt to the expectations of an American classroom and is part of the way the ESOL teacher ensures that one culture is not privileged over another in the learning environment.

Cultural differences in communication styles will also potentially affect ELL students' reading and writing. If students already have a strong background in literacy from previous schooling in their home/native language, they may be accustomed to reading/writing texts that communicate ideas in a different way than is customary in English. As an example, the essay structure most common in the United States generally calls for a clearly stated opinion supported by evidence to support the writer's point of view. In some cultures, this structure can be construed as overly forceful, especially the idea that a student would present him/herself as an authority on a topic. In such cases, the ESOL teacher will not only need to help students build language proficiency but also their understanding of the style of communication expected in English.

Skill 3.4 How to create culturally diverse and inclusive learning environment

(See also 3.1, 3.2, and 3.3.)

As noted previously, teachers and schools wield great influence in setting the tone towards language learning in general and towards ELL students in particular. Addressing the socio cultural and social-emotional factors that affect language acquisition is an essential component in maximizing opportunities for learning and academic achievement.

Some evidence-based strategies that ESOL teachers can use to create inclusive environments in the classroom include:

- Engaging in positive interactions with students
- Using appropriate modes of address (addressing students by their preferred names and pronouncing those names correctly)
- Establishing classroom communication ground rules to promote respect
- Using inclusive language
- Reflecting on teaching practices and personal attitudes

Recognizing the cultural diversity of the school community within the curriculum is a key step towards building a culturally inclusive school community. This can take many forms. In a language arts curriculum, multicultural literature is an easy way to incorporate rigorous, high-quality teaching materials while also celebrating the diversity of American society. Schools can also make the holidays, traditions, and celebrations of different groups part of school life. This enriches the school community and, at the same time, shows that every cultural group has something to contribute to the culture of the school.

Another component to consider when creating a learning community that is culturally inclusive is to involve parents and the wider school community. As Dodd & Konzall (2002) demonstrated, strong community involvement builds stronger schools.

Taking the time to share information with parents and other family members not only helps to enhance understanding and open communication, it can also provide more support for students than the school alone would ever be able to provide.

Communicating about assessment methods and results is important, but so is communicating about instructional practice so that stakeholders understand the goals and the strategies for meeting goals. Stakeholders can then more effectively help develop student strengths and meet student needs. When teachers communicate clearly, consistently and meaningfully with parents and families, colleagues, administrators and English language learners themselves, all stakeholders are more likely to work together towards the common goal of helping learners achieve communication, academic and social/emotional success.

See Skill 6.5 for strategies and information about communicating with parents and the wider community.

OBJECTIVE 4   STANDARDS BASED ESOL INSTRUCTION: APPROACHES AND RESOURCES

Skill 4.1   Characteristics, goals and research on ESOL models and program effectiveness; historical and research bases of past and current ESOL models and methodologies

Second language teaching methodologies have been adapted and transformed by important researchers, linguists, educators and theorists over the years. Some of the methodologies are based on second-language acquisition theories (see Objective 2) and some are created as an alternative to those theories. Below are summaries of some of the most important ESOL methodologies, their goals, their strengths and weaknesses and their lasting impact on ESOL education.

Method and Year	Goals	Classroom Practices	Strengths, Weaknesses & Impact
Grammar Translation Method 1800s - present Originally used to study Latin	Read literature in its original form; learn a language as an intellectual endeavor or to develop mental discipline	Study and drill grammar rules; Vocabulary; Translating sentences into L2 and L1	No oral/aural practice; no interaction; no self-expression Impact: Learning grammatical rules as a starting point.
Direct Method 1900s Popularized again in 1970s by Berlitz	Immerse students in L2 the way that children are immersed in L1; Good pronunciation; Good oral communication	Realia; oral interaction; very little study of grammar or rules; everyday vocabulary; visual aids; instruction in L2; no translation Teacher must be fluent in L2	Weak on grammar; hard to differentiate; hard to do in public schools (budget, class sizes, teacher and time) Impact: Introduced concept of realia; learn the language and not about the language

Audio-lingual Method 1930s - 1960s	Learn a language by building blocks; rules and practice from sound to sentence with rewards (Behaviorist)	Learning phonemes, morphemes and syntax; oral drills and repetition in pronunciation and intonation; teacher directed	Focus is on listening and speaking - not enough on reading and writing; form is emphasized over meaning; not enough on communicative competence; more passive learning Takeaway: Oral drills and pronunciation and intonation help with oral and aural communication skills
Community Language Learning 1970s	Part of the Humanistic approach to language learning - learners must feel comfortable and be empowered Learners pass through all stages of development	Teacher as facilitator; students sit in a circle and whisper in L1 what they want to say in L2. Teacher responds in L2 and student repeats. This process continues and teacher records dialogues and writes on board and class analyzes.	Needs small group; needs learners from same home language group; needs bilingual teachers; better for beginners; not for children but better for adults Takeaways: empowered learners; teachers as facilitators

The Silent Way 1960s	Learner autonomy; Student discovery; Pronunciation; Focus on how students learn and not how to teach; Trial and error Scaffolding	Teacher is silent most of the time; Students 'discover' for themselves; Manipulatives help students communicate with each other; Constant observation as assessment	Loss of interest in manipulatives; limited communication topics; process takes too long; need lots of space; decontextualized Takeaways: trusting classroom relationships; formative assessment; pronunciation techniques
Total Physical Response	1st language students learn by listening and physically responding - 2nd language will too; Physical movement helps learning	Imperative drills with physical responses	Okay for beginners; after that run out of language and imperatives; lack of student expression Takeaway: useful for teaching new vocabulary (esp. w/children)
The Natural Approach 1980s Krashen and Terrell	Making language acquisition more natural; reducing learner's anxiety; more exposure to input; based on Krashen's learning theories	Teacher centered; steady flow of comprehensible input, content, games, and problem-solving; students don't have to speak at the beginning in L2	Difficult for children who struggle; silent period makes it difficult to assess progress Takeaways: students are engaged;

			comprehensible input; allows for easy integration of speaking, listening, reading, and writing
Communicative Language Teaching 1990s to present	Presentation, practice, and production help students learn, practice and produce language (anxiety free); Know how to communicate in authentic situations	Combination of grammar, functions, dialogues, structures, and strategies; Students more active participants in their learning	Not as much of a focus on grammar and rules, rote-learning, or drilling to help w/accuracy Takeaways: Authentic learning; collaborative activities; incorporation of many 'methods'

These methodologies all came as a result of scientific research and study with children in first and second language learning to try to increase language proficiency by addressing the challenges of the programs that preceded them. At this point, many schools incorporate aspects of the different methodologies that work for them and their students, the particular classes they offer, and the expectations and standards that the school requires. Using formative assessment with these methodologies allows teachers to adapt instruction when needed. (See Skill 5.3 for more information on aligned assessment used to adapt instruction).

In combination with the ESOL methodologies above, there are three main instructional models that are widely used in the United States: ESL or EAL classes; sheltered instruction models; and dual-language programs (including dual immersion). These models do not determine the methodologies, per se. Instead they are more about how to organize student groupings to maximize proficiency and learning. Elements of most of the methodologies above can be used in the three main instructional models below:

ESL/EAL

Goal: Bringing students to proficiency in English as quickly as possible. Often used at the beginning English levels.

Sheltered Instruction

Goal: Bringing students to proficiency in English language and content-area knowledge. Focuses on English literacy in the content areas rather than mechanics of English.

Dual Language

Goal: Build on L1 skills to transition to L2: Part of the school day in English and part in home language. Teacher(s) speak both languages. Dual immersion consists of ½ students who are native English speakers and ½ who speak another language. Both groups become bilingual and both groups can learn from each other.

Finally, many states and schools are now using a standards based curriculum for ELLs and native-English speakers. Standards-based ESOL curricula encompass instruction, assessment, grading and reporting of assessments/grades. The Common Core is an example of a standards-based curriculum in that it describes standards or benchmarks for students at different grade levels in different classes. These standards or benchmarks consist of skills students are expected to master (including language proficiency skills) and content-knowledge that students are expected to know and understand. ESOL and content-area teachers use these standards to plan instruction and assess students using the standard as the goal. Assessment uses the language of the standards as does grading and reporting of assessment results. Standards-based ESOL instruction can incorporate diverse instructional methodologies and can work with any ESOL program model.

Skill 4.2 How to plan standards-based instruction (assessment-driven and differentiated)

Understanding the Standards
Teachers should know, understand and work towards the achievement of district, state and national learning standards for ELLs. The Every Student Succeeds Act (ESSA), signed into law in 2015, requires all states to adopt English language development standards. Many states have adopted or aligned the Common Core learning standards, and many use the WIDA English Proficiency Standards. Some school districts may have additional learning standards. ESOL teachers need to incorporate all required standards into instruction and assessment practices in order to support English language learners in becoming proficient in English and academically successful.

Assessment
After understanding the standards thoroughly, the next step is to determine the levels and needs of the ELLs. This can be done through a variety of formal and informal assessments in content-areas and in reading, writing, listening and speaking. Teachers can use the results of these assessments to plan and guide instruction.

Data-driven instruction and inquiry is an approach based on assessing and analyzing student data in order to adapt instructional plans to maximize student learning during the year and not just from one year to the next. With assessment of appropriate student performance tasks, teachers use data to close the gaps. Teachers (and administrators) should assess where students are and where they need to be by collecting and analyzing data to determine how to take action to help students throughout the year.

Key questions when using data-driven assessment to plan instruction are:

Where is the data being stored?
Assessment data needs to be stored in a place and in a format that is easily accessible to ESOL teachers (and others involved in assessing the student, if required). In order to benefit from data-driven assessment, it is not enough to merely collect the data - it has to be used. In order to use it, teachers have to know where to find it and must be able to move efficiently between assessment data and instructional planning apps, programs, or notebooks.

What are the goals for the student?
With every assessment, whether formal or informal, there are proficiency, knowledge and/or skill goals for each student. It is essential that assessments allow students to demonstrate what they know, what they have learned, or what they can do. For this to happen, the goals of the assessment must be clear to the English language learners. It also helps to have individual student goals easily accessible when analyzing assessment data.

What standards/progressions are met/not met?
Several competencies and skills in this book describe the need for teachers to demonstrate knowledge and understanding of state standards and progressions, including the Common Core and language proficiency standards. When using data-driven assessment to identify student needs and help guide instruction, ESOL teachers would benefit from having the standards and progressions easily accessible. This information can help teachers decide whether to re-teach a lesson (or a part of a lesson) with the whole class, with groups of students, and/or with specific students who have not yet met the standards.

What is the plan?
Making a plan is essential in order to truly use assessment data to help English language learners. The plan should include actions that both ELL students and ESOL teachers need to take, as well as outlining the formative and/or summative assessments that will be used to measure progress.

When ESOL teachers use consistent formative assessment, it keeps them focused on student progress and gives them the opportunity to plan appropriate instruction that meets students' needs. It also keeps parents, administrators, counselors and other colleagues informed as students develop their English language skills.

Planning and Designing Instruction
Finally, the teacher must design a course of study that will enable students to reach the necessary level of achievement, as displayed in their final assessments or exit behaviors. Teachers should teach with the students' developmental levels in mind.

Different approaches should be used to ensure that these students get multiple opportunities to learn and practice English and still learn content.

In choosing materials, teachers should also keep in mind that not only do students learn at different rates, but they bring a variety of cognitive styles to the learning process. Prior experiences influence the individual's cognitive style, or method of accepting, processing, and retaining information.

Many students will need certain concepts explained in greater depth; others may pick up on those same concepts rather quickly. For this reason, teachers will want to adapt the curriculum in a way that allows students the opportunity to learn at their own pace, while keeping the class together as a community. The more creative a teacher is with the ways in which students can demonstrate mastery, the more fun the experience is for students and teachers. Furthermore, teachers reach their students more successfully as they tailor lesson plans, activities, groupings, and other elements of curriculum to each student's need.

To maximize student learning, fluency and achievement, ESOL teachers need to align goals for learners so that as their English language proficiency develops, so does their content-area learning and output. By using data-driven inquiry, formative assessment and by getting to know each learner, teachers can personalize teaching and learning so that students can meet content and language goals in multiple ways.

It is very important that teachers choose, adapt and design instructional materials that are relevant and aligned with state learning standards. In helping students meet these standards, teachers need to be able to scaffold instruction and differentiate instruction for a range of English Language Learners.

The following are three primary ways to differentiate:

- Content—the specifics of what is learned: This type of differentiation does not mean that whole units or concepts should be modified. However, within certain topics, specifics can be modified.
- Process—the route to learning the content: This kind of differentiation means that not everyone has to learn the content using the same method.
- Product—the results of the learning: Usually, a product is the end result or assessment of learning. For example, not all students are going to demonstrate complete learning on a quiz; likewise, not all students will demonstrate complete learning on a written paper.

Two keys to successful differentiation are:

- Know what is essential in the curriculum and in the learning standards. Although certain things can be modified, other things must remain intact in a specific order. Disrupting central components of a curriculum can actually damage a student's ability to learn something successfully.
- Know the needs of the students. While this can take quite some time to figure out, it is very important that teachers pay attention to the interests, tendencies, and abilities of their students so that they understand how each student will best learn.

The effective teacher takes care to select appropriate activities and classroom situations in which learning is optimized. The classroom teacher should coordinate instructional activities and classroom conditions in a manner that enhances group and individual learning opportunities. For example, the classroom teacher can organize group-learning activities, placing students in situations in which cooperation, sharing ideas, and discussions occur. Cooperative learning activities can assist students in learning to collaborate and share personal and cultural ideas and values in a classroom-learning environment.

For English language learners who may be struggling with language proficiency and/or with content/skill-based standards, culturally relevant materials can help motivate, inspire and connect to students' prior experience/knowledge in a meaningful way. For example, for those who may have difficulty with reading, a novel that deals with culturally familiar experiences may allow ELLs to focus on comprehension. Novels dealing with unfamiliar experiences can force a beginning ELL student to simultaneously grapple with language and subject-area skills through textual content that is new and unrelatable.

In addition, the WIDA English Language Development Standards cover some research-based essential action strategies for effective instruction with ELLs. A few are adapted below:

- Create and utilize language proficiency profiles for each student.
- Design language teaching and learning with attention to the sociocultural context.
- Create meaningful, language-rich, and safe environments for English Language Learners that provide them with differentiated language practice and use. This means providing ample time for students to practice who need more and appropriate challenges for students who need less. That way all students are working to their potential and no students 'finish' before others.
- Use instructional supports and scaffolds.
- Communicate and plan with other teachers in order get to know students' strengths and challenges outside of your classroom. This can help in planning personalized learning opportunities inside it.

Helping Students Help Themselves
For students with limited proficiency in English, some content can be difficult, and teachers need to implement ways to make it accessible for these students. For this purpose, teachers should encourage their students to use graphic organizers such as webs, mind-maps, Venn diagrams, and charts to help them better comprehend challenging texts. These visual tools help ELLs visualize and organize information, summarize and interpret texts and promote active learning.

The goal is that each student, through his or her own abilities, will relate to one or more techniques and excel in the learning process. While all students need to have exposure to the same curriculum, not all students need to have the curriculum taught in the same way. "Differentiation" is the term used to describe the variations of curriculum and instruction that can be provided to an entire class of students.

When students are encouraged to be metacognitive learners, their ability to take responsibility for and personalize their own learning increases. This results in students becoming more active learners and has a positive effect on English language and content-area learning.

Skill 4.3 Criteria and methods for selecting, applying and designing resources

Before looking at materials and resources, the ESOL teacher must have key standards and goals in mind. With good planning, teachers know what skills and knowledge they want students to have for each unit, lesson or module. With these goals in mind, and after identifying student needs, interests and learning styles, teachers will have more of a framework for what types of materials/resources they want to use.

Many schools have sets of textbooks, texts, curricular materials and resources available for ESOL teachers. Some will be mandatory and some will be optional. Some may be out of date and/or there may be no budget for supplies and teachers will have to choose their own resources. Either way, every ESOL teacher needs to have clear criteria and methods for selecting, applying and designing resources that help ELLs meets standards for content-area skills and knowledge and for English language proficiency.

The next step in the process is to choose the materials to use in the classroom that help ELLs reach these standards or performance outcomes. It can be helpful to think about the questions that Robinett (1978 pp. 249-51) created as a checklist for choosing a textbook. Even though many schools do not use textbooks, schools often use worksheets, learning packets, and other instructional texts to frame a unit or series of content-area lessons or language goals. Some of the following questions can help ESOL teachers choose which resources to use and how to use them.

Approach: If you are using a textbook, does the approach match the approach of your school, classroom, curricula, and standards in terms of learning and language theories?

Language Skills: Are the four skills (reading, writing, speaking, and listening) integrated?

Content: Is the language authentic? Does it lead to authentic use of language with the students? If this is a student text, does it match the proficiency level of the students?

Quality of Practice: Will the activity/resource provide opportunities for students to practice in a variety of ways (i.e., guided, less guided and independent)? Are the student directions clear? Are there review exercises so that students are able to spiral back to and reinforce what they have learned?

Vocabulary: Is word and word study an important part of the text? Is the vocabulary relevant?

Format: Does the formatting of the text enhance the content or the skills students will be learning? Or, at the very least, not distract from it? This question is equally important with online materials as well as print. If the print quality is poor and/or if the webpage is so full of images and ads that it is difficult for students to read, then it might be better to choose another resource.

Accompanying Materials: Does the text come with materials that help students learn and understand like games, flashcards, audio/visual? Can you supplement and design these yourself? Are there materials to support and/or extend learning to help the teacher differentiate instruction?

If the answer to any of the above questions is a no, then the ESOL teacher may also choose to adapt and supplement the resource if it is still a valuable one. Adaptations and supplements can make the materials more differentiated, more engaging and more likely to result in learner proficiency in language and content-area goals.
In addition to textbooks or lessons directed at students and teachers, there are also a variety of ESOL materials that can be used in the classroom to develop literacy and content-area skills/knowledge (e.g., print forms, digital media, audio, visual, performance, games, simulations, etc.).

The ESOL teacher needs to know how to choose and adapt these types of texts for ELLs. Graves (2003) created an acronym, SARS, to describe a method for selecting, applying and designing resources for English language learners.

Select: Select the goal or aim for the lesson, unit or program and what parts of the texts you have that you want to use.

Adapt: Adapt your lesson or course for time, space, and students in your class.

Reject: Reject the parts of text or materials that are irrelevant; you don't have to use everything in the texts.

Supplement: Supplement the texts and materials you use with other materials that you design or use so that students are engaged, so that the focus is on what students need to learn, and so that students will want to learn.

With adapted checklists and techniques, a knowledge of the standards and of the students, the ESOL teacher is in a good position to choose, adapt and design materials and resources that will enable her/his students to learn to their potential.

Skill 4.4 Using resources for standards-based and content-area learning

Language learning proficiency encompasses the language specific to various disciplines as well as the mastery of grammar structures and vocabulary. When students learn ways of thinking as well as ways of talking about big ideas supported by rich content in specific texts, they will achieve more in the content area and in language learning in general.

Recent research in this area has come up with useful insights that can be applied across both grade level and language classroom settings in order to support ESL students' English language and literacy development. For ELL students, language and literacy development is a key objective of all grade level curricula to ensure success both inside and outside of the school setting.

These insights can be synthesized into seven key instructional criteria for designing and conducting instruction to support English language learners' language and literacy development (Enright, 1991).

1. *Collaboration:* Instruction should be organized for students to have many opportunities to interact and work cooperatively with each other and with teachers, family members, and community members. During collaborative activities, teachers and students actively work together in order for learning to take place. This cooperation entails organizing learning activities that require communicating and sharing, such as discussion groups, student partners, or student-teacher dialogue journals. Collaborative activities also include interacting with people outside of the classroom, such as interviewing the school drama club for the class newspaper or working with a parent or an elder to report on a special family tradition.

2. *Purpose:* Instruction is organized so that students have multiple opportunities to use authentic oral and written language to complete tasks and have real-life goals and purposes. An example of purposeful composition and questioning activities would be students writing letters to city officials to invite them to a class election forum and then interviewing them about school issues. Teachers can and should provide opportunities for shared social communication, fun (songs, games, etc.), academic purposes (research), and creative purposes (poetry, stories, etc.). These various forms of communication ensure that students learn both language and content.

3. *Student interest:* Instruction is organized to both promote and follow students' interest. This does not mean that the instructional goals are changed, but the focus is on organizing activities that combine students' interests and purposes with curriculum topics and objectives.

4. *Previous experience:* Instruction is organized to include students' previous experiences in the new learning. This includes tapping students' previous language and literacy experiences in their first language and English and also their already-developed knowledge and cultural experiences. This approach entails relating new concepts and materials to students' background experiences, such as brainstorming ideas before reading a text or connecting previous class activities and learning to new ones. An example would be including histories and folk tales from ESL students' families and native countries in reading group instruction or having students collect authentic speech and literacy data from their homes and neighborhoods to be studied in class.

5. *Support:* Instruction is organized so students feel comfortable and take risks in using English. The classroom atmosphere should be supportive, which provides challenging but safe opportunities for students to learn English. The activities are

adapted to students' current language and literacy capabilities or *zones of proximal development* (Vygotsky, 1978) in the second language, which also provides scaffolding of the newly acquired skills.

6. *Variety:* Instruction is organized to include a variety of learning activities and language forms and uses. This means that students are exposed to a wide range of oral and written English that they are expected to use in the classrooms and their daily lives. Organization for variety includes the instructional practices of collaboration, learning purposes, student interests, and familiar and unfamiliar student experiences within classroom learning activities.

7. *Integration:* Instruction is organized to integrate the various programs and resources available for supporting ELLs' language and literacy development so that they complement each other. This may include integrating the students' in-school and out-of-school experiences; integrating content and language instruction; integrating the four language skills of reading, writing, listening, and speaking; and integrating the students within the classroom through cooperative learning.

Academic tasks tend to increase their cognitive demands as students progress in their schooling, but the context becomes increasingly reduced. ELLs who have not developed Cognitive Academic Language Proficiency or CALP (see 1.4 for more detail) need additional teacher support to achieve success. Contextual support in the form of realia, demonstrations, pictures, graphs, etc. provide the ELL with scaffolding and reduce the language difficulty level of the task. Both content and ESOL teachers should incorporate teaching academic skills in their lessons. The following are essential elements to include in teaching academic English:

1. Integrate listening, speaking, reading, and writing skills in all lessons for all proficiencies.
2. Teach the components and processes of reading and writing.
3. Focus on vocabulary development.
4. Build and activate prior knowledge.
5. Teach language through content and themes.
6. Use native language strategically.
7. Pair technology with instruction.
8. Motivate ELLs with choice.

See Objectives 8, 9 and 10 for instructional strategies specific to listening and speaking, reading and writing and content-area knowledge.

Skill 4.5 Using technology to enhance effective teaching and learning

Educational technology can increase learning opportunities for English language learners. Developing effective and adequate management and instructional strategies is crucial to integrating technology in multiple ways in the ESL/ENL classroom. Competent use of computers prevents ELLs from "academic and social marginalization" (Murray & Kouritzin, 1997, p.187). It may allow them to have more control over the direction of their learning by controlling their time, speed of learning, autonomy, choice of topics, or even their own identity (Hoven, 1992).

Technology can provide English language learners with prompt feedback, individualized learning, and a tailored instructional sequence. It can meet specific student needs, increase their autonomy, allow for more responsibility, promote equal opportunities in a nonsexist environment, encourage student cooperation with peers, and encourage them to make decisions (Burgess & Trinidad, 1997).

Technology integration, defined by Reilly (2002), affects curriculum development and teaching practice. It is one way to move teaching from teacher- to learner-centered. To allow for greater success rates for ELLs, teachers need to integrate technology to advance student learning because technology activities, such as using the Internet or working as a team on a project, provide students with opportunities to enhance and extend the regular learning to higher levels of cognitive involvement. The effect of engaging English language students through technology can be multilayered. When technology is used as part of a model that involves students in complex authentic tasks, the results can be student-centered cooperative learning, increased teacher-student and peer interaction, and more positive attitudes toward learning, allowing greater interaction and sense of responsibility as a team.

The Internet can enrich the learning process if teachers design thoughtful learning activities and assessments that incorporate it. These activities can accelerate content learning by addressing relevant information that is not solely dependent on learning English. Through experiences such as these, ELLs have the opportunities to participate in an engaging learning environment and learn at higher levels. With technology, these students can control and self-direct their learning and get immediate feedback. They no longer depend on direct teacher instruction, which often limits the student to passive listening and watching the teacher.

While the direct teacher control is evidently lower in technology-based classrooms, the instruction is ever more demanding on the teacher. The teacher becomes a facilitator, rather than a "deliverer or transmitter of knowledge" (Padrón & Waxman, 1996, p. 348). Teachers scaffold their students' learning experiences to build high-quality instruction.

The following are some activities using technology that are intended to support learner knowledge construction:

1. Collaborating with others around the world
2. Utilizing educational applications of the internet
3. Creating multimedia projects (Hartley & Bendixen, 2001)

When students are engaged in activities like these, they are constructing their own knowledge with the teacher as the facilitator of the process. It is essential that teachers encourage students to be thoughtful and reflective about their technology use. It is also ideal if teachers who use technology extensively in the classroom infuse digital and media literacy throughout content and language based learning so that students apply critical thinking skills to digital media texts and textual interactions.

Incorporating technology effectively into a fully content- and skill-based curriculum requires a good understanding of lesson objectives and how those objectives can be met using the technology. While teachers should definitely consider technological integration as an important aspect of their work in any subject and at any grade level, teachers should not include technology simply for the sake of technology. The best approach, considering that all subjects can potentially be enhanced with technology, is for the teacher to consider a variety of lessons and units and decide which focus areas can be enhanced with technological tools.

It is important to remember that as with all other learning, technological learning must be developmentally appropriate. Concerns about excessive screen time and the importance of face-to-face interaction, especially with young students, are important factors to consider. Developing effective management and instructional strategies are essential components of successful technology use in the classroom.

Some examples of using technology to support English language learning include:

Blogging
Blogging can empower students as they express their ideas to a wider audience than just those in the classroom. They can practice different types of writing skills in different genres for different audiences and receive authentic feedback. In addition, many people use blogs to reflect on their experiences to others and this can be a good process for ELLs as they write about their learning experiences. They can also look back on previous writing to see the ways in which they have changed.

Videos
Videos can be good ways of engaging English language learners before a lesson or of explaining a more complicated concept. They are also great ways for students to demonstrate what they have learned; parameters for video assignments can be adapted for different subject-areas and performance outcomes. There are dozens of websites with videos for English language learning as well as websites with videos, commercials, etc. that ESOL teachers can use to build collaborative communication activities.

Online discussion forums
Online discussion forums can be created for any subject. Students can discuss problem-solving strategies, stories, art, or current events. Instructional activities can be real-world problem based. Students can be involved in collaborating on research and sharing what they have learned as they investigate solutions.

These are just a few of the examples of the ways in which technology can be used to enhance effective teaching and learning.

OBJECTIVE 5.0 CONCEPTS AND ISSUES RELATED TO ASSESSMENT

Skill 5.1 Different types of assessment (as well as indicators of their quality)

As a teacher of English Language Learners, it is important to advocate for the use of appropriate assessment tools for students. Commonly used norm-referenced tests are potentially problematic when being used with ELL students because of the bias inherent within them.

Norm-referenced tests seek to determine whether a test-taker performed better or worse than an 'average' student. The performance of the hypothetical 'average' student is determined by analyzing the performance on the test of a sampling of students of the same age and grade. In the development of the norm-referenced tests and the process of norming the tests themselves, test creators generally select their norm group from amongst the target population for the test. Because they are generally not from the intended population for the test, ELL students (and even sub-groups of American students) taking a norm-referenced test in the United States will often be at an inherent disadvantage.

For example, even an ELL student with strong English reading skills may have great difficulty answering a series of reading comprehension questions related to a passage dealing with the US government. The student may be, for example, unfamiliar with references to Congress or election campaigns that other students would take for granted. The unfamiliar terminology and context could make it impossible for the ELL student to answer questions correctly that would otherwise be at her/his reading level.

Criterion-referenced tests, in which students must demonstrate certain skills or knowledge, can also be problematic. As an example, a criterion-referenced test of students' math skills could provide inaccurate results when used with ELL students if the questions on the test involve extensive reading. The language skills needed to understand the question may make it difficult or impossible for an ELL student with outstanding math skills to solve a problem.

In these cases, the **validity and reliability** of the testing are undermined by the student's lack of contextual knowledge (in the case of the norm-referenced example) and language skill (in the case of the criterion-referenced example). Results would not reflect the student's reading comprehension or math level - the express purpose of the test. Validity refers to the most important characteristic of any test - do results on the test measure what they say they measure? When working with ELL students, validity takes on particular importance because the test used could produce valid results with native speakers but invalid results with their ELL peers.

Reliability refers to the reproducibility of results. A reliable test would be expected to produce similar results each time a student takes the test. In the example above, the student's score could be substantially different when taking the same test if the test uses a large bank of randomly generated questions. The student may score substantially higher if the s/he does not encounter questions for which s/he does not possess background knowledge. In this case, the test is not a reliable measure because the results could vary tremendously depending on which questions the student encounters.

Tests like the Peabody Picture Vocabulary test and the Woodcock-Muñoz Language Survey are examples of norm-referenced assessment tools. The Peabody test assesses a student's receptive vocabulary and potential scholastic aptitude but is not intended for students whose first language is not English. Because the images used in the test are representations of 'mainstream' culture, any student not from the dominant/majority cultural group may perform below his/her level because of cultural background - not ability.

Similarly, the Woodcock-Muñoz Language Survey is designed to be a measure of overall proficiency in reading, writing, speaking, and listening. However, it is normed for American students from Hispanic backgrounds. Therefore, it would be a useful assessment for some ELL students but not for others.

The most essential thing to remember about norm-referenced tests is their validity. As noted by Kim and Zabelina (2015), "[i]f the cultural or linguistic backgrounds of the individuals being tested are not adequately represented in the norming group, the validity and reliability of the test are questionable (Padilla and Borsato, 2008)."

Validity and reliability take on even greater importance if the purpose of testing is to determine placement in special programs, evaluation for potential learning disabilities, or planning for interventions. ESOL teachers play an invaluable role not only in testing but also in ensuring that appropriate tools are used. Translation of a norm-referenced test does not remove potential bias.

Validity and reliability are also considerations in graded classroom assignments and summative assessments (like tests, final projects, and end-of-unit assessments). If, for example, an ELL student has to produce a project presenting his/her findings on a science experiment and the teacher marks the student down for grammar and lexical errors, this can undermine the validity of the test. Again, a valid assessment measures what it is intended to measure. In this example, the project is supposed to determine the student's content-area knowledge - not his/her English writing proficiency. This does not mean that a teacher cannot include writing as part of the project assessment (especially since the involvement of all teachers in building language competency is valuable), but the writing component should be separate from the grade for content understanding. One way of addressing validity in this case would be to use a rubric for assessment, assigning a grade for content knowledge and another for writing.

Reliability can be affected by the subjectivity of the scoring, the construction of the assessment, and/or the way it is administered. In the previous example, the student who was marked down because of errors related to language development could demonstrate a high level of competency on a different type of assessment (such as a multiple-choice test) in which language production is not a factor. The objectivity of the assessment was compromised by the focus on correct language use rather than on content knowledge.

Similarly, if a graded assessment in a history class is an oral presentation, many ELL students would be at an inherent disadvantage because it may be very difficult to demonstrate mastery of the content in a presentation. The construction/administration of the assessment interfere with the intended purpose of the assignment.

At times, ESOL teachers play an important role in supporting and advising content-area specialists about assessment. They may have to advocate on behalf of their students to ensure that assessments are reliable and valid measures of what a student with limited English proficiency can do.

Within the classroom, formative, ongoing assessments play an important role in understanding student progress both in terms of language proficiency and content-area knowledge. These take many forms ranging from observation to checks for understanding and short quizzes. This type of assessment is important for both the teacher and student to mark progress and identify areas for further development.

(See 5.3 for more details on formative assessment.)

Performance-based assessment (or simply, performance assessment) is a useful tool in any classroom but is particularly well suited to the ESOL classroom. Performance assessments are considered more 'authentic' in that they require students to put knowledge and skills in action to complete a task. In contrast to a multiple-choice test, in performance assessments students combine different elements of what they have learned to create something original. Students process information, use skills, and often have to make critical decisions in order to do the task.

Varela, O'Malley and Valdez Pierce (1996) noted several key characteristics of performance assessment. These include:

- Responses are **constructed** using multiple resources;
- Prompts or tasks are **open-ended** and have no 'right answer';
- Tasks are **authentic** and often involve real world situations;
- Tasks **integrate** different language skills (speaking, reading, writing, etc.) and often different content-area skills;
- The **process and the final product** are assessed; and
- **Depth of mastery** is the goal rather than breadth.

A few examples of performance assessments include:

- Projects
- Demonstrations
- Oral interviews
- Constructed responses using evidence
- Portfolios

In the case of ELL students, all of these would be valuable ways of demonstrating and documenting language development.

Skill 5.2 Purposes of assessment and how to communicate assessment results to stakeholders

Assessment in ESOL programs, as in all elements of a school program, serves many purposes. Data from assessment is useful not only in determining student progress but also in determining effective instructional strategies. Making a plan is essential in order to truly use assessment data to help English language learners. The plan should include actions that both ELL students and ESOL teachers need to take, as well as outlining the formative and/or summative assessments that will be used to measure progress.

When ESOL teachers use consistent formative assessment, it keeps them focused on student progress and gives them the opportunity to plan appropriate instruction that meets students' needs. It also keeps parents, administrators, counselors and other colleagues informed as students develop their English language skills.

One of the most important functions of assessment is in determining student placement in an ESOL program.

Program Placement and Program Exit
In the case of students in the early stages of English language acquisition, placement in an English Language Development (ELD) program is often a simple choice. Students with very limited speaking and aural comprehension skills are easy to classify. For many students with more experience with English, however, that decision is not as straightforward. Some students have strong oral language skills but have not had sufficient time to develop literacy skills and CALPs.

A student in this situation might seem ready to handle the demands of the academic program without support. However, the student would find it difficult to maximize learning opportunities and would likely struggle academically. In this case assessment is essential to determine whether a student should be placed in a program that provides English language support. Without assessment to determine placement (and subsequent program support) the student in this example would likely not maximize his/her learning potential

In deciding to exit a student from programs designed to support language development, it is also essential to use proper assessments. A student may be succeeding academically even without full English language proficiency. This is not enough to exit a student since the ultimate goal of any ELD program is to ensure that all students have the greatest chance of maximizing their learning potential. An early exit could jeopardize that. Knowing and using your school/district/state's exit protocols is essential.

Determining Instruction
Assessment of all types can be used to adapt instruction to meet the needs of students. Standardized testing results can be used to pinpoint specific areas for growth in reading (e.g., vocabulary) or math (e.g., algebraic concepts). Teachers can use this information to target instruction for specific skills and concepts.

Within the classroom, formative assessments are excellent ways to check for student understanding of new skills and content. Instruction can be adapted to address specific students who may need additional support. Flexible groupings make it possible to target teaching to those who need it. When using data-driven assessment to identify student needs and help guide instruction, ESOL teachers would benefit from having applicable standards and progressions easily accessible. This information can help teachers decide whether to re-teach a lesson or a part of a lesson with the whole class, with groups of students and/or with specific students who have not yet met the standards.

Standards
In a standards-based environment, assessment procedures and tools are closely tied with adopted standards for both English language development and content-area knowledge and skills. This ongoing assessment helps determine whether students are making adequate progress towards grade-level standards. This information is generally the primary basis of reporting achievement in standards-based schools.

DISTINCTION BETWEEN ELL AND STUDENTS WITH DISABILITIES
One way to serve students with disabilities and the ELL student is to accurately assess their disability or limitation. Differentiating between ELLs with learning disabilities from those who are simply struggling with learning a second language can be problematic. Many of the problems associated with second language learning are also identified as learning difficulties: for example, should processing difficulties, behavioral differences, reading difficulties, and expressive difficulties (Lock & Layton, 2002) be associated with the difficulties of second language learning or with learning difficulties? While some learning difficulties can be partially identified by observation over a period of time or by the lack of academic improvement (Gersten & Baker, 2003), they are also often typical of ELLs struggling with the complexities of language and a new school environment.

Therefore, it is of critical importance to assess the student of concern using a variety of testing procedures. Chalfant & Psch (1981) recommend using a Teacher Assistance Team (TAT) consisting of regular classroom teachers who meet with the referring teacher to discuss problems, brainstorm possible solutions, and develop an action plan. After the plan has been implemented, the TAT and the referring teacher have a follow-up meeting to evaluate the results and to develop other recommendations if necessary. The TAT ultimately decides whether or not the student should be referred for a special education evaluation.

Suggestions concerning the testing procedure are:

- Tests that are not biased based on race or culture
- Tests conducted in both the student's primary language (not translated, but designed to assess speakers of the language) and English
- Identify student using observations from school, home, and community
- Alternative assessments combined with formal assessments
- Criterion-referenced assessments
- Curriculum-based assessments
- Portfolio of student's work

- Informal assessments: rubrics, dynamic assessment (test-teach-test), learning logs, self-evaluations
- Comparison of student's cultural teaching style (e.g., teacher centered) with the school's teaching style (e.g., student centered)

Communication of Assessment Data

(See also 6.4 and 6.5.)

Communication of assessment data is essential if it is to be useful. All stakeholders involved in a child's education need access to assessment data. Other teachers need to be aware of ELL students' language development in order to plan instruction and assessment to best meet the needs to all students. Administrators need accurate data as well in order to maintain and support programs. Finally, families have a legal right to be informed of their children's academic and language progress.

When teachers communicate clearly, consistently and meaningfully with parents and families, colleagues, administrators and English Language Learners themselves, the stakeholders are more likely to work together towards the common goal of helping learners achieve communication, academic and social/emotional success. Communicating about assessment methods and results is important, but so is communicating about instructional practice so that stakeholders understand the goals and the strategies for meeting goals. Stakeholders can then more effectively help develop student strengths and meet student needs. See also 6.4 and 6.5 for specific approaches to sharing information and building stakeholder involvement.

Skill 5.3   Importance of regular, aligned assessments and use to inform and refine instruction

(See also 5.2.)

Assessment is the gathering of information in order to make decisions. In education, assessment has often focused reporting on student performance, progress, and behavior. Rather than simply reporting this information as a grade or other measure of performance, this data has tremendous potential to make teaching more effective.

Teachers should know, understand and work towards the achievement of district, state and national learning standards for ELLs. Learning standards for English language development are required by the Every Student Succeeds Act (ESSA) signed into law in 2015. In addition, some school districts may have additional learning standards. ESOL teachers need to incorporate district, state and national standards into instruction and assessment practices in order to support English Language Learners in becoming proficient in English and academically successful.

When working with English Language Learners, some teachers make the mistake of focusing exclusively on language development or focusing only on content-area comprehension. To maximize student learning, fluency and achievement, ESOL teachers need to align goals for learners so that as their English language proficiency develops, so does their content-area learning and output. By using data-driven inquiry, formative assessment and by getting to know each learner, teachers can personalize teaching and learning so that students can meet content and language goals in multiple ways.

Assessment data can also be used to:

- Help in the selection of appropriate learning materials;
- Set goals with individual students;
- Decide what skills need re-teaching;
- Create and utilize language proficiency profiles for each student;
- Create meaningful, language-rich, and safe environments for English; language learners that provide them with differentiated language practice and use. This means providing ample time for students to practice who need more and appropriate challenges for students who need less. That way all students are working to their potential and no students 'finish' before others;
- Use instructional supports and scaffolds; and
- Communicate and plan with other teachers in order get to know students' strengths and challenges outside of your classroom. This can help in planning personalized learning opportunities inside it.

Making these types of decisions is easiest when the teacher has multiple sources of information or data points. Standardized tests, summative classroom assessments, and formative assessments together provide ESOL teachers with insights about student needs and development.

Skill 5.4 How to interpret standardized assessments results for English language learners

(See also 5.1.)

When interpreting standardized assessment results, it is particularly important in the case of ELL students to consider issues of validity and reliability. As noted previously, standardized tests that are norm-referenced may not provide accurate information on the knowledge or skills of language learners. This is because the norm group that performance is compared against likely does not reflect the linguistic or cultural background of the ELL students.

Criterion-referenced tests, meanwhile, measure student performance against a series of already defined criteria, most often a set of learning standards. These criteria can be related to skills (e.g., solve algebra problems) or knowledge (e.g., grade level vocabulary). Whereas norm-referenced tests rank students, criterion-referenced tests describe whether a student has/has not met certain criteria (e.g., is on grade level, can pass to the next level).

Results on a norm-referenced test almost always form part of a bell curve with a small group of students at the high and low ends of the bell curve and a large group in the middle (or average). These scores are commonly reported as a percentile representing where the student is ranked in comparison to others. A score in the 50th percentile, for example, would place the student in the center of the bell curve.

With criterion-referenced results, all students could theoretically 'pass' a test by achieving a certain score based on their number of correct answers.

Issues of **validity and reliability** (see 5.1) are essential in interpreting standardized test results for ELL students. Students may still need to take such tests because of district or state requirements, but the results must be interpreted with an understanding of potential problems with the resulting data. ESOL teachers play a key role in advocating for appropriate interpretation of such data.

TEACHER CERTIFICATION STUDY GUIDE

OBJECTIVE 6.0   IMPACT OF NATIONAL LAWS AND POLICIES ON ESOL INSTRUCTION; PROFESSIONAL DEVELOPMENT AND SCHOOL/COMMUNITY PARTNERSHIPS

Skill 6.1   Understand legal decisions and legislation on ESOL programs

Teachers should know and understand legislation and case law on ESOL programs as they work towards the achievement of standards for English language learners and English language learners with disabilities.

Case law and legislation regarding bilingual education, minority language rights and testing requirements have an impact on ESOL education and English language learners. The impact is most significant in the areas of educational rights and English language teaching accountability on the part of states, districts and schools.

Case Law and Legal Decisions

Meyers vs. Nebraska (1923) This case gave schools the right to provide heritage language (or foreign language, as it was called in the law) instruction on school premises. It was based on a case in which German community members were teaching Bible studies in German after school but in the school building. Nebraska tried to pass a law that would prohibit any school from allowing foreign language instruction until after 8th Grade. This law was ruled unconstitutional on the grounds that the 14th Amendment prohibited discrimination against language minorities. Schools were not required to provide foreign language instruction but if they wanted to offer it on the premises, separate from the regular school day and regular classes, they could.

Title VI of the Civil Rights Act of 1964 established that schools, as recipients of federal funds, cannot discriminate against ELLs: "No person in the United States shall, on the grounds of race, color, or national origin, be excluded from participation in, be denied the benefits of, or be subjected to discrimination under any program or activity receiving Federal financial assistance."

In 1968, congress passed the **Bilingual Education Act,** which provided funding (in the form of grants) for school districts to implement programs for ELLs to "participate" in academic activities. Schools were not required to provide bilingual education, but if they wanted to, they could receive a grant to buy resources, train teachers and create opportunities to involve parents in the process.

Lau v. Nichols (1974): A 1969 class action suit filed on behalf of the Chinese community in San Francisco alleged that the school district denied "equal educational opportunity" to their children because the classes the children were required to attend were not taught in the Chinese native language. The Supreme Court ruled in favor of the plaintiffs, and determined a set of requirements that academic programs must provide, called the Lau Remedies, which applied to all school districts. The essence of these requirements is that school districts need to be able to identify and evaluate national-origin-minority students' English skills, provide them with appropriate instruction, decide when to mainstream them and determine the professional standards of the teachers who work with them. These remedies later became federal law as part of the Equal Opportunities education act of 1974.

The Bilingual Education Act was amended 4 times after 1974 (1978, 1984, 1988 and 1994) to provide more funding, more autonomy for school districts, and to make programs more systematic.

In **Castaneda v. Pickard** (filed in 1978 but not settled until 1981), a federal court established three specific criteria schools must use to determine the effectiveness of bilingual education programs:

- A program for English language learners must be based on pedagogically sound educational theory that is recognized by experts in the field.
- The program must be implemented effectively with resources provided for personnel, instructional materials, and space.
- The program must produce results that indicate the language barrier is being overcome.

In the past 40 years there have been many rulings and laws that both supported and eroded support for bilingual education.

In 2002, with the introduction of No Child Left Behind, the Bilingual Education Act became the English Language Acquisition, Language Enhancement, and Academic Achievement Act.

Standardized Testing, Accountability and Legislation
In December 2015, the Every Student Succeeds Act (ESSA) was signed into law, replacing No Child Left Behind. The ESSA is a reauthorization of the Elementary and Secondary Education Act of 1965. The ESSA made some changes to the testing data required for ELL students and left the number of tests intact (including the National Assessment of Educational Progress, English language proficiency tests and required state states in content areas). The National Assessment of Educational Progress (NAEP) keeps an ongoing record of school performance and while in general participation is voluntary, all schools that receive Title I money must participate. This includes low socioeconomic and minority students, which includes a large percentage of ELLs.

Rather than requiring that all results for students learning English be included in a school's cumulative data, the ESSA allows schools to develop a plan for phasing in the inclusion of their results. Further, ESSA requires schools to report in great detail on the progress of ELL students. They must:

- Report on the number of ELLs meeting academic standards (even for four years after exiting any learning programs in place for ELL students);
- Determine their own policies and procedures for entering and exiting language programs;
- Assess English language learners within 30 days of enrollment; and
- In addition, English language proficiency must be a factor in determining school ratings.

Skill 6.2 Strategies for pursuing professional goals and growth opportunities

Most ESOL instructors know that what is considered good teaching practice has evolved over the years as understanding of language acquisition and attitudes towards bilingualism have changed. It is important to stay informed about current research-based teaching practice in order to provide the best possible learning opportunities for students. The term research-based refers to ideas and practices that have been systematically tested through experimentation or observation. Furthermore, the observed outcomes have been analyzed and often subjected to further testing with results published in peer-reviewed journals.

As new information emerges in the fields of linguistics and language teaching, successful ESOL teachers are able to adapt and improve their teaching practice. Professional journals like TESOL and TESL-EJ explore and explain issues and ideas in English language teaching. Results are published for additional review and provide teachers with insight into effective teaching methodology. In addition, online communities allow teachers to share information and ideas about innovative teaching practices that best support ELL students.

Participating in professional development activities, both formal and informal, can be important ways to improve teaching practice. Conferences (online and in-person) offer opportunities to share resources and to find out about current research into effective ESOL pedagogy. Membership in professional organizations usually provides opportunities to find out about conferences and to receive regular updates about research.

In addition to taking advantage of professional development opportunities, effective ESOL instructors foster and develop metacognitive strategies in their students and apply these strategies to their own teaching practice. When ESOL teachers reflect on how they are teaching, they can be more effective teachers. Part of being a metacognitive teacher is taking time to reflect on teaching experiences and making a conscious plan to improve elements of teaching practice - e.g., what is the best way for me to teach this particular standard/content or language skill to this particular group of learners at this particular time?

Being a metacognitive ESOL teacher means being a more effective teacher because it entails making personalized and 'just in time' adaptations to teaching plans. Reflective teachers are better able to make decisions to improve student learning because they are more aware of the many decisions they make that affect instruction and learning.

Reflective educators who examine their impact on colleagues and students are more likely to hone their teaching practice and make progress towards meeting their own professional growth goals. This, in turn, has an impact on student progress and the overall professional environment in which English language learning takes place. Moreover, metacognitive ESOL teachers are able to set more appropriate goals for professional development to refine teaching practice.

Skill 6.3 Collaborating with colleagues

It is important, particularly when second language learners have multiple teachers, such as in middle or high school, that teachers communicate and collaborate in order to provide a greater level of consistency. It is particularly difficult for second language learners to go from one class to the next, where there are different sets of expectations and varied methods of instruction, and still focus on the more complex elements of learning language.

When students have higher levels of anxiety due to the learning of a second language, they will be less likely to focus on the language; rather, they will be focusing on whatever is creating their anxiety. When teachers reinforce common expectations and understand each other's differing expectations, they are better able to lessen this anxiety and smooth the transition between classes.

Another important reason for teachers to collaborate, particularly with the ESOL specialists, is to ensure that students are showing consistent development across classes. Where there is inconsistency, teachers should work to uncover what it is that is keeping the student from excelling in a particular class. In a cooperative teaching environment, the ESOL teacher might work with the classroom or subject-area teacher to develop curriculum and instructional strategies that best meet the needs of all students. Collaborative or partnership teaching "builds on the concept of cooperative teaching by linking the work of two teachers, or indeed a whole department/year team or other partners, with plans for curriculum development and staff development across the school" (Bourne, 1997: 83).

There are a number of essential elements for effective collaboration between language and content-area teachers (see, for example, Davison, 1992; Hurst and Davison, 2005). These elements include: the need to establish a clear conceptualization of the task; the incorporation of explicit goals for ESL development into curriculum and assessment planning processes; the negotiation of a shared understanding of ESL and mainstream teachers' roles/responsibilities; the adoption of common curriculum planning policies and processes; experimentation with diversity as a resource to promote effective learning for all students; the development of articulated and flexible pathways for ESL learning support; and the establishment of systematic mechanisms for monitoring, evaluation and feedback (Davison,, 2001).

Extensive cooperation between ESOL specialists and classroom teachers enables the sharing of information about student strengths and weaknesses. This facilitates opportunities for improving instruction as well as better communication with students and their families.

Skill 6.4 Serving as an ESOL resource in the community

(See also 5.2.)

ESOL teachers play an important role in creating an environment in which all stakeholders (students, families, teachers, and administrators) work together to support the learning of ELL students. Especially when communication is difficult because of language barriers, the commitment of the ELL teacher to bridging the gap can make a significant impact in bringing all stakeholders together to work towards supporting the academic, linguistic, and social/emotional development of the student.

By modeling effective teaching practices and sharing resources both with colleagues and families, the ESOL teacher can help to maximize the learning opportunities available to all students. Support to classroom or content-area specialists can be invaluable in helping them to foster a supportive learning environment and in establishing a strong relationship to their students with limited English proficiency.

Skill 6.5   Understand role of family and community in ELL development

The ESOL teacher plays a key role in ensuring that students' families are involved in the educational program. An essential component of this is the facilitation of communication between students, families, and all teachers. Language barriers may prevent families' (and students') full participation in the learning community.

Often in schools, parents, grandparents, and other people involved in children's lives, want to take a more active role in the educational process. It is important to provide opportunities for stakeholders to come into the school and participate in activities designed to encourage their participation in the schooling of their children. During these programs, it is important to share information about the methodologies and strategies being implemented to support students. In this way, the public can begin to understand the methodology and programs used in ESOL instruction.

Parents who understand how their children are progressing and the different elements of the academic program are better able to support their learning. Similarly content-area teachers often benefit from the information provided by ESOL teachers about students' English language development. This information provides an invaluable context for understanding the simultaneous elements of an ELL student's route towards academic success - language and content learning.

Parents should be provided with ongoing information about their child's language progress and development including the opportunity to attend a meeting with teachers and/or other school staff. Communicating about assessment methods and results is important, but so is communicating about instructional practice so that stakeholders understand the goals and the strategies for meeting goals. Stakeholders can then more effectively help develop student strengths and meet student needs.

Some strategies for educating parents and family members include:

- Open house style events
- Parent workshops on various topics
- Newsletter pieces or paragraphs
- Individual parent meetings
- Inviting parents to observe lessons

- Information shared during social times where parents are invited into the school

Communicating general information about English and appropriate English language instruction is important. It is just as important to share specific information about students with parents, other school personnel, and the community. Once the teacher has gathered sufficient information on the students, s/he must find appropriate methods to share this information with those who need the data. Again, depending on the audience, the amount and type of information shared may vary. Some ways to share information with parents/guardians include:

- Individual parent meetings
- Small group meetings
- Regular parent updates through phone calls, email, or other messaging tools
- Charts and graphs of progress sent home
- Class blogs or portals on learning management systems

ESOL teachers can also encourage students and their families to make full use of public resources such as the local public library, including its online resources. This will help families expand their own knowledge and understanding of additional resources and programs available to them. Teachers can encourage students and families to visit museums (which often have educational outreach programs), parks and the local YMCA and YWCA (or similar organizations). Museums, parks and community centers can be supportive spaces for ELLs and their families in addition to providing them with recreational and educational opportunities.

The same cultural, environmental, social and psychological factors that may affect a student's English language development are relevant in effective communication between the teacher, the student, and the student's family. For example, based on their own cultural experience, some parents may be reluctant to ask teachers questions if they perceive the teacher as an authority figure who should not be questioned. Others may not attend meetings with the teacher or school events if they find these situations to be intimidating because of their own limited English skills. In neither case is parents' lack of communication due to a lack of interest in their children's educational progress.

Since effective communication between the school and the home is an important factor in students' academic success, recognition of these factors is an important part of finding ways to communicate with all stakeholders in a child's education. Anticipating questions and creating a FAQ (frequently asked questions) to share with parents may help get conversations started. Similarly encouraging parents to send in questions before meetings (to avoid having to ask them directly) can also break the ice. Use of home language when possible to reach out to parents can help draw parents into the school community. Encouraging groups of parents to reach out to others in their home language is another way to connect the institution and ELL students' homes.

DOMAIN 3	INSTRUCTION AND ASSESSMENT OF ENGLISH LANGUAGE LEARNERS
OBJECTIVE 7	RESEARCH BASED PRACTICES IN ESOL INSTRUCTION

Skill 7.1 Creating, organizing and managing a student-centered learning community

To meet the varied needs of ELL students, differentiating instruction becomes extremely important. With differentiated instruction, the teacher seeks to develop learning opportunities that allow students with diverse needs, abilities, and learning styles to access essential learning. This may involve creating extra opportunities for practice, re-teaching, planning multiple activities, and overall flexibility in the ways in which the teacher approaches each student's needs.

It is important to note that differentiation is not the same as individualized instruction. "Every student is not learning something different; they are all learning the same thing, but in different ways. And every student does not need to be taught individually; differentiating instruction is a matter of presenting the same task in different ways and at different levels, so that all students can approach it in their own ways" (Irujo, 2004).

Students may vary in their cultural background, language, interests, learning styles/preferences, prior experiences, and learning readiness. Differentiated instruction is responsive to these differences. Important characteristics of this approach include:

- Ongoing assessment of student needs;
- Flexible grouping;
- Meaningful, authentic activities whenever possible;
- Flexibility in the learning environment; and
- Flexibility in learning activities and in the ways in which students demonstrate their learning.

This approach to instruction has the benefit of responding to students' individual needs, increasing student opportunities to perform, and developing students' personal sense of relevance and achievement. Furthermore, it leads to fewer teacher-dominated activities. Students work individually, in pairs, or in small groups on tasks and projects that cater to their different ability levels and learning styles. A number of activities can be used to help ELLs in language acquisition.

Teachers can also make use of multiple intelligence approaches to teaching the same lesson. ELLs can benefit from a variety of instructional methods that cater to their different learning preferences or styles. For example, some English language learners will benefit from the opportunity to learn through hands-on activities. During such activities, students learn while discussing, investigating, creating, and discovering with other students. In time, students gain background knowledge regarding the subject they are learning and start making their own decisions, leading to less teacher support and more student-centered interactions. (Cooperstein & Kocevar-Weidinger, 2004).

Needs Analysis
A necessary first step in planning is to conduct needs analyses that identifies the proficiency level and language needs of the students involved. This helps when modifying and adjusting instruction so it will be more conducive to learning. Furthermore, attention should be given to the methodology used in class to cover the course materials. With respect to proficiency level, beginning level students require practice of material in controlled situations moving to more free expression activities. Relatively advanced learners may need to polish or refine already developed skills and can be encouraged to involve themselves in less structured activities on their own.

Prior Knowledge, Language Literacies and Cognition/Metacognition
Moll (1988) discusses the value of the funds of knowledge that students bring to the classroom. These funds of knowledge are student's prior knowledge that can inform their acquisition of English. This knowledge regarding students' lives can be incorporated into lessons and content for course work. It also helps in choosing topics that would be of interest to the students and in engaging them in the learning process. For example, a teacher can plan a unit in which students pick an area of the city they want to learn more about. Students research their selected topics and then prepare reports or projects. Parents and family members can help students and become part of this research. Graves (1998) observes that teachers who seem to know each of their students and take an active interest in them are most successful. Teachers should also be in contact with the parents and involve them in their children's learning.

Literacy development is affected not only by the individual student's educational background but also by the linguistic background of their families. With respect to individual ESOL students, it is paramount to note that some adolescent ELLs may need to learn to read for the first time, while others are building second or third language literacy with already developed first language literacy (Peregoy & Boyle, 2000).

Literacy requires a number of cognitive and metacognitive skills that students can transfer from their first language to their second or third language. In addition to this, students literate in their first language have more funds of knowledge or prior knowledge to comprehend the content of the text. The educational background of the ELLs gives them the advantage of transferring their first language literacy skills to their second language and using their prior literacy knowledge to understand new information. With respect to writing, research has shown that students who lacked first language literacy strategies displayed a similar lack of strategies for writing in their second language.

Mohan and Lo (1985) suggest that students who have not developed good strategies in their first language will not have developed strategies to transfer to their second language. Conversely, transfer of knowledge from L1 literacy helps students build literacy in their new language.

Chamot and O'Malley (1994) stated that teachers need to be aware of their students' approaches to learning and plan ways to expand the students' repertoire of learning strategies. According to Arreaga-Mayer (1998), language-sensitive content instruction based on effective and efficient learning strategies must (a) be effective for culturally and linguistically heterogeneous learning groups; (b) lead to high levels of student and student-student active engagement in learning; (c) foster higher-order cognitive processes; (d) enable students to engage in extended discourse in English; (e) be feasible to implement on a small-group or class-wide basis; (f) be socially acceptable to teachers, students, and parents; and (g) be responsive to cultural and personal diversity.

ESOL instruction is more engaging, meaningful and effective when it is based on knowledge of English language learners' strengths, needs, interests and experiences.

The first step in personalizing instruction is for ESOL teachers to assess English language learners' proficiency in literacy and oracy. In addition, teachers might also take into account a learner's:

- Age and grade level
- Level of home language proficiency
- Social-emotional well being
- Comfort levels with group work and independent work
- Proficiency and comfort level with the four core skills (reading, writing, listening, and speaking)

After analyzing assessment data, teachers can make action plans for individuals and groups of students. Aspects of instruction that can be personalized include:

- Teaching tools and resources (including technology and media)
- Production tasks
- Revising communicative, academic literacy and content-based goals

An important part of any personalized action plan for students, particularly for students who are not meeting language literacy or content-area goals, is for the ESOL teacher to communicate with families and with the students themselves about learning or performance gaps and about the strategies teachers are going to use to support ELLs development.

The WIDA English Language Development Standards cover some research-based essential actions strategies for effective instruction with ELLs.

A few are adapted below:

- Create and utilize language proficiency profiles for each student.
- Design language teaching and learning with attention to the sociocultural context.
- Create meaningful, language-rich, and safe environments for English Language Learners that provide them with differentiated language practice

and use. This means providing ample time for students to practice who need more and appropriate challenges for students who need less. That way all students are working to their potential and no students 'finish' before others.
- Use instructional supports and scaffolds.
- Communicate and plan with other teachers in order get to know students' strengths and challenges outside of your classroom. This can help in planning personalized learning opportunities inside it.

Finally, when students are encouraged to be metacognitive learners, their ability to take responsibility for and personalize their own learning increases. This results in students becoming more active learners and has a positive effect on English language and content-area learning.

Skill 7.2   Apply research-based practices that promote English language development (e.g., comprehensible input, regular feedback and integration of skills)

ASCD recently published the results of a survey of 32 exemplary/effective ESL programs and identified several practices that had a positive impact on ELL students' language and academic proficiency. Applying the following practices can help the ESOL teacher improve learning in the classroom and out.

The inclusion of student-directed activities (see 7.1)

Activities that focus on helping ELLs understand and not just memorize.
To help students understand, tasks and topics have more success when they are engaging and to some extent related to student interests, goals or 'want to know". Teachers should try to choose engaging and authentic topics and tasks for study. ESOL teachers can then structure consistent routines, reviews of materials, and explicit teaching of tasks and skills (see below). In addition, by using metacognitive strategies (See 2.5) students are more likely to learn, understand, and remember what they are learning.

Student understanding of new concepts may be enhanced through instruction that uses routines, embeds redundancy in lessons, provides explicit discussion of vocabulary and structure, and teaches students metacognitive skills (August & Hakuta, 1997). Although not specific to reading instruction, these practices can be used in the teaching of reading.

Plenty of opportunity for guided and independent practice
In many ESOL models, especially the Communicative Language Teaching (CLT) model, the lesson moves from presentation (teacher-directed), to practice (guided and independent) to production (performance task). The opportunity to practice new skills and new vocabulary is an essential part of helping ELLs achieve proficiency. Ideally there is enough time in the lesson for students to do some guided practice with others, as a whole class, or in small groups. This can be followed by independent practice so that they can try to apply what they have learned. When it is time for production, learners will feel more confident, have a bigger knowledge base and be more likely to take risks with their learning.

Aligned, consistent, formative and summative student assessment (see 5.1, 5.2, and 5.3)

Integration of core skills (reading, writing, listening, speaking)
Though there are times in which it may be necessary to teach specific skills in isolation (e.g., when a student continues to struggle with a particular grammatical structure in his/her writing), in general it is far better to approach language acquisition holistically by integrating reading, writing, speaking, and listening. This approach encourages more natural interactions with language and exposes ELLs to authentic language. Chamot and O'Malley (1994) demonstrate that content and language learning can be integrated with their Cognitive Academic Language Learning Approach (CALLA).

The integrated approach offers many benefits: it is often more engaging for students, offers opportunities for ELLs to communicate with their peers, and shows English as a 'living' language (as opposed to learning skills in isolation). It also allows teachers to evaluate student progress towards content and language standards. Integration of skills is beneficial for all English language learners, regardless of their proficiency level (Genesee et. al., 2006).

The integration of the four skills provides an effective context for writing so that the use of one leads naturally to the use of another, as in real life. In this way, the learners will see how writing relates to certain communicative needs just as the other skills do. For example, students need to participate in classroom conversations by articulating their opinions, sharing their observations, making comparisons, etc., through speaking and writing. They need to listen to the topic, take notes, discuss with their classmates, and read about the topic, which requires the integration of all four skills.

English language learners also need to engage in real-life communicative situations, so classroom activities should be organized in a way to make them use all four skills. Students should not only speak with the teacher but also with other students. As an example, students can listen to peers and try to comprehend what each speaker is saying. The listener can then react by writing down for a reader her/his version of the information s/he has just heard. This sequence of activities helps students connect listening, speaking, reading, and writing. There is thus very little opportunity for the student to 'translate' his/her idea from his/her native language into English. Instead, the students will be relying more on their knowledge of English.

An example of integrating skills for a writing assignment is to use the following Prewriting techniques. Prewriting techniques can give students opportunities to use reading, writing, listening and speaking to help them explore and get started with their ideas on a given topic or to develop a topic for a writing activity based on communicative classroom activities.

Brainstorming

- Brainstorming allows students to work together in the classroom in small groups and say as much as they can about a topic. This process helps them generate ideas to use for their individual brainstorming on paper. This activity involves the use of both speaking and listening skills to produce effective writing.

Guided Discussion

- Another way to get students to talk about a topic or to focus on specific aspects of a topic is to provide guidelines for group or whole class discussion. This technique has the advantage of helping the students beforehand with the vocabulary and sentence forms that they might need in their discussion, making use of all the four skills to guide students in their writing process.

Other activities that can incorporate combinations of the four skills students include:

- Interviews
- Creating movies, podcasts, posters
- Skits
- Dictation
- Note-taking
- Storytelling

Task-based instruction, another model for integrating the four communicative skills of language arts, involves increasingly complex learning tasks that require students to use language in authentic cooperative tasks such as projects, plays, or writing. These cooperative tasks simultaneously reinforce and build on ELLs' language skills. For example, in creating a book talk with a partner, students read, speak with partners, write a script, speak and listen.

The explicit teaching of task-specific skills

Teaching ELLs how to complete a task includes helping them set goals, modeling how to complete the task and providing informative feedback. These steps can help students move from more dependent to greater independence in academic tasks. By teaching explicitly, teachers not only help ELLs learn how to do the tasks but also how to talk about them using academic language. For example, for reading tasks, explicit instruction in decoding, vocabulary and comprehension strategies can help ELLs make significant progress in all four-skill areas. An additional aspect of explicit skill teaching is for ESOL teachers to show students connections and relationships between ideas so that they are better able to understand and apply what they have learned.

Cognitive skills and learning strategies (**see 7.3**) are also part of task-specific skills that students would do before during and after a task.

For comprehensible input (See 2.1)

A combination of the above practices with comprehensible input (language just beyond the comfort level of ELL students) will be the most effective ways for ESOL teachers to apply research-based practices to improving the proficiency, content-area knowledge, skills and confidence of English language learners.

Skill 7.3 Strategies for exceptional students

It is important for ESOL teachers to understand that English language proficiency can be both independent from and interrelated to students' cognitive and academic levels. Some English language learners are intellectually gifted, some may have learning disabilities, and some may have both. Just like native English speaking students, ELLs may have multiple exceptionalities.

English language learners, who have had their education interrupted face the dual challenge of learning grade-level content and learning the basic tenets that support grade-level content. For ELLs, the challenge is daunting as they must also learn English at the same time.

Cognitive strategies/processes
Cognitive processes are used by the learner to organize and direct second language acquisition. Examples of these processes are: problem-solving, method of approaching the learning of new information, and choices regarding what to ignore and what to notice (Díaz-Rico, Weed, 1995). Developing these skills leads to language acquisition, but these skills also bridge languages and serve to enhance cognition in the first language.

Memorization of the words and rules of a second language is insufficient to integrate the second language into the learner's thought patterns. L2 learners use cognitive processes to form rules, which allow them to understand and create novel utterances. The creation of novel utterances, whether grammatically correct or not, offers proof that the L2 learner is not simply mimicking chunks of prescribed language, but rather is using cognitive processes to acquire the second language. People use their own thinking processes, or cognition, to discover the rules of the language they are acquiring.

Planning what actions to take when confronted with an academic (or social) challenge demonstrates understanding of the problem and the ability to confront it. By engaging the cognitive skills, the student can plan where and how to search for information, how to organize it and how to present the information for review.

Organizational skills may show differences in different cultural contexts. Teachers cannot assume their students know these skills. Even the most basic organizational skill concepts must be reviewed or fully taught if necessary. For explicit Teaching of Skills (see 7.2).

Teaching specific learning skills and strategies can support ELL students in learning the language structures necessary to both understand and express learning in different disciplines while also helping them to master and integrate new content-area knowledge. For students with limited or interrupted formal school experiences, these can be essential tools.

Strategies to consider include explicit teaching of skills in the following areas:

- Note-taking - Students need to learn to synthesize large chunks of information presented orally or in writing in order to remember and apply essential ideas.

Note-taking strategies vary tremendously, and different students will respond better to different methods.
- Research - All students will need to do research in different subject areas. This is a challenging process that includes searching for information, selecting what is relevant, synthesizing it into usable 'chunks', and integrating it into writing or projects. Students need methods for finding, saving, and annotating. Some students will find this easiest with traditional paper/pen and a notebook while others will benefit from digital tools (like Evernote or Diigo) that allow them to save sources and then annotate them. Research is a cross-disciplinary skill that should be used in multiple classes, but the ESOL teacher will play a special role in supporting ELL students.
- Studying - Students may need to practice reviewing for a test or preparing for an assessment. Teachers can assist students with creating flashcards (digital or paper) or learning ways of review (quizzing oneself/a partner, reviewing notes, etc.).
- Test-taking - Particularly in an era of high stakes testing, students may need guidance on how to pace themselves during assessments, when to skip items for later review, how to create an outline, or simply following procedural directions.
- Building vocabulary - For ELL students in particular, content area vocabulary can pose a challenge. Students may need support in learning how to categorize words, how to use new terms in context, or even the importance of looking up unfamiliar words to determine meaning.
- Comprehension - Inference is an important part of reading comprehension. For students learning English, extra time is often needed to develop skills for recognizing implied meaning.

Differentiating Instruction
To meet the varied needs of ELL students, differentiating instruction becomes extremely important. With differentiated instruction, the teacher should seek to develop learning opportunities that allow students with diverse needs, abilities, and learning styles to access essential learning. This may involve creating extra opportunities for practice, re-teaching, planning multiple activities, and overall flexibility in the ways in which the teacher approaches each student's needs.

It is important to note that differentiation is not the same as individualized instruction. "Every student is not learning something different; they are all learning the same thing, but in different ways. And every student does not need to be taught individually; differentiating instruction is a matter of presenting the same task in different ways and at different levels, so that all students can approach it in their own ways" (Irujo, 2004).

Students may vary in their cultural background, language, interests, learning styles/preferences, prior experiences, and learning readiness. Differentiated instruction is responsive to these differences. Important characteristics of this approach include:

- Ongoing assessment of student needs;
- Flexible grouping;
- Meaningful, authentic activities whenever possible;

- Flexibility in the learning environment; and
- Flexibility in learning activities and in the ways in which students demonstrate their learning.

This approach to instruction has the benefit of catering to students' individual needs, increasing student opportunities to perform, and developing students' personal sense of relevance and achievement. Furthermore, it leads to fewer teacher-dominated activities. Students work individually, in pairs, or in small groups on tasks and projects that cater to their different ability levels and learning styles.

ELLs can benefit from a variety of instructional methods that cater to their different learning preferences. For example, some English language learners will benefit from the opportunity to learn through hands-on activities. During such activities, students learn while discussing, investigating, creating, and discovering with other students. In time, students gain background knowledge regarding the subject they are learning and start making their own decisions, leading to less teacher support and more student-centered interactions. (Cooperstein & Kocevar-Weidinger, 2004).

ELLs with exceptionalities
Students may arrive at a new school with special education needs undiagnosed or with families not sharing previous academic or cognitive data with the school. ESOL teachers, together with parents and other school staff, should endeavor to assess and support ELLs who they think may need additional learning supports.

To identify ELLs with exceptionalities, school personnel should try to get the whole picture of the student, which can include assessments in aptitude and ability, achievement in subject areas, recommendations from parents, teachers and students, portfolios, how quickly the ELL is progressing in English language acquisition, and student persistence and interests. The sooner ELLs with exceptionalities are identified, the more likely it will be that students will succeed because the school can provide differentiated and more effective teaching strategies for the learner(s).

It is essential that teachers and other school staff are careful not to misdiagnose students who are struggling with English as students who are learning disabled. When testing English language learners for placement in specialized classes, you must be certain that the tests used are both reliable and valid (**see also 5.1**). Reliability can be established using multiple assessment measures, objective tests, multiple raters, and clearly specified scoring criteria (Valdez-Pierce, 2003). For a test to be valid, it must first be reliable (Goh, 2004).

ESOL teachers should communicate with other colleagues and school staff about students' progress in different classrooms and school settings. This will help provide ELLs of all cognitive and academic levels with the best opportunities for English language proficiency and content/subject area knowledge and skill achievement.

Student-centered classrooms that use assessment to drive and modify instruction will be better able to work with gifted ELLs to set new learning goals and to push them to achieve at highest possible level.

Learning disabilities refer to physical, emotional, cognitive, or social components that severely limit what is considered to be "normal" functioning behavior. Children who fall into this category can be one or more of the following: emotionally challenged; hearing, vision, or speech impaired; or intellectually challenged. One similarity between second language development and learning disabilities is comprehensive diagnostic testing before placement.

The ESOL specialist bears a large responsibility for ensuring that ELLs are assessed fairly and accurately. For the long term educational and emotional well-being of ELL students, the ESOL educator may have to advocate for adequate testing, observation, and opportunities to make sure that students acquiring English are not improperly designated as having a disability.

Topics to investigate in determining whether an ELL student has a learning disability include:

- History of language delay in his/her native language;
- Difficulty in developing literacy skill in his/her native language;
- A family history of reading difficulties;
- Specific language weakness in his/her first language; and
- Relatively little progress relative to ELL peers after participating in reading interventions designed for ELL students.

In the education of students with exceptionalities, assessment is used to make decisions about the following:

- Screening and initial identification of children who may need services
- Diagnosis of specific learning disabilities
- Selection and evaluation of teaching strategies and programs
- Determination of the child's present level of performance in academics
- Classification and program placement
- Development of goals, objectives, and evaluation for the IEP
- Eligibility for a program
- Continuation of a program
- Effectiveness of instructional programs and strategies
- Effectiveness of behavioral interventions
- Accommodations needed for mandated or classroom testing (See 6.1 for information on laws regarding accommodation).

Skill 7.4   Vocabulary instruction

Research continues to highlight the role that vocabulary development plays in English language literacy and subject-based learning. ESOL teachers can use evidence-based methods to guide them in vocabulary instruction such as:

- Teaching vocabulary every day in all parts of the curriculum in all four of the learning modalities (reading, writing, listening, speaking);
- Ensuring that words studied are meaningful to students;
- Providing plenty of time after introducing words for review, practice and use;

- Identifying words within reading programs that need more intensive instruction for English Language Learners;
- Working with other teachers at grade level or subject area when designing important vocabulary lessons and/or reading about evidence-based approaches to vocabulary instruction;
- Ensuring that reading vocabulary lists emphasize important words and not just decoding;
- Working to create some word lists that are common to many subjects, and if not, making word lists available to subject-area teachers to help students practice;
- Striving to teach short and intensive word lists that are meaningful, rather than longer lists that cannot be truly learned (this can be per week or per day); and
- Teaching conversational/social words as well as academic. English language learners need both.

Research has shown that the same 1000 words (approximately) make up 84 percent of the words used in conversation and 74 percent of the words in academic texts (*The Nation*, 2001). The second most frequently used 1000 words increases the percentages to 90 percent of the words used in conversation and 78 percent used in academic texts. The ELL needs to understand 95 percent to achieve comprehension of higher-level academic texts. ELLs need to acquire the 2000 most used words and work on academic content words at the same time. In order to help students acquire the vocabulary they need for school, consider the following.

- Vocabulary development for ELL students is increased using the same methods used with native speaker beginning readers: ample exposure to print, word walls, realia, signs on objects around the room, and so on.
- Older children may take advantage of all these methods in addition to studying true and false cognates, creating personal dictionaries, journal writing between themselves and their teacher, and using learning strategies to augment their vocabulary.
- Other strategies, from Peregoy and Boyle (2008) are:
  - Activate the prior knowledge of the ELL.
  - Repeat the new word in meaningful contexts.
  - Explore the word in depth through demonstrations, direct experience, concrete examples, and applications to real life.
  - Have students explain concepts and ideas in writing and speaking using the new words.
  - Provide explicit strategy instruction so that students can independently understand and use the new words.

In addition, ESOL teachers build academic language proficiency with their ELLs by introducing academic language that consists of more than just content area vocabulary. English language learners benefit from consistent reinforcement of academic vocabulary so that they don't just memorize the words for an assessment and then forget them. Assessment is a key part of this process and teachers should work hard to ensure that they are assessing ELLs' academic vocabulary knowledge in a meaningful way.

OBJECTIVE 8   ORAL AND AURAL LANGUAGE DEVELOPMENT

Skill 8.1   Assessment of oral and aural development

Assessment of Listening Skills

ESOL teachers should choose methods used for teaching listening skills by first deciding on a clear purpose for the assessment. Using lengthy cumulative assessments that might be appropriate for evaluating students at the end of a course or unit might not be appropriate for assessing ELLs when they are engaged in learning a new skill and need constructive feedback. The first step, in choosing a listening assessment then, is to have a clear purpose in mind.

Some purposes for listening assessments:

- Assessing a set of listening skills and students' strengths and weaknesses at the beginning of a course
- Assess students' mastery of a specific listening skill
- Assess students' progress towards listening standards at the end of a term or important time period

It is essential that the assessment measure only the skill(s) that the ESOL teacher is assessing so that the assessment accurately reflects the ELLs proficiency, mastery and progress.

Typically, during a listening test, students listen to a passage and then answer multiple-choice questions that assess various levels of literal and inferential comprehension. The assessment can be broken down into three parts; the listening stimuli, the test questions and the test environment. It is important that the listening stimuli models the language the students are expected to encounter in the classroom, in various media, or in conversations.

In order to engage the students, the passage should be relatively short and interesting. Furthermore, the topic of the passage should be based on experiences common to all students. Any kind of bias should be avoided, for example, material slanted for or against one sex, or a particular geographic, socioeconomic, or racial/ethnic background. Similarly the topic should not be context-dependent, i.e., it should not, for example, be about a holiday that only a few students would be familiar with.

The test questions, or multiple-choice items should focus only on the most important aspect of the passage and should measure a specific set of skills. There is also an alternative to a multiple-choice test. ESOL teachers can use a performance assessment that requires students to select a picture or perform a task based on oral instruction. For example, students might hear a description of a few scenes and choose pictures that match the description or they might be given a map and asked to follow a route described orally.

Finally, the testing environment for listening assessment should be free of external distractions. If stimuli are presented from a recording, the sound quality is of importance. If a test administrator presents stimuli, the material should be presented clearly, with appropriate volume and rate of speaking.

Once ESOL teachers choose an assessment based on purpose, they need to ensure that they have designed or selected an aural assessment that is valid, reliable, and fair. (See skill 5.1 for more on bias and assessment.)

Assessment of oral proficiency

As with the assessment of aural skills, ESOL teachers should:

- Have a clear purpose in mind;
- Consider the three parts of the assessment (performance, directions, environment); and
- Strive to create an oral assessment that is valid, reliable and fair for ELLs.

Assessment of speaking skills should evaluate the communicative ability of the English language learner. Rather than focusing on the number of errors an ELL student might make, assessment should emphasize the student's overall ability to communicate ideas clearly. If there are errors in grammar, for example, but the overall message is clear, a student could still do well on the assessment. The errors may be an area for future growth but not a cause of 'failure'. Assessment methods that focus on the message conveyed by the learners are more accurate in evaluating oral proficiency.

There are formal and informal methods for assessing the oral proficiency of English language learners. For example, students could deliver a speech and the teacher can provide feedback using an evaluation form. Peer evaluation is another method of assessment of speaking skills. For example, student evaluators might outline the main points of a presentation in order to demonstrate their ability to follow the speech.

The student evaluators can orally sum up their reactions to the performance before the rest of the class (though care must be given to ensure that feedback is appropriate and does not intimidate the speaker). They fill out evaluation forms provided by the teacher for the presenter to read and consider. Other students in the class also fill out the evaluation forms and ask the presenter follow-up questions. The teacher uses these evaluation sheets as part of the assessment.

In order to help build speaking proficiency, ESOL teachers can conference with English language learners after student or teacher evaluations and ensure that the student understands strengths and challenges, and has some strategies in place for improvement. Ideally, teachers and students would have another, smaller assessment or performance task where students could check their progress and strategies.

Another method of assessment of speaking skills is self-evaluation. With all the digital media tools available for project-based work, this can be quite easy to do. This method involves recording students during their initial performances and allowing them to evaluate themselves. Students listen to or watch their recorded projects and evaluate themselves according to the same criteria that the teacher and peer evaluators use. After that, the student performers select a portion of their talk and transcribe it in detail. In their initial performance, they focus on communication, but at this point they can focus on trying to make their speech more effective (similar to editing in the writing process). At this stage, the teacher could focus on both fluency and accuracy so students could understand that both are important for effective communication.

These evaluations could be used in various types of classroom activities, helping students gain confidence in their own ability to evaluate language. This method also leads to an opportunity for real spontaneous interactions as the evaluation process is discussed among the students and is important to everyone involved.

Apart from these informal methods of assessment, there are some formal methods ESOL teachers can use to evaluate students in terms of general oral proficiency. There are testing instruments that focus on the message produced by the students. Apart from this one-time assessment, there are other summative assessments that focus on different types of skills needed to convey a message. For this purpose, many task types are used, such as describing a picture or diagram, giving directions, storytelling, expressing opinions, etc., according to the purpose of the assessment.

Portfolio assessment intends to examine students' oral abilities over an extended period of time. The purpose is to produce a record of each student's progress on a variety of tasks over the course of a given unit of study. This type of assessment could also serve as a diagnostic measure of students' major strengths and weaknesses. The tasks may include describing a picture, summarizing orally, interviews, information gap exercises, role-plays, etc. To create a complete profile of the students' performance, a number of different tasks are included.

In these assessments, it is extremely important that students have the opportunity to practice and be familiar with a particular evaluation technique before being evaluated. Likewise, the teacher should also be familiar with the evaluation criteria of each technique used. In short, a variety of techniques should be utilized in order to evaluate students' overall performance.

Skill 8.2   Instruction to promote listening skills

Listening is now not considered a 'passive' skill, but a dynamic process, which can make a lot of demands on language learners.

For beginning students, Total Physical Response by Asher (1982) allows ELLs to participate without forcing speech in the beginning of their introduction to the English Language. TPR consists of the instructor issuing commands that are carried out by the students using high-quality pictures to illustrate concepts or vocabulary. The popular children's game *Simons Says* can be used after vocabulary items have been introduced in the classroom for a slightly different way to achieve the same goals.

Keeping in mind the complex nature of processing spoken language, a combination of bottom-up and top-down approaches have been recommended in order to help learners develop a solid foundation of English language listening skills.

Bottom-up processing refers to detailed analysis of the language by the listener to identify the intended meaning of the message. In this type of analysis, the focus might be on specific word choices, phrasing, and references by the speaker to determine meaning. **Top-down processing** relies on the listener's bank of prior knowledge and expectations. Prior knowledge allows the learners to make predictions about the incoming message on the basis of the context in which the interaction is taking place. Top-down processing involves prediction and inference on the basis of the listener's background knowledge regarding the participants in the situation, their roles and purposes, the typical procedures adopted by the participants of the interaction, and their consequences.

The aim of these tasks is to give opportunities to analyze selected aspects of both language structure and language use. These tasks also encourage the development of some listening strategies to facilitate learning, and the emphasis is on aural perception. Activities can focus on one or two points at a time and would include focus on a variety of features of grammar, pronunciation, vocabulary, discourse markers, sociolinguistic features, and strategic features (Canale & Swain, 1980).

Specific activities can include the following:

1. Analysis of some of the features of "fast speech" through the use of tasks that will help students learn to cope with rapid, natural, contextualized speech;
2. Analysis of phrasing and pausing points can be used to facilitate listening as well as "chunking" the input into units for interpretation;
3. Analysis of both monologue "speeches" and dialogue exchanges with attention to discourse organizational structures;
4. Describing and analyzing sociolinguistic dimensions, including participants and their roles and relationships, settings, purpose of the communication and its expected outcomes;
5. Describing and analyzing communicative strategies used by speakers to deal with miscommunication, communication breakdowns, and distractions (Morley, 1991); and
6. Other listening activities can include identifying word divisions, identifying stress, identifying intonation, dictation, repetition, etc.

Using both bottom-up and top-down approaches, ESOL teachers can use the above types of perception tasks to promote beginning English language listening proficiency.

Skill 8.3 Instruction to promote speaking skills

The teaching of speaking skills has moved away from a focus on perfect accuracy towards a focus on fluency and communicative effectiveness. This has transformed the kind of activities used by the teachers in the classroom into activities that promote the students' ability to understand and communicate real information. They also provide opportunities for them to engage in interaction that is as close as possible to real life situations.

TPR, the Natural Approach and LEP

Though TPR (Total Physical Response) is primarily used to develop receptive language skills. As the student progresses, it can be used as a structured introduction to language production. Students can write out the imperatives and then practice speaking them before moving on to the stage when they will be demonstrating, taking turns with partners, and leading and giving instructions. Just as the teacher uses TPR to prompt students, ELL students with increased proficiency can use TPR to prompt their peers (and teachers) and to tell stories.

In Krashen and Terrell's (1983) Natural Approach, ELLs are actively involved in listening to comprehensible input and start speaking by making simple choices, answering yes-no questions, and playing games. Students are introduced to new vocabulary through these experiences and move from seeing/listening to pointing/drawing, to writing, to reading aloud, to producing original speech based on what they have seen, heard and read. This maintains the comfort levels of ELLs while moving them forward in speaking skills.

Similarly, the Language Experience Approach (LEA) is an instructional technique used to encourage spoken responses from ELL students after they are exposed to a variety of first-hand sensory experiences (Badia, 1966). LEA develops and improves the students' reading and writing skills by using their ideas and language.

Structured Activities

Structured activities for beginning ELLs can promote confidence in speaking and accuracy at the same time. Using clearly structured activities provides a form that novice English speakers can imitate and repeat in simple communication. Such controlled activities can be provided with a context, so they could have some of the elements of a communicative activity. This would help the beginner level student focus on accurate structure within a communicative context. An example of this is the structured interview, where students question each other and answer, exchanging real information while at the same time repeating and producing specific structures (e.g., yes-no, or where/when/who questions).

Some language games can also provide students with controlled practice. However, it is important to model the language structures for the beginning students. Games can help students focus on and repeat specific structures as well as perform natural, "authentic" tasks.

Observation Activities

Observation activities for ELLs give students the opportunity to record both verbal and nonverbal interactions between native speakers or advanced speakers of the target language. This helps students become aware of the language spoken in an authentic setting. It also allows students to observe how people greet each other, make requests, interrupt each other, respond to each other, disagree, or receive compliments. A follow-up activity could be a role-play created by the students to show the verbal and nonverbal behaviors appropriate in a particular situation.

To enhance communicative competence, it is paramount to provide students with a relaxed classroom environment in which they feel comfortable and confident. It allows the students to take risks and produces more interactions. The teacher should also provide the students with situations as close as possible to real life in which they can communicate with one another. The speaker's focus is on the communicative task itself, for which they collaborate to achieve mutual understanding and modify their language according to the demands of the situation.

Group Work Activities
Interactive group work is also important to lessen students' anxiety and lower their affective filters. Anxiety can seriously impede the learning process. Different group sizes (pairs, small groups, and large groups) provide opportunities for students to practice the different thinking and oral skills that are unique to each group type. When students' affective filter is lowered, they are more likely to take risks and engage in meaningful conversations without the fear of mistakes. Students also develop social skills by interacting in a variety of small group situations that aim to resolve a problem or give directions, advice, etc.

Skill 8.4   Development of listening skills for academic purposes

Educational psychologists posit that verbal learning becomes easier when information can be chunked into meaningful patterns and then related to existing meaning structures - *schemata*. Carrell and Eisterhold (1983) discovered that background knowledge in the listener's mind is of two types: content schemata and formal schemata. Content schemata include familiarity with the topic, cultural knowledge, and previous experience with a field. Formal schemata deals with people's knowledge of discourse forms: text types, rhetorical conventions, and the structural organization of prose. Both content and formal schemata can help listeners in comprehension.

Based on schema theory, especially when developing listening skills for academic purposes, it is important to make ELLs familiar with the topic under discussion and the structure and type of text under consideration. Preparing students in this way taps into their schemata and previous experiences. This front-loading of connections can aid ELLs in listening comprehension and help them develop skills to become academically and socially proficient English language listeners.

Usually when we listen to something, we have certain expectations and a purpose for listening. We have some idea about the content, formality level, etc. in the discourse that we are about to hear. Some ideas are based on "script competence", which is the knowledge the listeners possess in advance about the context or the subject matter of the discourse. These expectations are often linked to the purpose for listening. People listen to specific information or details depending on the purpose or the task at hand (enjoyment, knowledge, persuasion, social or expression).

Listening for gist is to get the general idea or meaning. This means ignoring the details and following the overall topic even if you do not understand every word – for example, listening to the news every day to get a general idea of what is happening in the world. Conversely, someone could understand all the words that form a news story, but without context about the situation being reported, s/he could easily not understand what was being said. Additionally, if a person listens only for enjoyment or entertainment (like listening to a conversation), he or she will only focus on the overall message.

On the other hand, *listening for details* means to get the specific facts. The focus is to selectively extract information to suit one's purpose. For example, if we want to know the answer to a question and expect to hear the appropriate response, this makes us listen for key phrases or words. When we ask a question like, "Where are you going?" we listen for the particular expression of place. Additionally, we look for specific information when watching a weather channel to plan a trip or to listen to the sports news to find out the outcome of a game.

Extensive listening means listening to the overall content of a long text, such as a film or a play. Likewise, *intensive listening* means trying to understand all the facts and information – for example, listening to a lecture about which a summary must be written. However, the skills required might change according to the purpose of the listener. If you listen to a lecture only to gain an overall knowledge of the topic, you will not indulge in intensive listening but will only look for the gist or the general meaning.

Listening purpose is an important variable. The processes and strategies employed by the listener change according to his or her purpose. Listening to a sequence of instructions for installing new computer software requires different skills and strategies than listening to a poem or a short story. Therefore, when designing learning tasks, it is important to teach students a range of listening strategies and skills.

Language use tasks (language for comprehension)
The aim of these tasks is to give students practice in listening to get information and to use it communicatively. These activities help learners to comprehend and use language in order to communicate effectively. Specific activities can include the following:

- Listening and performing operations (constructing a figure, drawing a map, etc.);
- Listening and solving problems (riddles, puzzles, challenges, etc.);
- Listening and transcribing (taking notes, etc.);
- Listening and summarizing information (giving the gist of a message, etc.); and
- Interactive listening and negotiating meaning through questioning answering routines (to get repetition of information, to verify information, to clarify information, questioning to get elaboration) (Morley, 1991).

These listening and language use tasks help students to build on their background knowledge in the second language as well as build strategies to facilitate successful communication. In short, all the above activity types help students to develop both top-down and bottom-up processing of information, which is essential in building effective listening skills and strategies.

Skill 8.5 Development of speaking skills for academic purposes

The Cognitive Academic Language Learning Approach (CALLA) launched by Chamot and O'Malley (1994) helps intermediate and advanced students understand and retain content area material as they are enhancing their English language skills. CALLA helps ELLs by giving instruction in the appropriate language areas (specialized vocabulary, syntax, phonology) while dealing with different content areas. Learning strategies that emphasize critical and creative thinking skills such as problem solving, inferencing, etc., need to be taught during these lessons since they are critical to success in the mainstream classroom.

Additionally, it is important to provide students with comprehensible input that is just above their proficiency level. For instance, for beginner level ESL students, comprehensible input would be in the form of short sentences, phrases, and relatively simple language segments which are integrated into activities of purposeful communication. These exchanges should be as authentic as possible and carried out in a meaningful context (activity/task). These activities and tasks can be adjusted to the levels and needs of the ELLs.

Similarly, second language learners should communicate in situations/exchanges that are as authentic as possible and should bring about a maximum of personal involvement in the communication. Students should also be provided opportunities to use the target language in social interactions, allowing the students to produce the language in varied contexts.

Ellis concluded that two-way exchanges of information show more benefits for ELLs partly because they require more negotiation of meaning. When learning cooperatively, participating in TPR races, or team drawing, students are focusing on comprehension and on producing the language in some form - whether by drawing, physical movement or communicating with other students.

The selection of appropriate activities depends on the level of the learners. For example, beginning level students need more controlled, structured practice and drills to move to slightly more complex communicative activities. On the other hand, advanced learners may be asked to engage in less structured activities on their own.

In classrooms where these strategies are in place, the teacher helps students build on what they already know, which helps them expand on their prior knowledge and retain information. Ideally, to promote more complex communication, the questions asked in the class should produce a variety of responses for which there is no right answer. Furthermore, students should be provided with ample opportunities where meaning is negotiated within a contextualized meaningful context.

Following are the examples of the kinds of activities that could promote speaking skills for academic purposes:

Participation Activities
Participation activities allow students to participate in some communication activity in a natural setting. One of these activities is the guided discussion, where the teacher

introduces a problem or a controversial topic. Students in small groups discuss the problem and try to come up with appropriate solutions. For more advanced classes, students can choose a topic and lead a discussion on it. This activity will help with elements ranging from turn-taking to topic control among the students as well as accuracy of grammar and pronunciation. Another activity is the interview, where students interview a native speaker about some meaningful or memorable experience in their lives. After the interview, the students organize the information collected to present it to the whole class. Other participation activities could include peer interviews, problem-solving tasks and project-based learning.

Performance Activities
In performance activities, language learners prepare for the activity beforehand and, for example, deliver a message to a group. Other performance activities in content-areas that involve preparation include seminars, speeches, short presentations, and debates. This could vary from a student's speech explaining an experiment to simply telling a story from their own experience. The follow-up activity could involve videotaping the students during their performances and having them evaluate themselves. This allows the students to focus on communication during their initial performance and in the follow-up session to deal with specific language features. This follow-up self-evaluation can promote greater accuracy in future while the initial activity allows students to focus on the ideas they wish to communicate.

Role-play and drama can be used for all language learners making varying demands on the learners according to their proficiency level and can be adapted for different content-area classes to reinforce learning. Role play and drama can also be practiced and rehearsed, providing ELLs with the time and space and structure they may need to perform with as little anxiety as possible.

Spontaneous performance activities become increasingly important as ELLs language levels progress, including participating in debates (formal and informal), improvised drama and role-play and incorporation question periods into seminars and formal presentations.

OBJECTIVE 9.0   ASSESS AND PROMOTE LITERACY DEVELOPMENT

Skill 9.1   Classroom-based assessment of reading development

Ongoing classroom-based reading assessment is a valuable tool not only for monitoring the developing literacy of ELL students but also for adapting instruction to meet the needs of students. The literacy demands at different grade levels become increasingly complex as students progress from understanding simple stories to reading for information and literary analysis. Increasingly complex vocabulary, greater emphasis on implied meanings, content specific vocabulary, and decontextualized readings are just some of the challenges that all students face but which are particularly noteworthy for ELL students.

Classroom assessments provide teachers with regular opportunities to determine the specific challenges facing individual students. Is a student who has done well with novels struggling with history/social studies readings? Perhaps s/he lacks contextual knowledge about the topic. Is an otherwise strong ELL student struggling with reading poetry? Perhaps the implied meanings or varied syntax of the poems are unfamiliar and can be addressed through partner work or some annotated examples.

Classroom assessments can take many forms and can be formal or informal, formative or summative. The following sections deal with some of the many types and purposes of different assessment tools.

- **Regular student observations:** Used to observe and evaluate student comprehension performance, regular student observations are probably the most flexible format. Teachers may observe students in class discussions, in literature circles with peers, or while completing tasks in class. Checks for understanding, whether written or oral, can be evaluated to check progress.
- **Student conferencing:** One-on-one meetings with students about maybe books they are reading or about progress on a project are effective ways to get a sense of student comprehension and reading challenges.
- **Authentic assessments:** Authentic assessments are designed to be as close to real life as possible so they are relevant and meaningful to the student. They can be formal or informal, depending upon how they are constructed.
- **Teacher-made and textbook assessments:** Many teachers use this type of assessment, pairing them with assigned readings. They can target specific reading skills suited to the text and or the unit of study. General comprehension, vocabulary development, inference, and symbolic language are just a few examples of what these can be used to assess.
- **Performance assessments:** An example of an authentic reading assessment might require students to follow written directions to complete a task.
- **Self-assessments:** Students often have very good insights into their reading. They can often be quite clear about whether they understood a text or what aspects of it were difficult.

For class-based assessments that involve multiple-choice questions, the following guidelines should be considered.

Reading items

The purpose of the test items should be to elicit reliable performance and reliable scoring. The items should be within the capabilities of the students and should make minimal demands on their writing skills. Those items should be avoided for which the correct response can be found without understanding the text. Also, paragraph numbers and line numbers should be added to the text if items need to make reference to them. It is very important to get the opinion of colleagues on the text and the test items.

Possible Techniques: The items should interfere as little as possible with the reading itself and avoid asking students to write answers in response to the reading passage.

Some of the methods used are:

- Multiple choice: Students are provided with choices from which they select the correct answer. True/False questions are also a variety of multiple choice.
- Unique answer: In this task type, there is only one possible correct answer. This might be a single word or number, or something a little longer. The test item may be a question, however, this form is not recommended for extensive use.
- Short answer/Guided short answer: Short answer items can be used when unique answer items are not possible. However, it may again be a problem that students are not able to express themselves through writing. Guided short answer items provide partial information to students so that they have only to complete sentences already given to them. For example: "Many universities in Europe used to insist that their students speak and write only _____. Now many of them accept _____ as an alternative, but not a _____ of the two." Hughes (1989)
- Summary cloze: In this technique, a reading passage is summarized and gaps are left in the summary for students to complete. Similar to guided answers, this is a more reliable way of testing reading comprehension than unique answer items.
- Information transfer: Another way of limiting the demands on students' writing ability is to ask them to perform successful completion of a reading task, transferring simple information in different ways, such as a table, following a route on a map, labeling a picture, or numbering a series of events.

There are also a number of formal reading assessments for classroom use (such as the DRA) that are intended to determine general reading level.

- **Informal Reading Inventories (IRIs):** Graded reading passages and comprehension questions
    - May include both narrative and expository passages
    - May include narrative and expository retelling checklists
    - May incorporate prior knowledge questions for each passage
    - Purposes:
        - Can be used to gauge oral reading comprehension
        - Can be used to assess silent reading comprehension

- Include passages read aloud by a test administrator to test listening comprehension

Factors to consider
There are several factors to consider when using classroom-based reading assessments. Assessing specific dimensions of English language proficiency is complex. For testing the reading abilities of English language learners, Hughes (1989) presents a framework, which includes content (operations, types of text, addresses, and topics) and criteria levels of performance.

Content
Operations: Operations include different levels of analysis that require attention. These comprise the macro-skills that cover the objectives of the course and the needs of the students and include:

- Identifying stages of an argument
- Identifying examples in support of an argument
- Scanning text to locate specific information
- Skimming text to obtain the gist

These also include micro-skills such as:

- Using content to guess meaning of unfamiliar words
- Identifying referents of pronouns, etc.
- Recognizing indicators in discourse, especially for the introduction, development, transition, and conclusion of ideas

There should be a balance of the macro and micro skills tested which reflects the relationship between the two levels of skill.

Types of text: The designer of the test should identify the type of text used for the test, such as textbook, novel, magazine, newspaper, academic journal, letter, poem, etc. Additionally, the use of authentic texts depends in part on what the test is intended to measure. It is possible to use authentic text at lower levels of abilities.

Addresses and topics: This element is related to test types and specifies the audience of a particular type of text. The range of topics can be mentioned in general terms.

Setting criteria levels of performance: In a norm-referenced approach to testing, student performance is evaluated by comparison with others. In criterion-referenced approach, it is specified what the candidate should know to achieve a specific level. However, it can be difficult with reading to provide interpretation of scores (e.g., what does a student know if s/he gets 60 or 70 %?). It would be best to use the test task itself to define the level (Hughes, 1989). For example, in order to pass, the student should be able to score a particular number of items correct (say 80 per cent). Additionally, while scoring, errors of grammar, spelling or punctuation should not be penalized if the student is able to successfully complete the task.

Setting the tasks

Selecting the texts:

- Keep the content and the criteria level in mind when selecting a text.
- Choose text of appropriate length. For example, scanning may require a longer passage (approx. 2000 words) as opposed to detailed reading.
- To obtain reliability, include as many passages as possible in order to give candidates ample chances to show performance level.
- Choose a text of interest to the students.
- Texts should be avoided that contain information that is part of the students' general knowledge, which would enable them to answer questions without reading the passage.

Skill 9.2   Classroom-based assessment of writing development

Developing written communication skills is obviously an essential element of developing English language proficiency. Classroom-based assessment of writing offers many of the same advantages as classroom reading assessment (See Skill 9.1). There are many ways of assessing student-writing skills.

Considerations for Classroom Assessments

For teachers concerned with assessing writing in the regular classroom, Weigle (2002) offers the following criteria:

- Evaluate out-of-class writing as well as in-class writing;
- Evaluate more than one writing sample;
- Build authenticity and interactiveness into timed writing tasks;
- Use scoring instruments (e.g. rubrics) specific to the assignment and to the instructional focus of the class; and
- Use assessment to provide useful feedback to the students.

Additionally, when designing and analyzing writing assessments, ESOL teachers should keep the following goals in mind.

1. Set writing tasks that are properly representative of the type of tasks that we should expect the students to be able to perform.
2. The tasks should elicit samples of writing that truly represent the student's ability.
3. Writing samples should be scored reliably. (Hughes (1989))

A well-structured writing test does the following:

Specifies all appropriate tasks and selects a sample
When preparing the test, it is essential that the tasks represent what we expect the students to be able to perform on the test. This should be identified before we start creating the test.

Focuses on writing
Writing tests for ELLs should not set tasks that evaluate students' intelligence, general knowledge, or good support for their opinions. Additionally, we should not make the instructions so difficult or long that the students have problems comprehending them.

Presents well-defined tasks
When responding to a task, students should know what is required of them and should not stray from the topic. However, teachers should be careful not to provide too much information in the instruction that can help students perform the task. For example, complete sentences should be avoided which could be used in the composition.

Presents tasks that can be scored reliably:

1) Holistic **scoring**: In this type of scoring, a single score is given to the writing piece on the basis of an overall impression. This helps to score quickly and therefore one piece of writing can be scored more than once to ensure reliability. However, this scoring system should be appropriate to the level of the candidates and the purpose of the test.

2) Analytic **methods of scoring**: This method of scoring requires a separate score for each of a number of subskills. The number varies according to the purpose of the test and may include grammar, vocabulary, mechanics, fluency (style of communication), and form (organization). This kind of scoring helps assess and diagnose all subskills as well as make the test reliable because each test is given a number of scores (one for each subskill). However, the scoring takes longer and the division into sub-skills might divert the assessment from the overall effort of the writing.

The choice of the type of scoring depends on the purpose of the test, but it is important that the scorers should be trained in using these scales. Additionally, each writing sample of the student should be scored independently by two or more scorers and should be recorded on separate sheets. A third member of the test team should search for any discrepancies in the scores given to the same piece of writing.

Portfolios
Writing portfolios are a particularly effective way to assess writing growth. Rather than a snapshot of performance on a given day, portfolios offer the long view of writing development. These can be particularly useful, especially since portfolios can now be preserved digitally through blogs and other online tools.

Pros of Writing Portfolio Assessment

Assessment is:

- **Integrative:** Combines curriculum and assessment which means evaluation is developmental, continuous, comprehensive, and fairer, representing program goals and reflecting writing progress over time, and genre
- **Valid:** Closely related to material taught and what students can do

- **Meaningful:** Students see portfolios as a record of work and progress
- **Motivating:** Presents a range of challenging writing experiences in different genres; students can see similarities and differences between assignments
- **Process-oriented:** Focuses on multi-drafting, feedback, collaboration, revision, etc.
- **Coherent:** Assignments build on each other rather than being isolated from each other
- **Flexible:** Teachers can adopt different selection criteria, evaluation methods and response practices over time, emphasizing different features of writing
- **Encourages reflection:** Students can evaluate their improvement and consider their weaknesses, which encourages greater responsibility and independence in writing
- **Formative:** Grading may be delayed until end of course allowing teacher to provide constructive feedback without the need for early, potentially discouraging, evaluation

Cons of Writing Portfolio Assessment

- **Logistic:** May produce considerable work for teachers
- **Design:** Grading criteria needs to be understood by all teachers
- **Reliability:** Need to ensure standardized grading by all raters across genres, portfolios and courses
- **Product variation:** Problem in fairly assigning a single grade to a collection varied in genre, complexity and quality, especially if assigned by a variety of teachers in different departments
- **Task variation:** Some tasks may be more interesting than others and therefore, elicit better writing
- **Authenticity:** Some students may get considerable outside help or plagiarize since portfolios may be compiled without close teacher supervision. Adapted from Hyland, 2002)

Skill 9.3 Strategies for promoting beginning reading and writing skills

Foundational literacy skills include demonstrating an understanding of print concepts (organization and features of print), phonological awareness (See Skills 1.1 and 1.2), knowing and applying phonics and word recognition (See Skills 1.1 and 1.2) and fluency.

Pressley (2008) discusses the mental processes of good readers and states that teachers need to understand what good reading entails. According to him, good readers rely on both decoding strategies and comprehension strategies to achieve their reading goals. A decoding focused strategy is considered a 'bottom-up' approach while a 'top-down' approach relies more on the reader's prior knowledge and experience. Both these processes should be taught to increase students' reading ability. A third 'interactive model' combines both approaches with readers drawing on both their prior experience and word knowledge to construct meaning (Ahmadi and Pourhossein, 2012).

Teachers should take the following strategies into account to design effective reading instruction programs.

1. **Phonemic awareness**: Phonemes are the smallest units of sound that combine to form syllables and words. For example, the word shut has three phonemes (sh-u-t) while skip has four phonemes (s-k-i-p). Therefore, phonemic awareness enables the learner to identify and manipulate these phonemes. Some English phonemes may be absent in students' native language and are more difficult to acquire. In this case, it is necessary to teach phonemic awareness with the vocabulary word, its meaning, and its pronunciation. Additionally, teachers could learn about the phonemes that exist or do not exist in their students' first language in order to provide them with effective instruction. Meaningful activities that focus on particular sounds and letters, such as language games and word wall, are useful as are songs and poems that help teach phonemes with rhythm and repetition.

2. **Phonics**: This is the understanding of the relationship between the phonemes and graphemes (the letters and spellings that represent sound in the written language). It helps readers read familiar words and decode unfamiliar ones. Instructional activities that develop students' phonemic awareness help them understand the systematic and predictable relationship between written letters and spoken sounds. Teachers can more effectively teach phonics if they have knowledge about their students' native language. For example, in Spanish the letters b, c, d, f, l, m, n, p, q, s, and t represent sounds that are similar enough to English that students may learn them with relative ease. However, the vowels look similar in English and Spanish but are named differently and have different sounds. Therefore, they may be more difficult for Spanish speakers to master when reading English (Peregoy and Boyle, 2000).

3. **Reading fluency**: Reading fluency is crucial for reading comprehension. A fluent reader not only reads words quickly and accurately but also comprehends them at the same time. Students can be taught fluency by reading passages aloud with explicit instruction from the teacher. The other way is for students to read silently on their own with less teacher guidance. However, accent should not be confused with lack of fluency, as students can learn to read fluently in English even with a native language accent.

4. **Vocabulary development**: Vocabulary development is crucial for reading comprehension. It is difficult for a reader to understand the content unless they know the meaning of most of the words in the text. Vocabulary development is particularly important for beginner ELL students both to support comprehension and to avoid frustration. Avoiding frustration will promote a more positive attitude towards reading. When a student sounds out a word, it helps to make sense of the word if they already know its meaning and are able to understand the sentence. Therefore, vocabulary needs to be taught explicitly as a part of the daily curriculum to help ELLs comprehend academic texts.

5. **Reading comprehension strategies**: Comprehension is an active process that requires a repertoire of strategies. These strategies help students engage with the text and monitor their comprehension. Brown (2008) notes that secondary students need a wide variety of strategies in order to tackle the complex reading required of them to succeed in and out of school. Students need to be taught explicitly how, why, and when to use these strategies. Pearson and Gallagher's Gradual Release of Responsibility Model (1983) for adolescence provides guidance with teaching strategies. Teachers explicitly describe the strategies they use while reading and demonstrate them to the students during read-aloud. Students model these strategies and later adapt them to suit their individual needs. This shifts the focus of responsibility from the teacher to the learner to help them adapt and internalize the strategies.

6. **Scaffolds before, during, and after reading**: "Scaffold" is the term used for teacher support for a learner through dialog, questioning, conversation, and modeling. A number of such reading strategies such as questioning, discussion, and writing are recommended for struggling readers. Roehler and Cantlon (1997) identified five types of scaffolding: (a) offering explanations, (b) inviting student participation, (c) verifying and clarifying student understandings, (d) modeling of desired behaviors, and (e) inviting students to contribute clues for reasoning through an issue or problem. Additionally, these reading strategies/ scaffolding activities should also be used in the content-area classroom in order for them to be effective.

7. **Knowledge about the learner**: Diagnostic assessment is necessary to determine the strengths and weaknesses of the students to provide effective instruction. If they know the history of their students' reading difficulties, it will help the teacher focus more on these problematic areas. Similarly, knowledge regarding the cultural and linguistic background of the students assists the teacher in selecting reading material for the class in accordance with their interests, cultural sensitivity, and acknowledgement of their cultural beliefs and values.

English language fluency is developed over time through extensive practice both in speaking and in reading. Ample opportunities should be given to ELLs to develop their speaking and listening abilities to help them achieve more oral fluency. Role-plays, skits, poems, singing, and interviews are good ways to increase oral fluency. Fluency in reading interacts with oral fluency. Wide exposure to print and reading will increase both reading fluency and oral fluency. The two are intertwined.

Fluent readers are able to grasp chunks of language, read for meaning (not word by word), decode automatically, and become confident readers who are able to self-monitor, while maintaining comprehension. Specific instruction devoted to these areas should improve fluency rates in slower readers. Promoting first language literacy and drawing connections to developing literacy in English will support ELLs' literacy development.

In some ways, we only learn to read once. Once we figure out how reading works in our native language, we can apply the same skills to a new language. Learning to read in a new language with a similar orthographic system (e.g., Spanish and

English) is easier than learning to read in a language with a totally different system of writing (such as Mandarin), but the skills are similar. It is important for ELLs to increase their vocabulary and knowledge of the structure of English, their new language. By building on what the ELL already knows with regards to literacy, language, and experiences in his or her native language, teachers will be able to improve the reading level of the ELL in English. For this reason, it is necessary to evaluate the ELL in his or her first, native, or heritage language in order to initiate the best reading instruction in English.

There may be a temptation to immerse new English language learners who are older in content-area English. Because of their age, it may seem unfair or juvenile to teach foundational literacy skills such as word recognition and fluency, but without mastery of these concepts, students will not fulfill their academic potential and high-level literacy will remain a challenge.

Students with strong literacy skills in their first language will likely move quickly past the foundational skills in English. For those who do not have those skills in their first language, however, it is important to take the time to ensure students master them. Only through mastery of these skills will students be ready to engage with complex literary texts, read and research for information, or follow complex procedural texts. Ignoring the foundational aspects of literacy does a disservice to ELL students.

Writing Skills

Just as the native English speaker has to manage many different skills to become a proficient writer, so must the ELL student. ELL students must develop clarity of thought and expression, use of different genres for different purposes in writing, and standard conventions of spelling, grammar, and punctuation. Since the characteristics of each type of writing may vary, it is not always easy to discuss writing stages. Students may develop proficiency more quickly in one text type than another. Because of the complexity of learning to express oneself in writing, it is particularly important to have a clear process of writing instruction for students who are simultaneously developing language skills in a new language.

The following set of writing traits with accompanying level descriptors, based on a writing matrix developed by Peregoy and Boyle (2008), offers a good guide to identifying characteristics of an English Language Learner's writing level. It encompasses three developmental levels and six traits.

- Trait 1: Fluency

Beginning Level: Writes one or two short sentences.
Intermediate Level: Writes several sentences.
Advanced Level: Writes a paragraph or more.

- Trait 2: Organization

Beginning Level: Lacks logical sequence or is so short that organization presents no problem.
Intermediate Level: Somewhat sequenced.
Advanced Level: Follows standard organization for genre.

- Trait 3: Grammar

Beginning Level: Basic word order problems. Uses only present tense form.
Intermediate Level: Minor grammatical errors.
Advanced Level: Grammar resembles that of native speaker of same age.

- Trait 4: Vocabulary

Beginning Level: Limited vocabulary. Needs to rely at times on L1 or ask for translation.
Intermediate Level: Knows most words needed to express ideas, but lacks vocabulary for finer shades of meaning.
Advanced Level: Flexible in word choice; similar to good native writer of same age.

- Trait 5: Genre

Beginning Level: Does not differentiate form to suit purpose.
Intermediate Level: Chooses form to suit purpose but limited in choices of expository forms.
Advanced Level: Knows several genres and makes appropriate choices similar to effective native writers of the same age.

- Trait 6: Sentence variety

Beginning Level: Uses one or two sentence patterns.
Intermediate Level: Uses several sentence patterns.
Advanced Level: Uses a good variety of sentence patterns effectively.

For beginning level students, the first steps in teaching writing skills in an ESL classroom center around the mechanics of the skill. This means letter recognition, letter discrimination, word recognition, basic rules of spelling, punctuation and capitalization, and recognition of whole sentences and paragraphs. Recognition and writing drills are the initial steps that help in the development of effective writing skills.

Three main types of recognition tasks are usually used at the early stages of learning:

1. *Matching tasks:* These are effective recognition tasks that are mostly in the form of games, puzzles, etc.
2. *Writing tasks:* At this early stage of writing, it is important to get learners accustomed to correct capitalization in English and to basic punctuation rules.
3. *Meaningful sound spelling correspondence practice:* Students write meaningful sentences (accompanied by pictures) which show sound-spelling correspondences. These sentences practice correct capitalization and punctuation rules as well as words that students have recently learned. These sentences may not be interesting but fulfill a definite purpose. Eventually, this language knowledge works as the basis for developing more meaningful and interesting texts.

Skill 9.4 Development of reading skills for social and academic purposes

As students progress in their literacy skills, the demands on them increase as well. More complex texts and more complex tasks based on what they read are part of the progression. Learning about the characteristics unique to different text types can be helpful for ELL students as they take the next steps in their literacy development.

Working with Literary Texts
Literary genres are collections of works with a similar theme or style. Some literary genres come under the huge umbrella of biography and nonfiction whereas others, like folktales, are further classified into fables, tall tales, fairy tales, and myths. Additionally, under fiction, there are other literary genres: historical fiction, mystery, realistic fiction, fantasy, science fiction, etc. Students should be made aware of these different genres and the different formats and styles that make them distinct. Learning about the features of new text types provides students with additional tools for understanding complex texts. For example, learning that an essay typically starts with the author's main point, continues on to incorporate his/her evidence or arguments, and then ends with a conclusion will help all students (but particularly ELL students) to identify main ideas, look for key points, or even to construct a clear contrary opinion. The concept of genre and its purpose becomes more complicated as children advance to a higher-grade level.

Informational Texts and Purposes for Reading
According to Shanahan (2008), people make decisions based on information that comes from multiple viewpoints in multiple formats (e.g., letters, essays, reports, advertisements, lectures) through various media (e.g., newspapers, television, websites, books, magazines). This is evident in content-area subjects as well. For example, historians supply evidence from multiple sources (e.g., film, newspapers, letters, interviews, fictional accounts) to prove their point of view regarding a historical event. The views regarding a particular event might change based on the era in which historians were doing the writing and who the historians were. Historians not only read multiple genres when collecting information but also write them (e.g., scholarly books, journals, articles, lectures). This is also true for other disciplines, such as science and mathematics. Students must also learn to gather information or present their own ideas in different genres and formats.

These multiple genres within a single topic make reading even more challenging for ESL learners. This struggle is magnified when these genres communicate contradictory purposes and messages depending on the author and the context. These genres and their purposes for writing change across disciplines; therefore, teachers need to make students aware of these differences so they can become critical readers. Shanahan (2008) suggests what teachers could do to help students to understand complex texts of different genres:

- Preteach potentially troublesome vocabulary.
- Provide information to build background knowledge. Use an anchor text or experience before reading a more difficult text.
- Teach students to use strategies that will help them to better interpret texts. This includes teaching the key features of different text types.

- Teach students about various genres and structures used in particular texts and how texts within those genres signal important information.
- Teach students information about the discipline in which they are reading as well as how experts in that discipline approach and use information in text to build upon existing knowledge.
- Set up cooperating group structures that allow students who are weaker readers to be supported in their reading by better readers.
- Find easier texts or annotate existing texts to make them easier if the difficult texts are so challenging that students become unmotivated, even with all of the support they receive.

Critical Literacy: The development of critical literacy skills in English Language Learners can increase levels of achievement in learning standards relating to their understanding of complex informational and literary texts. The instructor can integrate the following strategies to promote critical literacy for L2 learners:

- Ask the L2 learners to consider the author's motivation for writing a certain newspaper or magazine article. Specifically, ask the learners to support their opinions and answers, using examples of tone, structure, and word choice.
- Ask the L2 learners to compare/contrast the photographs, topics, and writing styles of an L1 and L2 newspaper. Specifically, ask the learners what the style of each may reveal about the different cultures or countries, whether these differences influence readership, and if the choice of advertising influences readership.

The critical piece of both activities is for the learners to not only consider the specific questions, but to also consider which values, ethics, and cultural factors influence their own thinking and responses. Most importantly, instructors need to introduce topics that are relevant to the L2 learner, as well as use codes. "Codes" are graphics, pictures, speeches, themes, issues, or realia from a specific culture that help stimulate discussion. "Simple, familiar, focused representations of complex, often emotionally charged issues or situations, codes can be structured for use with low level learners" (Van Duzer and Florez, 2001). Providing English language learners with opportunities to engage with texts that prompt them to examine values, morals, and biases of individuals, groups and the new culture(s) can help promote critical literacy skills.

Graphic Organizers and Mind Maps: Graphic organizers and mind maps can help students evaluate and comprehend more complex informational texts by helping English Language Learners visualize raw data. These can be used by the teacher for simplification of complex materials, numerous data, and complicated relationships in content areas. Students use them to analyze data, organize information, and clarify concepts. Examples are: pie charts, flow charts, bar diagrams, Venn diagrams, family trees, spider maps, organizational charts, and strip maps. Still other graphic organizers are webbing, concept mapping, passwords and language ladders, and brainstorming.

- With webbing, students learn to associate words or phrases within a topic or concept.

- By using concept maps, students learn the relationships between the different elements of a topic and how to organize them from the most general to the most specific. This is different from webbing, where relationships between words or phrases are shown, but not ranked.

Passwords and Language Ladders: Words of the Day and Language Ladders are motivating ways to teach chunks of language to ELLs. The Word(s) of the Day is language needed for daily student life in school. After the words or phrases are explained, they are posted on the board, and must be used before leaving the room or participating in some activity. Language ladders are associated words, such as different ways to say hello or good-bye.

Brainstorming: Brainstorming consists of students contributing ideas related to a concept or problem-centered topic. The teacher initially accepts all ideas without comment. Students then categorize, prioritize, and select proposed ideas for further investigation.

For vocabulary study, see Skill 7.4

Reading Comprehension Strategies: Successful readers use reading strategies in each of the three distinct phases of reading—pre-reading, reading, and post-reading—to successfully understand a text (Peregoy and Boyle, 2008). Teachers can use pre, during and post-reading strategies to build English Language Learners' reading comprehension skills.

- Pre-reading: Build background knowledge through anticipation guides or field trips, motivate the reader with structured overviews or films, and establish the purpose using experiments or pictures.
- During reading: Read based upon the established purpose, using learning logs or annotating texts to record information, to improve comprehension by Directed Reading-Thinking Activities and asking questions, and to utilize background knowledge by studying headings and subheadings and answering questions.
- Post-reading: Help the student with organizing and remembering information through activities such as art work, maps, or summaries and to use the information in reporting, making a film, or publishing.

Skill 9.5 Development of writing skills for social and academic purposes

The next step focuses on the basic process-oriented tasks that incorporate some language at the morphological and discourse level. Therefore, these activities focus on both accuracy and content of the message. This step caters to a wide range of proficiency levels, depending on the specifications of the task.

These include:

1. *Practical writing tasks:* These writing tasks have a predictable format, which makes them suitable for focusing primarily on spelling and morphology. These

include various types of lists, notes, short messages, simple instructions, etc. This step caters to beginning and intermediate level students.

2. *Emotive writing tasks:* These are concerned with personal writing, which includes letters to friends and narratives describing personal experiences, as well as personal journals and diaries. These writing activities are suitable for intermediate and advanced learners but can also be used at the beginning level in a limited manner. For example, letters can be limited to the level of structure and vocabulary knowledge of the students as they increase in their proficiency level. It is necessary to provide students with specifications for the tasks in order for them to respond according to their proficiency levels.

3. *School-oriented tasks*: The function of writing in school is the most important aspect of students' writing. A lot of individual learning takes place when students are writing assignments, summaries, answers to questions, book reports, research papers, or a variety of essay-type passages. The teacher could be the audience of these writing tasks, but eventually the students should be engaged in activities that convey information to multiple audiences across multiple genres (Shanahan, 2008). At an early stage of ESL learning, the assignments should be short and limited. Answers might be single phrases or sentences, and summaries could be just listing main ideas. However, at a higher proficiency level, the activities can require more complex structure and organization skills catering to multiple audiences and also skills involving writing across different genres (e.g., research papers, scientific journals and magazines, newspaper articles, etc.).

Appropriate task selection involves a variety of factors, but it is also important to use a variety of writing tasks at all levels of student learning. Writing is a vital communication skill, and it also requires the learner to plan and think about the process. Therefore, the learner focuses on both linguistic accuracy and content organization.

In early studies of developing writing skills in all learners, the focus of research was on the product produced by the writer. However, Emig's (1971) L1 research changed the focus from product to process. This has become the focus of the research design for conducting research in both L1 and L2 writing process. Similar to Emig's research, L2 composition specialists Zamal (1976) and Raimes (1979) recommended treating L2 writing as a process in the L2 classroom. This approach focuses less on surface-level errors and achieving correctness, but stresses process-oriented pedagogy. In a process-oriented writing class, the teacher provides students with a wide range of strategies for composing texts. This approach focuses on what the writer does (planning, revising, etc.) instead of only on what the final product looks like (grammar, spelling, etc.).

One way of addressing different language levels is to characterize writing tasks along a continuum from *controlled* to *guided* to *free* which starts with maximum teacher-controlled activities and builds to tasks that require students to supply content, organization, and language structure. A controlled task may require students to make changes to an existing text or to write based on teacher-supplied model text. An example of a guided writing task, which allows more freedom to the student than a controlled task, is to ask students to produce a short text by answering directed yet open-ended questions.

Finally, free writing tasks ask students to produce complete texts in response to a variety of writing prompts. Free writing can also be encouraged with less emphasis on the correctness of grammar or form by having students keep a journal.

The focus of all writing should be to allow students to learn and practice the skills of producing good writing. Regardless of the kind of writing task, prewriting is important at the beginning. The goal of the teacher should be to present students with a variety of prewriting strategies and help them figure out which one works best for them for the task. Some examples are:

- Brainstorming
- Listing
- Free writing
- Clustering

After this first step, the teacher needs to work with students to help them revise and improve their original written task, especially at the free writing stage. This drafting process is an essential part of the writing process where students learn to revise and to work through a series of drafts before considering a paper finished. Knowledge of a student's writing level for particular traits can help guide instruction. Mini-lessons, one-on-one instruction, and individualized goals can help ELL students address specific elements of their writing in different genres and styles.

Another stage that requires a lot of attention is responding to student writing. This is a complex process which requires teachers to develop or adopt strategies which help foster student improvement. Moreover, students should also be trained to use the feedback in ways that will improve their writing. This feedback should not only be on surface level errors but on the relevance of the idea to the topic and also on strategies students should utilize in producing better essays. These strategies should be taught explicitly to the students (prewriting, revising, organizing, etc.) for them to implement during the writing process.

There are many ways of providing teacher feedback:

- Oral teacher feedback in the form of individual or group conferences
- Written comments or suggestions on students' drafts
- Modeling the traits of good writing using exemplars or model texts
- Peer response in which students read or listen to each other's papers for the purpose of providing insight. This could be done in groups or pairs. The teacher can provide guidelines to the students so they remain focused on the task at hand.

The above stages are important in the writing process and should be implemented effectively by the teacher. The writing of the composition as well as the feedback stage of the writing process are crucial in improving the writing abilities of all learners but especially those developing fluency in English.

To keep students engaged in a writing task, it is important for the writer to be interested in the task. Therefore, these tasks need a purpose other than just *language practice*. Personal topics (such as autobiography, hobbies, preferences, problems) allow students to convey real information. However, when topics move away from personal narratives, it is helpful to specify the communicative purpose of the topic. A topic like, "*A vacation on a cruise ship is a wonderful experience*" can be changed to "*Write an advertisement for a cruise ship to convince people to take a cruise.*" While selecting a topic, it is necessary to consider how to make it meaningful for both the reader and the writer This way the writer will put more effort and interest into his/her writing in order to communicate real meaning.

The organization of written discourse in English is culturally determined to a large degree. Therefore, students who write well in their first language cannot simply rely solely on their prior writing skills when writing in English. Students have to learn not only how English sentences are formed but how paragraphs and longer pieces are constructed. In written English, we generally state our topic and elaborate on our statement by adding supporting details such as facts, examples, descriptions, illustrations, reasons, causes, effects, comparisons, and contrasts. This may not be true in the student's L1.

Additionally, multiple texts are used across all subject areas to convey "multiple viewpoints in multiple formats (e.g., letters, essays, reports, advertisements, lectures), through various venues (e.g., newspapers, television, postcards, websites, books, magazines)…" (Shanahan, 2008).

Shanahan (2008) further postulates that adolescents need instruction to use effective strategies in writing about the same topic in multiple ways and for multiple purposes. Students need to learn to keep the audience in mind as well as the kind of writing they are engaged in. They can use the techniques mentioned below to help them identify these factors beforehand.

Organizing thoughts in writing is a process in itself. A number of strategies can be used to teach students these skills. They allow the students to make choices with the purpose of the task in mind. Following are some techniques that would help students develop organization skills.

Outlines
There are two basic types of outlines:

- An outline the writer makes before writing the text
- An outline the writer makes of what s/he has already written

An outline that is developed before writing the text should be brief and made after extensive discussion, list-making, brainstorming, and other prewriting activities. It helps to guide the writer in developing the text. Similarly, an outline that is made after the first draft is written helps the writer analyze his/her work and see what needs to be done to make the text clearer to the reader. A technique to teach this skill would be to give the students a reading passage and ask them either to discuss and make their own outline of what has been written or to complete the skeleton of a given outline.

Analysis

Outlining is one way to help students examine a text closely. Additionally, students should analyze a reading passage and ask questions about a piece of writing regarding not only what the writer has written but also how s/he has written it. Some techniques to teach this skill are:

- Students are given short paragraphs and asked to read one sentence of each. Then they are asked to discuss in pairs or in groups which one sentence best expresses the paragraph it belongs to and why.
- Give or read students a paragraph without its topic sentence or the concluding sentence. Then ask the students to choose from the choices provided and give reasons for their choice. If the students are advanced, they could discuss the passage and write their own sentences.

Models

Model paragraphs or texts should not be used for students to imitate mechanically, but they should be used as a resource for the writer. For example, the students might read a passage comparing two bicycles and then write their own composition comparing two cars, following the organizational and structural pattern of the model. Explicit instruction that draws attention to the features of specific text types will help students learn the features of important forms like essays, research projects, etc. Rather than following the model step-by-step, students use their prior analysis of the form as a resource to help deal with problems that may emerge in the process of their own writing. For example, if the student is not sure how to best organize an argument, the model can be used to analyze, manipulate, and shed a light on what path to take.

Research based projects are extremely important both as a writing form and for success in different academic disciplines. Completing research projects can pose additional challenges for English language learners because of the reading and analysis required to complete them. Integrating information gleaned from different sources into a project can be particularly difficult for students in the early stages of vocabulary and literacy development in English.

Teachers can support students as they address the challenges of researching a topic by assisting them in selecting texts, curating resources that are directly connected to the project, or by helping students break down key information within a text. These scaffolding strategies should be used with the goal of helping the learner move towards independence. These strategies can be targeted to support students with the challenges of reading or to allow them to focus on the process of writing, depending on the teacher's perception of student need.

OBJECTIVE 10 CONTENT-AREA LEARNING AND ACCESS TO THE CORE CURRICULUM

Skill 10.1 Classroom-based assessment of content-area learning and concept development

ELL students are constantly working simultaneously to build language proficiency and to learn content-area knowledge and skills. Though in many cases language limitations may make some content-related material difficult to master, progress towards standards achievement must still be assessed. The ESOL teacher plays an important role in helping to ensure that content-area teachers use assessments that accurately assess ELL student growth and understanding in their subject area.

Care must be taken in designing content-area assessments when they are used with ELL students. In analyzing both formal and informal assessment data, ESOL teachers should carefully consider whether content-area performance tasks provide native speakers and ELLs equal opportunities to succeed. The construct of a content-area performance task should not necessarily involve a high level of English language proficiency. If it does, it might make it difficult for ELLs to perform well, even if they have considerable knowledge and skills in the content-area. This puts ELLs at a disadvantage. Linguistic demands need to be clear and fair, if testing content-area knowledge and skills.

Other possible assessment areas for consideration include the ways in which students are asked to demonstrate knowledge and skills. Providing ELLs (and all students) with multiple opportunities and ways to demonstrate their knowledge and skills is more likely to produce better performance outcomes. Similarly, carefully consider the weighting of test items. If some items are weighted heavily because they require longer written responses, this could put ELLs at a disadvantage, as these written tasks will require more English language skills in order to express content-area knowledge.

Finally, the language used in the assessment should be linguistically accessible for both assessment directions and items/questions to give native speakers and English language learners equal opportunities to express what they know.

Skill 10.2 Principles, features and applications of content-based and sheltered approaches to content instruction

Though ELL students, particularly in the early stages of English language development, face challenges in learning content, research-based theories and strategies can maximize content-area learning. The following language learning theories support specific instructional strategies. Many of these theories overlap in theory and in practice.

Theory: Language learners will learn authentic language and gain a truer picture of the complexities and richness of English when used as a real means of interacting and sharing among people

Strategy: Integrated Language Teaching

The two main types of integrated language teaching are Content-Based Instruction and Task-Based Instruction. Both of these approaches require students to use language authentically to obtain information and to communicate information. Content-based instruction requires students to practice all the language skills in a highly integrated, communicative way while learning content (Oxford, 2001). The three main models of content-based instruction are:

- Theme-based models: Language skills are integrated in the study of themes or broad topics (e.g., cities, recycling, homelessness)
- Adjunct model: Language and content courses are taught separately but closely coordinated
- Sheltered model: English is simplified to ELL's level of proficiency while teaching content. (Oxford, 2001)

Task-based learning is another way of achieving Integrated Language Teaching. Students are guided through tasks (Prabhu, 1987) formulated so that they are as realistic as possible.

Three main trends in tasks are:

- Communicativeness: Learning is achieved through activities promoting real conversation between learners.
- Tasks: Learners who use language in a meaningful way to carry out tasks will learn language.
- Meaningfulness: Learners need to find meaning in the task for the learning tasks to be most effective.

Theory: When learners are instructed through content-based instruction such as mathematics, science, social studies, etc., they tend to achieve a much higher proficiency level in the target language than if they were only instructed in the target language through ESL methods.

Strategy: The Cognitive Academic Language Learning Approach (CALLA) integrates the following tenets:

- The L2 learners' actual grade level in the main subject areas of mathematics, science, and social studies etc., should be the deciding factor for content.
- The L2 learners should be exposed to and gradually acquire the specific language used when studying in the subject areas, such as: add this column of numbers; determine "x" in this algebraic problem; identify the properties of this cell, etc.
- The L2 learners should be encouraged to use higher-level cognitive processes such as application, analysis and synthesis.

The CALLA teacher needs to first introduce basic literacy skills. If possible, these should be introduced in the native or heritage language of the child. For older students, the Language Experience Approach (see 8.3 and 10.2) has proven effective. Another technique to use with older students is to have them read such everyday items as signs, menus, ads, and recipes because there is an immediate association with these materials and the need to learn to read (Chamot & O'Malley, 1994).

Some examples of methods to help ELL students begin developing basic English literacy before transitioning to more academic English include:

- Creating illustrated autobiographies: ("All about Me" or "The Story of My Life") can help ease ELLs into the academic challenges of a new school and culture. Students use as much English as they can and draw pictures to illustrate other points. This is an integrative activity because ELLs are not singled out, but are part of the group.
- Dialogue journals: Can be used with students of all ages. Provide all students with blank journals and allow them to draw or write in the language of their choice. The instructor should respond to the journals periodically. Journals are an excellent way to develop a personal relationship with the students while at the same time introducing literacy to the class.
- Themes: Such as "Where We Were Born" or "Family Origins" make good starting points to bring in home cultures and activate prior knowledge of all students. (Adapted from Peregoy and Boyle, 2008)

Theory: Students can learn content while developing their English language skills

Strategy: Sheltered Content Teaching

In sheltered content teaching, students from diverse linguistic backgrounds are grouped together allowing content instruction through English adapted to the proficiency level of the students. Emphasis is on content, though English language learning is also expected. Specifically Designed Academic Instruction in English (S.D.A.I.E.) is one example of this type of instruction. Sheltered content teaching—which is based upon the theories of Krashen (comprehensible input and affective environment) and Cummins (Basic Interpersonal Communication Skills—BICS and Cognitive Academic Language Proficiency--CALP) are indispensable components of Sheltered Content Teaching.

Some of the features of Sheltered Content Teaching would be:

- Comprehensible input
- Assessing prior knowledge
- Scaffolding
- Hands-on activities
- Visual clues (realia, word lists, pictures, models, gestures, body language)
- Cooperative learning
- Reduced language demands (teachers monitor their syntax, rate of speech, and language structures)
- Cultural affirmation and multicultural appreciation
- Graphic organizers
- Active learning with higher order thinking skills

- Teacher as a facilitator of learning

Depending on student population sizes and staffing levels, schools often employ different models of programs to support ELL students' content-area learning. Some programs focus on 'push-in' with specialist teachers working with ELL students in content-area classes while others are 'pull-out', working with English learners in special classes. Still others combine push-in and pull-out. They generally share as goals the intent to teach English language learners to communicate in social settings, engage in academic tasks, and use English in socially and culturally appropriate ways. Some of these models are:

Content-based instruction: Instruction in English that attempts to develop language skills and prepare ELLs to study grade-level content material in English. This has an emphasis on language, but with gradual introduction to content areas, vocabulary and basic concepts.

Structured English immersion: The goal is English proficiency. ELLs are pulled out for structured instruction in English so that subject matter is comprehensible. Used with sizeable groups of ELLs who speak the same language and are in the same grade level or with a diverse population of language minority students. There is little or no first/home language support. Teachers use sheltered instructional techniques and often have strong receptive skills in the students' native or heritage language.

Submersion with primary language support: The goal is English proficiency. Bilingual teachers or aides support the minority students in each grade level who are ELLs. In small groups, the ELLs are supported by reviewing the content areas in their primary language. The teachers may use the L1 to support English content classes.

A number of program models have been developed to meet the needs of language minority students involving the integration of language and content instruction. In this approach, the second or foreign language is used as the medium of instruction for mathematics, science, social studies, and other academic subjects; it is the vehicle used for teaching and acquiring subject- specific knowledge. The focus of the second language classroom should be on something meaningful, such as academic content, and modification of the target language facilitates language acquisition and makes academic content accessible to second-language learners.

Integrated language-and-content instruction offers a means by which ELL students can continue their academic or cognitive development while they are also acquiring academic language proficiency. In **theme-based programs**, a language curriculum is developed around selected topics drawn from one content area (e.g., the democracy) or from across the curriculum (e.g., pollution and the environment). The theme could be a week or two long and focuses on language taught in a meaningful way. The goal is to assist learners in developing general academic language skills through interesting and relevant content.

There are a variety of strategies to teach the integrated approach to language teaching of which the four most important are (Crandall, 1994):

1. Cooperative learning: In this method, students of different linguistic and educational backgrounds and different skill levels work together on a common task for a common goal to complete a task pertaining to the content being taught in the classroom. The focus is also on an implicit or explicit language feature that the students acquire through negotiation of meaning.

2. Task-based or experiential learning: Appropriate contexts are provided for developing thinking and study skills as well as language and academic concepts for students at different levels of language proficiency. Students learn by carrying out specific tasks or projects that they complete with a focus on the content, but learning language and academic skills as well.

3. Whole language approach: The philosophy of whole language is based on the concept that students need to experience language as an integrated whole. It focuses on the need for an integrated approach to language instruction within a context that is meaningful to students (Goodman, 1986). The approach is consistent with integrated language and content instruction, as both emphasize meaningful engagement and authentic language use, and both link oral and written language development (Blanton, 1992). Whole language strategies that have been implemented in content-centered language classes include dialogue journals, reading response journals, learning logs, process-based writing, and language experience stories (Crandall, 1992).

4. Graphic organizers: These frameworks provide a "means for organizing and presenting information so that it can be understood, remembered, and applied" (Crandall, 1992). Graphs, realia, tables, maps, flow charts, timelines, and Venn diagrams are used to help students place information in a comprehensible context. These tools enable students to organize information obtained from written or oral texts, develop reading strategies, increase retention, activate schema as a prereading or pre-listening activity, and organize ideas during the prewriting stage (Crandall, 1992).

An approach to teach vocabulary and to build prior knowledge about the content for readers is the **language experience approach**. Pressley (2008) states that good readers make use of background knowledge to make inferences that are necessary for understanding a text. This process helps readers create new knowledge from the text (*top-down processing*). In light of this view, the language experience approach supports children's concept development and vocabulary growth while offering many opportunities for meaningful reading and writing activities. It also helps in the development of shared experiences that expand children's knowledge of the world around them. In this approach, students' attention is focused on an experience in their daily life such as taking a class walk to collect leaves, blowing bubbles, making popcorn, apple picking, or experimenting with magnets. Students are involved in planning, experiencing, responding to, and recording the experience. The teacher initiates a discussion eliciting narrative from the students while providing appropriate vocabulary. In the end, the students compose oral individual or group stories that the teacher writes down and reads with students.

WIDA identifies three primary types of strategies that teachers may employ to support ELL students. These are sensory (e.g., word walls, math manipulatives, audio books), graphic (e.g., Venn diagrams, graphic organizers, tables or word webs), and interactive (partner or group work, cooperative learning strategies, mentors).

In designing learning opportunities, the ESOL teacher must be responsive to the needs of learners. Flexibility in the use of materials and in instructional practices will ensure that students can maximize learning and progress in language acquisition. Employing these methods will allow students to build social language skills while also developing communicative skills for academic purposes.

Skill 10.3 Instructional strategies to make academic language and content-area concepts accessible (i.e., authentic uses of language and scaffolding)

As noted previously, the linguistic demands of academic language and content-related concepts can be particularly difficult for students with limited proficiency in English. Learning content while simultaneously learning language is a daily challenge for ELL students. There are, however, a number of strategies to make this process easier. Most are good practices for making content more accessible for native speakers as well, but the focus here is on supporting English language learners.

Vocabulary
Increasingly complex vocabulary is one of the features of both academic language and content-area learning. ESOL teachers can help English language learners develop academic language by frontloading vocabulary. When students are given explanations and new vocabulary they need in upcoming reading (or content classes), they are better able to handle the academic demands placed upon them. By using examples of the word in its context, asking students to decide if the word is used correctly, and asking them to draw pictures of the word, students are actively engaged in the learning process.

Similarly, annotating complex texts is an effective method of supporting ELL students. In this way they can focus on understanding readings without having to stop to look up unfamiliar words.

Modeling
Because the academic language uses specific to certain subjects (i.e., literary essays, lab reports for experiments, etc.) are often not encountered outside of class, they may be totally unfamiliar to ELL students. ESOL teachers can provide ELLs with opportunities to learn and use forms of English language necessary to express content-subject specific academic language functions (e.g., analyzing, comparing, persuading, citing evidence, making hypotheses). ELLs need opportunities to debate, write written reports, make hypotheses, etc., but in most cases, these structures will have to be taught explicitly. Citing evidence and making hypotheses are academic skills used throughout an academic's life and need to be taught beginning with simplified reports or research papers.

Teachers need to provide models of the language activity/structure they are teaching and demonstrate it to the students. The teacher can list the specific vocabulary and rhetorical structures used on the board for illustration. These forms could be copied and distributed to the class.

Mixed groupings

It is also useful to provide authentic opportunities for ELLs to use the English language for content-related communicative purposes with both native and non-native speakers of English. ELLs need the opportunity to practice English regardless of their level. By grouping ELL students with native speakers and other nonnative speakers of English they are practicing language and the social elements of communication. Many ELLs have content knowledge but may have difficulty expressing it, whereas a native speaker may not have the content knowledge necessary to complete a task. Both students benefit when working in small groups on assigned tasks.

Other strategies

It is important to implement powerful instructional strategies that actively engage students from linguistically and culturally diverse backgrounds instead of allowing them to be passive participants or observers. Krashen (1981, 1982) states that students must be instructed at a level slightly *higher* than their competence level, i.e. $i + 1$. He believes that for a student to learn, the input must be comprehensible.

Chamot and O'Malley (1994) stated that teachers need to be aware of their students' approaches to learning and how to expand the students' repertoire of learning strategies. Supporting students' metacognitive development through reflection on the learning process is a good way to encourage new learning strategies. Working with students to identify new ways of studying, taking notes, or organizing ideas before writing are just three examples.

Arreaga-Mayer (1998) puts forward constructs for effective instruction to linguistically and culturally diverse students:

Challenge
- Implicit (cognitive challenge, use of higher-order questions)
- Explicit (high but reasonable expectations)

Involvement
- Active involvement of all students

Success
- Reasonable activities that students can complete successfully.

Scaffolding/cognitive strategies
- Visual organizers, adequate background information, and support provided by teachers to students by thinking aloud, building on and clarifying their input

Mediation/feedback
- Strategies provided to students for understanding/using feedback

o Frequency and comprehensibility of feedback is important

Collaborative/cooperative learning
- o Opportunities for students to work together, solve problems, and complete projects

Techniques for second-language acquisition/sheltered English
- o Extended discourse
- o Consistent language
- o Incorporation of students' language

Respect for cultural diversity
- o Respect and knowledge of cultural diversity

Additionally, **peer-mediated instruction** is effective in promoting higher levels of language and academic learning and social interaction. Research has shown that cooperative, peer-mediated instruction contributes more to content mastery than do whole-class instruction, workbook activities, and question-answer sessions. This method gives ELLs opportunities to actively practice a concept, the amount of discourse produced, the degree of negotiation of meaning, and the amount of comprehensible linguistic input. The essential components of peer-mediated learning strategies are: (a) cooperative incentives, (b) group rewards, (c) individual accountability, and (d) task structures.

In this method, students of varied academic abilities and language proficiency levels work together in pairs and small groups toward a common goal. In these groups, the success of one student depends on the help of the others. In peer-mediated instruction the learning task assigned to groups varies, but the format of learning always includes interaction and interdependence among the students.
Similarly, **peer tutoring** is a method developed to improve the acquisition and retention of basic academic skills. In this method, students are either paired randomly or matched by ability or language proficiency to partners each week. Student's roles are switched during the daily tutoring session, allowing each child to be both the tutor/teacher and the tutee/student. Students are trained in the procedures necessary to act as tutors and tutees. The four basic components of this method are:

- Weekly competing teams (heterogeneous grouping)
- Highly structured teaching procedure (content material, teams, pairing, error correction, system of rewards)
- Daily, contingent, individual tutee point earning and public postings of individual and team scores
- Direct practice of functional academic and language skills to mastery

Content-based instruction (CBI) integrates L2 acquisition and the basic content areas of math, science, social studies, literature, etc. The most current research continues to find validity in the following:

- Learners do not learn L2 through singular instruction in the language's rules; they learn from meaningful interaction in the language.

- Learners will gain proficiency in a language only if they receive adequate input; i.e., language that is heard or read will start to make sense to a learner when they can build upon previous knowledge as well as understand context and cues.
- Although conversational fluency in L2 is a goal, speaking is not sufficient to develop the academic cognitive skills needed to learn the basic content areas.

When speaking, instructors should:

- Speak slowly, but naturally, taking care to enunciate without raising the volume;
- Use short sentences when explaining a concept or instructions; and
- Use instructional strategies like repeating or rephrasing;
- Write new vocabulary, expressions, or idioms on the board for further reinforcement.

When solving word problems in math, the instructors should first:

- Work through a word problem with the student step-by-step; and
- Demonstrate various strategies for problem solving.

When providing contextualization, the instructor should:

- Use facial expressions and gestures;
- Use realia (cultural objects);
- Use visual cues, such as photos, drawings, videos, etc.; and
- Use graphic organizers.

When giving directions, the instructor should:

- Simplify complicated tasks by giving specific instructions such as, "Open to page 107. Read the story. Once you have finished, wait for the class to finish reading."
- Periodically check for comprehension during the lesson.
- Provide opportunities for learner interactions.
- Create cooperative learning groups, which are essential for English language learners with varying levels of proficiency; heterogeneous groupings help to improve academic performance, especially if ELLs have the opportunity to clarify concepts and ask questions in their primary language.

When checking for understanding, the instructor should:

- Ask the learners to clarify the first, second, and continuing steps of a process.
- Ask a "who," "what," "when," "where," or "whose" question.
- Ask for clarification from the learner.

When correcting an error, the instructor should:

- NEVER embarrass or humiliate an English Language Learner.

- Avoid corrections when possible and simply accept the ELL's efforts at language. Model the language correctly without comments.
- Keep error correction to a minimum at first.
- Emphasize that making mistakes and being corrected is a basic part of any learning process, especially when learning a language.
- Focus on what a learner is trying to communicate rather than on how correct the communication is.
- Restate the question or sentence correctly when the error interferes with understanding.

Included with the preceding strategies are several reminders. Always announce and write down the objectives for a particular unit, use handwriting that is readable, develop consistency through daily routines, list step-by-step instructions, and use blended instructional approaches, whenever possible.

One of the great challenges of middle school and high school teachers is to make content accessible to students with limited proficiency in English. As subject-area content becomes more complex, ELL students may need even more support to make the content accessible. Teachers can offer tools like **graphic organizers**, infographics and charts to help support student comprehension of written materials or content from discussions. As students' language skills develop, they should be encouraged to employ these tools independently to support their own understanding. As noted in Skill 3.5, these visual tools help ELLs visualize and organize information and promote active learning. Not only does the use of graphic organizers encourage creativity and high-order thinking skills, but it also helps students summarize and interpret texts.

In addition, ESOL teachers can:

- Use or create materials that simplify the language of abstract concepts by retelling content information in easier English. Depending on the proficiency level of the students, teachers should use simple sentence structure and high frequency verbs.
- Select materials that help students build connections and associations in order to access background knowledge or previously taught information. This can be accomplished through teacher-prepared outlines and study guides.
- Present students with written as well as aural messages. Outline what you are saying on the chalkboard.
- Allow students' use of native language for English language and concept development.
- Model think-alouds to increase student comprehension. *Think-alouds* are oral demonstrations of the teacher's own cognitive processes or the strategies they use to comprehend a text. Students then try to incorporate these strategies to help themselves in the learning process. Teachers explicitly teach these strategies until the learners are able to use them independently.

Some English language learners (ELLs) know very little English but have a rich content background in their primary language. Other ELLs may have acquired intermediate or advanced English skills but still have gaps in their content knowledge. In order for ELLs to become successful overall students, they need to learn both English and grade-level content. ESL teachers support the teaching of **content area subjects** in the classroom. They can adopt certain strategies that will give additional support to ELLs in their learning of content-area subjects such as math, science, literature, etc.

Some of the strategies are as follows:

- *Introducing a text before reading*: Pre-reading activities may be designed to motivate student interest, activate prior knowledge, or pre-teach potentially difficult concepts and vocabulary. This is also a great opportunity to introduce comprehension components such as cause and effect, compare and contrast, personification, main idea, sequencing, and others. Some pre-reading activities could be showing a film on a related topic, conducting an experiment, going on a field trip, etc.
- *Cooperative learning strategies:* Cooperative learning is particularly beneficial for any student learning a second language. Cooperative learning activities promote peer interaction, which helps the development of language and the learning of concepts and content. It is important to assign ELLs to different teams so that they can benefit from English language role models. ELLs learn to express themselves with greater confidence when working in small teams. In addition to picking up vocabulary, ELLs benefit from observing how their peers learn and solve problems. There are a number of such group activities that help students gain content and language at the same time. An example is *team jigsaw* in which each student in a team is assigned one-fourth of a page to read from any text (for example, a social studies text), or one-fourth of a topic to investigate. Each student completes his or her assignment and then teaches the others or helps to put together a team product by contributing a piece of the puzzle. Another example is a literature circle for teaching literature.
- *Explicit teaching of reading comprehension skills:* English language learners often have problems mastering science, math, or social studies concepts because they cannot comprehend the textbooks for these subjects. Teaching comprehension strategies help students apply these skills to all subject areas. These skills include: summarizing, sequencing, inferring, comparing and contrasting, drawing conclusions, self-questioning, problem solving, relating background knowledge, and distinguishing between fact and opinion.
- *Multicultural literature* can be an effective tool to teach literacy skills in an English language classroom. It helps to acknowledge the diversity of cultures in the classroom, where students feel proud of their own culture as well as learn about other cultures. Multicultural literature not only celebrates different cultures but also helps students relate to the text at hand. Students are able to activate their background knowledge, thus improving their comprehension of challenging texts.

Skill 10.4 **Instructional strategies to develop ELL students' development of learning skills and strategies (e.g., critical thinking skills) to support content-area learning**

All students face the challenges of learning new content in different subjects, but for ELL students, this challenge can be compounded by the additional need to learn new vocabulary and new language structures (**as noted in 10.3**). Teaching specific learning skills and strategies can support ELL students in learning the language structures necessary to both understand and express learning in different disciplines while also helping them to master and integrate new content-area knowledge. For students with limited or interrupted formal school experiences, these can be essential tools.

Strategies to consider include:

- **Note-taking** - Students need to learn to synthesize large chunks of information presented orally or in writing in order to remember and apply essential ideas. Note-taking strategies vary tremendously, and different students will respond better to different methods.
- **Research** - All students will need to do research in different subject areas. This is a challenging process that includes searching for information, selecting what is relevant, synthesizing it into usable 'chunks', and integrating it into writing or projects. Students need methods for finding, saving, and annotating. Some students will find this easiest with traditional paper/pen and a notebook while others will benefit from digital tools (like Evernote or Diigo) that allow them to save sources and then annotate them. Research is a cross-disciplinary skill that should be used in multiple classes, but the ESOL teacher will play a special role in supporting ELL students.
- **Study skills** - Students may need practice in how to review for a test or prepare for an assessment. Teachers can assist students in creating flashcards (digital or paper) or learning ways of review (quizzing oneself/a partner, reviewing notes, etc.).
- **Test-taking** - Particularly in an era of high stakes testing, students may need guidance on how to pace themselves during assessments, when to skip items for later review, how to create an outline, or simply following procedural directions.
- **Building vocabulary** - For ELL students in particular, content area vocabulary can pose a challenge. Students may need support in learning how to categorize words, how to use new terms in context, or even the importance of looking up unfamiliar words to determine meaning.
- **Comprehension** - Inference is an important part of reading comprehension. For students learning English, extra time is often needed to develop skills for recognizing implied meaning.

All of these skills and strategies play a role in any student's long-term academic success.

REFERENCES

"Academic Language and ELLs: What Teachers Need to Know." *Academic Language and ELLs: What Teachers Need to Know | Colorín Colorado*. Web. 13 Jan. 2017.

Alderson, J. 1992. Guidelines for the evaluation of language education. In: Ellis, R. 1997. The empirical evaluation of language teaching materials. ELT Journal Vol. 51, No. 1 Jan.

Allen, V.G. (1994) Selecting materials for the instruction of ESL children. In: Zainuddin (2007).

Au, K. H. 1993. Literacy instruction in multicultural settings. Orlando, FL.: Harcourt Brace.

------ 2002. Multicultural factors and effective instruction of students of diverse backgrounds. In A. Farstrup and S. J. Samuels (eds.) *What research says about reading Instruction*. Newark, DE: International Reading Assn. Coral Gables: U of Miami. 392-413.

Banks, J. A. 1988. Multicultural Leader. Vol. 1, No. 2. Educational Materials & Services Center. Spring.

Baker, K. 1998. Structured English Immersion: Breakthrough in Teaching Limited-English-Proficient Students. Phi Delta Kappan, Nov. pp199-204.

Barton, L. 1997. Quick Flip Questions for Critical Thinking. Dana Point, CA: Edupress.

Bebe, V.N & Mackey, W.F. 1990. *Bilingual schooling and the Miami experience*. Coral Gables, FL University of Miami. Institute of Interamerican Studies. Graduate School of International Studies.

Bennett, C. 1995. Comprehensive multicultural education: Theory and practice (3rd ed.). Massachusetts: Allen & Bacon.

Berko Gleason, J. 1993. *The Development of Language* (3rd ed.) New York: Macmillan.

Bialystok, E. (ed.). 1991. *Language Processing in Bilingual Children*. Cambridge: CUP.

Blakey, E. & Spence, S. 1990. Developing Metacognition (ED327218). ERIC Clearinghouse on Information Resources. Syracuse, NY.

Brisk, M. E. 1998. Bilingual Education: From compensatory to quality schooling. Mahwah, N. J. Lawrence Erlbaum.

Brown, H. Douglas. *Teaching by Principles: An Interactive Approach to Language Pedagogy.* Englewood Cliffs, NJ: Prentice Hall Regents, 1994. Print.

Burstall, C., Jamieson, M., Cohen, S. and Hargreaves, M. 1974. *Primary French I the balance.* Slough: NFER.

California Department of Education. Testing & Accountability. CELDT Questions and Answers. http://www.cde.ca.gov/ta/tg/el/celdtfaq.asp Rev. 11/03/09.

Candlin, C. 1987. In Batstone, R. 1994. *Grammar.* Oxford: OUP.

Chalfant, J.C. & Pysh, M.V. 1981. Teacher assistance teams—A model for within building problem solving. Counterpoint. Nov. p 16-21.

Chalfant, J.C., Pysh, M.V. & Moultrie, R. 1979. Teacher Assistance Teams: A Model for Within-Building Problem Solving. Learning Disability Quarterly. v2, n3 Summer, p. 85-96. Council for Learning Disabilities.

Chamot, A.U. and O'Malley, J. M. 1994. *The Calla Handbook.* Reading, MA: Addison-Wesley.

Clay, Marie M. *What Did I Write?:.* London: Heinemann Educational, 1975. Print.

Collier, V.P. 1989. "How long? A synthesis of research on academic achievement in second language." *TESOL Quarterly*, 23. 509-531.

-----. 1992. A synthesis of studies examining long-term language minority student data on academic achievement. *Bilingual Research Journal*, 16 (1-2). 187-212.

-----. 1995. "Acquiring a second language for school." Directions in Language & Education. Washington, DC: NCBE. 1(4), 1-10.

Conflict Research Consortium. Online Training Program on Intractable Conflict (OTPIC) Conflict Management and Constructive Confrontation: A Guide to the Theory and Practice. University of Colorado Revised July 20, 1999. http://conflict.colorado.edu

Crawford, J. 1998. Ten Common Fallacies About Bilingual Education. ERIC Clearinghouse on Language & Linguistics. Washington, D.C. Nov. ERIC Id ED424792.

Criteria for Evaluating Instructional Materials: Kindergarten Through Grade Eight. Reading/Language Arts Framework for California Public Schools. California Department of Education. 2007.

"Critical Literacy." *Critical Literacy*. Web. 13 Jan. 2017.

Cruz, J. 2005. Second Language Acquisition Programs: An Assessment of the Bilingual Education Debate. McNair Scholars Journal: Vol. 9, Iss. 1, Art. 6. http://scholarworks.gvsu.edu/mcnair/vol/iss1/6

Cummins, J. 1981. Bilingualism and Minority Language Children. Toronto: Institute for Studies in Education.

Cummins, J. 1984. Bilingualism and special education: Issues in assessment and pedagogy. San Diego: College-Hill.

Cummins, J. 1998. Rossell and Baker: Their case for the effectiveness of bilingual education. The Journal of Pedagogy Pluralism & Practice. Issue 3, Vol. 1: Fall.

Cummins, J. & Genzuk, M. 1991. Analysis of final report longitudinal study of structured English immersion strategy, early-exit and late-exit transitional bilingual education programs for language-minority students. California Association for Bilingual Education Newsletter, 13.

Curry, D. 1989. Illustrated American Idioms. Washington, DC. English Language Program Division. Bureau of Educational and Cultural Affairs. USIA.

"Defining Emergent Literacy: Developing Lifelong Readers." *Concordia Nebraska Online*. Web. 13 Jan. 2017.

Díaz-Rico, L.T. and Weed, K.Z. 1995. Language, and Academic Development Handbook: A Complete K-12 Reference Guide. Needham Heights, MA: Allyn and Bacon.

Diaz-Rico, L.T. 2008. Strategies for Teaching English Learners. 2nd ed. Boston: Pearson.

Dodd, Anne W., and Jean L. Konzal. *How Communities Build Stronger Schools: Stories, Strategies, and Promising Practices for Educating Every Child*. New York: Palgrave, 2002. Print.

Dulay, H. and Burt, M. 1974. "You can't learn without goofing" in J. Richards' (ed.) Error Analysis, Perspectives on Second Language Acquisition. New York: Longman.

D. W. Carnine|J. Silbert|E. J. Kame'enui|S. G. Tarver. "Reading Development: Chall's Model." *Education.com*. 01 May 2014. Web. 13 Jan. 2017.

Ellis, R. 1985. Understanding Second Language Acquisition. Oxford: OUP.

------ 1994. The Study of Second Language Acquisition. Oxford: OUP.

"English Language Development (ELD) Standards." *WIDA English Development (ELD) Standards*. Web. 13 Jan. 2017.

Entwhistle, N.J. and Entwhistle, D. 1970. The relationships between personality, study methods and academic performance. British Journal of Educational Psychology. Vol 40(2). doi.apa.org. 132-143.

Fillmore, L.W. 2001. Scott, Foresman ESL:Accelerating English Language Learning. In: Zainuddin (2007).

Friend, M. and Bursuck, W. D. 2005. *Models of Coteaching: Including Students with Special Needs: A Practical Guide for Classroom Teachers*. (3rd ed.) Boston, MA: Allyn and Bacon.

Garcia, E. 1994. *Understanding and Meeting the Challenge of Student Cultural Diversity*. Boston: Houghton Mifflin.

Garinger, D. 2002. Textbook Evaluation. TESL Web Journal Vol. 1, No. 3.

Genesee, F. 1987. *Learning through Two Languages: Studies of Immersion and Bilingual Education*. Cambridge, MA: Newbury House.

------ (ed.) 1994. *Educating Second Language Children: The Whole Child, the Whole Curriculum, the Whole Community*. Cambridge: CUP.

Grellet, F. 1981. *Developing Reading Skills*. Cambridge: CUP.

Gersten, R. & Baker, S. 2000. What we know about effective instructional practices for English-Language Learners. Exceptional Children, 66(4) June, p. 454-470.

Gersten, R. & Baker, S. 2003. English-Language Learners with Learning Disabilities. In H. L. Swanson, K. R. Harris & S. Graham (eds.) Handbook of Learning Disabilities. (pp. 94-109). NY: Guilford.

GOLLNICK, Donna M. *Multicultural Education in a Pluralistic Society.* Pearson/Merrill/Pr. Hall, 2006. Print.

Grasha, A. F. 1996. Your teaching style. Pittsburgh, PA: International Alliance of Teacher Scholars.

Gregorc, A.1982. An adult's guide to style. Maynard, MA: Gabriel Systems.

Gurel, Sarah M. (2004) Teaching English Language Learners with Learning Disabilities: A Compiled Convergence of Strategies. College of William and Mary. School of Education, Curriculum and Instruction.

Harris, M. and McCann, P. 1994. *Assessment*. Oxford: Heinemann.
Jerald, C.D. 2006. School Culture: "The Hidden Curriculum". The Center for Comprehensive School Reform and Improvement. Issue Brief. December. www.centerforcsri.org

Heywood, D. 2006. Using Whole Discourse Tasks for Language Teaching. www.jalt-publications.org/tlt/chaprep/ Jan.

Holdaway, Don. "Shared Book Experience: Teaching Reading Using Favorite Books." *Theory Into Practice* 21.4 (1982): 293-300. Print.

"How We Teach English Learners: 3 Basic Approaches." *NPR*. NPR. Web. 13 Jan. 2017.

Hruska-Reichmann, S. & Grasha, A.F. 1982. The Grasha-Reichmann Student Learning Scales: Research findings and applications. In. J. Keefe (Ed.). Student learning styles and brain behavior. Reston, VA: NASSP.

Hyland, K. 2002. Teaching and Researching Writing. Harlow, England: Pearson.

Kamenetz, Anya. "What's Going on Inside the Brain of a Bilingual Child?" *MindShift*. Web. 13 Jan. 2017.

Keirsey, D. 1998. Please understand me II. Del Mar, CA: Prometheus Nemesis.

KH Kim, D Zabelina. Cultural Bias in Assessment: Can Creativity Assessment Help? The International Journal of Critical Pedagogy, 2015

Kolb, D. A. 1976. The learning style Inventory technical manual. Boston: McBer.

Kramsch, C. 1998. *Language and Culture*. Oxford: OUP.

Krashen, S. 1981. *Second Language Acquisition and Second Language Learning*. Oxford: Pergamon Press.

------1982. *Principles and Practice in Second Language Acquisition*. Oxford: Pergamon Press.

Lambert, W. and Klineberg, O. 1967. Children's views of foreign peoples: A crossnational study. New York: Appleton. (Review in Shumann, J., Affective factors and the problem of age in second language acquisition, *Language Learning* 25/2. 1975. 209-235).

Lambert, W. E. 1990. Issues in Foreign Language and Second Language Education. In: Proceedings of the Research Symposium on Limited English Proficient Students' Issues. (1st, Washington, DC. September 10-12. ED 341 269. Fl 020 030.

"Landmark Court Rulings Regarding English Language Learners." *Landmark Court Rulings Regarding English Language Learners | Colorín Colorado*. Web. 13 Jan. 2017.

Language Development in Children. Child Development Institute (https://childdevelopmentinfo.com/child-development/language_development/#.WGdUApJ-hr1)

Larsen, D. and Smalley, W. 1972. *Becoming Bilingual, a Guide to Language Learning*. New Canadian: CT. Practical Anthropology.

Larsen-Freeman, D. 1997. Chaos/complexity science and second language acquisition. *Applied Linguistics*, 18 (2). 141-165.

Leshinsky, J.G. 1995. Authentic listening and discussion for advanced students. Englewood Cliffs, NJ: Prentice-Hall Regents.

Lock, R.H. & Layton, C. A. 2002. Isolating Intrinsic Processing Disorders from Second Language Acquisition. Bilingual Research Journal. v 26n2 p. 383-94. Summer

Long, M. 1990. The lease a second language acquisition theory needs to explain. *TESOL Quarterly*. 24(4). 649-666.

Ludke, Karen M,Ferreira, Fernanda Overy, Katie. Singing can facilitate foreign language learning. *Memory & Cognition*, 2013; DOI: (10.3758/s13421-013-0342-5)

The Map of Standards for ELS. 2002. 3rd ed. West Education.

McArthur, T. ed. 1992. *The Oxford Companion to the English Language*. Oxford: OUP. 571-573.

McCarthy, B. 1983. The 4-MAT system: Teaching to learning styles with right-left mode techniques. Oak Brook, IL: Excel.

McClelland, D., Atkinson, J., Clark, R. & Lowell, E. 1953. *The Achievement Motive*. New York: Appleton, Century, Crofts.

McDonough, J. and Shaw, S. 1993. *Materials and Methods in ELT: A Teacher's Guide*. Blackwell.

McKay, S. L. 1987. Teaching Grammar: form, function, and technique. New York: Prentice Hall.

McLaughlin, B. 1990.The development of bilingualism: Myth and reality. In A. Barona & E. Garcia (eds.) *Children at Risk: Poverty, Minority Status and other Issues in Educational Equity*. Washington, D.C.: National Association of School Psychologists. 65-76.

Mitchell, Rosamond, and Florence Myles. *Second Language Learning Theories*. London: Hodder Education, 2010. Print.

Mitchell, V. 1990. Curriculum and instruction to reduce racial conflict. (ED322274). ERIC Clearinghouse on Urban Education. NY, NY.

Murphy, J. M. 1998. The eight disciplines. Grand Rapids, MI: Venture Management.

Naiman, N., Frolich, M., Stern, H., and Todesco, A. 1978. *The Good Language Learner*. Toronto: The Modern Language Centre, Ontario Institute for Studies in Education.

National Center for Research on Cultural Diversity and Second Language Learning. 1999. Two-Way Bilingual Education Programs in Practice: A National and Local Perspective. Center for Applied Linguistics, Online Resources: Digest. July.

National Center on Education and the Economy. 2001. California Performance Standards.

Nieto, S. 1992. "We Have Stories to Tell: A Case Study of Puerto Ricans in Children's Books." In Harris, V.J. (Ed.), Teaching Multicultural Literature in Grades K-8. Norwood, MA: Christopher-Gordon Publishers.

Nunan, D. 1989. *Designing Tasks for the Communicative Classroom*. Cambridge, CUP.

Nunan, David. *Practical English Language Teaching*. New York: McGraw-Hill/Contemporary, 2003. Print.

O'Malley, J. M. and Pierce, L. V. 1996. *Authentic Assessment for English Language Learners*. Longman.

Ovando, C.J., Coombs, M.C., and Collier, V.P. eds. 2006. *Bilingual and ESL Classrooms: Teaching in Multicultural Contexts* (4th ed.) Boston: McGraw-Hill.

Oxford, R. 2001. Integrated skills in the ESL/EFL classroom. Center for Applied Linguistics. Online Digests. Sept. EDO-FL-01-05.

Padilla, Amado M., Borsato N. Issues in Culturally Appropriate Psychoeducational Assessment. Research Gate. January 2008. (https://www.researchgate.net/publication/242580525_Issues_in_Culturally_Appropriate_Psychoeducational_Assessment)

Penfield, W. and Roberts, L. 1959. *Speech and Brain Mechanisms*. New York: Atheneum Press. (reviewed in Ellis, R. 1985).

Peregoy, S.F. and Boyle, O.F. 2008 *Reading, Writing, and Learning in ESL. 5th ed*. Boston: Pearson.

Prabhu, N. S. 1987. *Second Language Pedagogy: A Perspective*. London: Oxford, OUP.

Pugach, M.C. & Johnson, L.J. 1989. The Challenge of Implementing Collaboration between General and Special Education. Exceptional Children. V56.

Pugach, M.C. & Johnson, L.J. 1989. Prereferral Interventions: Progress, Problems, and Challenges. Exceptional Children. V56.

Quiocho, A. and Ulanoff, S.H. 2009. Differentiated Literacy Instruction for English Language Learners. Boston: Allyn & Bacon.

Reading/Language Arts Framework for California Public Schools. Kindergarten through Grade Twelve. 1999. Sacramento: CA DOE.

Reid, J. The learning style preferences of ESL students. *TESOL Quarterly*, 21(1): 86-103.

Rennie, J. 1993. ESL and Bilingual Program Models. Eric Digest. http://www.cal.org/resources/Digest/rennie01.html

Richards, Platt, and Weber. 1985. quoted by Ellis, R. The evaluation of communicative tasks in Tomlinson, B (ed.) *Materials Development in Language Teaching*. Cambridge: CUP. 1998.

Rinvolucri, M. 1984. Grammar Games: Cognitive, affective and movement activities for EFL students. Cambridge, CUP.

Rinvolucri, M. and Davis, P. 1995. More Grammar Games: Cognitive, affective and movement activities for EFL students. Cambridge, CUP.

Rochman, H. 1993. Against Borders: Promoting Books for a Multicultural World. Chicago, IL: American Library Association.

Rosansky, E. 1975. The critical period for the acquisition of language: some cognitive developmental considerations. In: Working Papers on Bilingualism 6: 92-102.

Rosenberg, L. Global Demographic Trends. F&D: Finance and Development Sept. 2006, Vol. 43, No. 3.

Rosenblatt, L. 2005. Making meaning with texts: selected essays. Portsmouth, NH: Heinemann.

Samway, K.D. & McKeon, D. 1999. Myths and realities: Best practices for language minority students. Portsmouth, NH: Heinemann.

Schiffrin, D., Tannen, D., and Hamilton, H., eds. 2003. The Handbook of Discourse Analysis. Wiley, John & Sons.

Schimel, J. et al 2000. Running from the Shadow: Psychological Distancing From Others to Characteristics People Fear in Themselves. Journal of Personality and Social Psychology. Vol. 78, No. 3 446-462

Schmidt, R. W. 1990. The role of consciousness in second language acquisition. *Applied Linguistics*, 11(2). 129-158.

Schumm, J.S., ed. 2006. *Reading Assessment and Instruction for All Learners*. New York: The Guilford Press.

Shoebottom, Paul. "The Factors That Influence the Acquisition of a Second Language." *The Factors That Influence the Acquisition of a Second Language*. Web. 13 Jan. 2017.

Sinclair, J. and Coulthard, M. 1975. Towards an Analysis of Discourse. Oxford: OUP. 93-94.

Slavin, R.E. and Cheung. 2003. *Effective Reading Programs for English Language Learners: A Best-Evidence Synthesis*. U.S. Dept. of Education. Institute of Education Sciences.

Slee, Phillip T., Marilyn Campbell, and Barbara A. Spears. *Child, Adolescent and Family Development*. Cambridge: Cambridge UP, 2012. Print.

Snow, C. and Hoefnagel-Hohle, M. 1978. Age Differences in Second Language Learning. In *Second Language Acquisition,* Hatch ed. Rowley, MA.: Newbury House.

Sonbuchner, G. M. 1991. How to take advantage of your learning styles. Syracuse, NY: New Readers Press. .

"Standards-Based Definition." *The Glossary of Education Reform*. 05 Dec. 2014. Web. 13 Jan. 2017.

Suid, M. & Lincoln, W. 1989. Recipes for Writing: Motivation, Skills, and Activities. Menlo Park, CA Addison-Wesley.

Taylor, O.L. 1990. Cross-Cultural Communication An Essential Dimension of Effective Education. Rev. ed. Chevy Chase, MD. Mid-Atlantic Equity Center.

Teachers of English to Speakers of Other Languages. 1997. *ESL Standards for Pre-K—12 Students*. Alexandria, VA.: TESOL.

Teaching Tolerance. n.d. *Anti-Gay Discrimination In Schools*. Southern Poverty Law Center, (http://www.tolerance.org)

Tharp, R. 1989. Psychocultural variables and constants: Effects on teaching and learning in schools. American Psychologist, 44(2). 349-359.

"Theories." *Theories | National Literacy Trust*. Web. 13 Jan. 2017.

Thomas, Adele. *Family Literacy in Canada: Profiles of Effective Practices*. Welland, Ont.: Éditions Soleil Pub., 1998. Print.

Thomas, W. P., and Collier, V. P. 1995. Language minority student achievement and program effectiveness. Manuscript in preparation. (in Collier, V.P. 1995).

Tollefsen, J. 1991. *Planning Language, Planning Inequality.* New York, Longman.

Tompkins, G. 2009. *Language Arts: patterns of practice*. 7th ed. Upper Saddle River, N.J.: Pearson.

Traugott, E. C. and Pratt, M. L. 1980. *Linguistics for Students of Literature*. San Diego: Harcourt Brace Jovanovich.

Trim, J.M. 1981. Council of Europe Educational Objectives. Adapted from the report of a working party of the British National Congress on Languages in Education.

Two-Way Immersion Education: the Basics. 2005. Center for Applied Linguistics. http://www.alliance.brown.edu/pubs/twi and http://www.cal.org/twi

United Nations Cyberschoolbus. 1996. Understanding Discrimination. cyberschoolbus@un.org

Unrau, N. 2008. *Content Area Reading and Writing*. 2nd ed. Upper Saddle River, N.J.: Pearson.

Ur, P. 1996. *A Course in Language Teaching*. Cambridge: CUP.

Valsiner, J. 2003. Culture and its Transfer: Ways of Creating General Knowledge Through the Study of Cultural Particulars. In W. J. Lonner, D. L. Dinnel, S. A. Hayes, & D. N. Sattler (Eds.), Online Readings in Psychology and Culture (Unit 2, Chapter 12), (http://www.wwu.edu/~culture), Center for Cross-Cultural Research, Western Washington University, Bellingham, Washington.

Vohs, J. 2009. Parents Place Pointers. Massachusetts Parent Information & Resource Center (PIRC). Northhampton, MA.

Vygotsky, L.S. 1986. *Thought and language.* Cambridge, MA: MIT Press.

Vygotsky, L.S. 2006. *Mind in society.* Cambridge, MA: Harvard University Press.

Watson, S. (2011) Learning Disability Checklist. www.About.com

Weir, C. 1993. *Understanding and Developing Language Tests.* Hemel Hempstead: Prentice Hall International.

Willing, K. 1988. "Learning strategies as information management: Some definitions for a theory of learning strategies". *Prospect* 3/2: 139-55.

Yokota, J. 1993." Issues in Selecting Multicultural Children's Literature." Language Arts, 70, 156-167.

Zainuddin, H., et al. 2007. *Fundamentals of Teaching English to Speakers of Other Languages in K-12 Mainstream Classrooms.* 2nd ed. Dubuque: Kendall/Hunt.

Zebroski, J. T. 1994. Thinking through theory: Vygotskian perspectives on the teaching of writing. Portsmouth, NH: Boynton/Cook.

Zwiers, J. 2007. *Building Academic Language. Essential Practices for Content Classrooms, Grades 5-12.* San Francisco: Jossey-Bass.

SAMPLE TEST

1. An ESOL teacher notices that a student is struggling to understand change in register when speaking with peers, with teachers and when approaching people she doesn't know to ask for information.

   In which of the following areas should a teacher work with the student? *(Skill 1.6)*

   A. Phonemic awareness and phonology
   B. Pragmatics and morphology
   C. Semantics and syntax
   D. English language variations

2. In addition to learning and practicing with phonemes, English language learners must also learn to recognize all of the following aspects of phonology, except: *(Skill 1.1)*

   A. How sounds influence communication
   B. How phrases and clauses influence communication
   C. How pitch and stress affect meaning
   D. How graphemes affect pronunciation

3. ESOL teachers should have a thorough understanding of pragmatics so that they can help students understand: *(Skill 1.5)*

   A. The effect of contemporary culture on language use
   B. The ways in which context impacts the interpretation of language
   C. Meaning which is "stored" or "inherent", as well as "contextual"
   D. The ways in which roots or bases determine the meaning of words

4. If one of your ELL students says, "I to school go," their error is one of: *(Skill 1.3)*

   A. Semantics
   B. Syntax
   C. Pragmatics
   D. Morphology

5. An elementary school ESOL teacher asks a beginning level ELL student where her pencil is. The student answers, "He is in my locker." Which of the following explanations should the teacher assume is the best explanation of why the student used the word 'he' instead of the word 'it'? *(Skill 1.3)*

   A. The student may be confused about what the word 'pencil' means
   B. The student's native language is one that marks objects as well as people by gender.
   C. The student doesn't understand the difference between inanimate and animate objects in general.
   D. The student is overgeneralizing rules for pronoun use as a result of fossilization.

NES ESOL

6. ESOL experts generally posit that phonographemic differences such as 'here' and 'hear' be taught explicitly. What is the best explanation for why this is important for intermediate level English language learners? (Skill 1.1)

   A. Sound-letter relationships in English are not always consistent.
   B. This is actually not true. Teaching about homophones is not encouraged for ESOL teachers anymore.
   C. Teaching figurative language and idiomatic expressions helps English language learners make sense of communicative input.
   D. It provides extra practice in reading words and sentences

7. A principal is observing an elementary school ESOL teacher during a reading lesson. After the observation, the principal suggests that the teacher do some morphemic analysis study with the students. What does the principal mean by 'morphemic analysis'? (Skill 1.2)

   A. Studying the order in which words occur in a sentence, e.g., SVO
   B. Studying the way words can have the same spellings but different meanings
   C. Studying the way in which speech sounds form patterns
   D. Studying the smallest unit within a language system to which meaning is attached

8. When ESOL teachers teach English language learners about English morphemic analysis, they are providing students with the tools necessary to: (Skill 1.2)

   A. Understand English grammar
   B. Understand English idioms
   C. Understand unfamiliar words
   D. Understand oral and written discourse markers

9. Use the text example below to answer the question that follows.

   "The plane leaves at 6:00 make sure you are at the airport before 4:00!"

   The exclamation above best illustrates which of the following grammatical errors? (Skill 1.3)

   A. A misuse of articles
   B. A run-on sentence
   C. A sentence fragment
   D. An inappropriate use of the imperative

10. Which of the following variables have an impact on discursive forms? (Skill 1.4)

    A. Mood, anxiety, and self-esteem
    B. Language, structure, context and topic
    C. Age, literacy history and aptitude
    D. Phonology, morphology and semantics

11. An ESOL teacher notices a student struggling to make friends. Other students have also complained to the teacher that the student is difficult to work with. The teacher has observed the student working in a small group and knows exactly what the problem is. What oral communication principle would the teacher work on with the student? *(Skill 1.4)*

    A. Taking turns in conversation.
    B. Choice of topic.
    C. Elaboration.
    D. Requesting and giving clarification.

12. Empty or perfunctory language is a feature of what type of discourse? *(Skill 1.4)*

    A. Academic discourse
    B. Poetic discourse
    C. Polite discourse
    D. Expressive discourse

13. When beginning to use textbooks with English language learners, which of the following discourse characteristics should the ESOL instructor teach? *(Skill 1.4)*

    A. Genre
    B. Passive voice
    C. Pronoun reference
    D. All of the above

14. Complete the following sentence with one of the answers below:

    An understanding of pragmatics helps ELLs with comprehension in social conversation and in reading content-area texts because: *(Skill 1.5)*

    A. Building contextual understanding is a scaffolding strategy that can help ELLs tackle new and unfamiliar content.
    B. Pragmatics helps ELLs recognize repeating patterns and develop decoding skills
    C. Pragmatics helps build productive and receptive vocabulary without depending on translation dictionaries
    D. Developing recognition of native English speaker's use of intonation, connotation and synonyms helps ELLs understand the meanings of words and sentences

15. The term diglossia: *(Skill 1.6)*

    A. Refers to the use of language restricted to a limited close circle of speakers
    B. Means speaking
    C. Is defined as the use of separate dialects or use of different language to communicate in different situations or groups
    D. Refers to a method of speaking when speakers do not share similar experiences or background

16. The acronym SPEAKING (setting, participants, ends, act sequence, key, instrumentalities, norms, genre) was used to explain knowledge that native language speakers have about the relationship between language and its social context (also known as communicative competence). Which of the following theorists is known for his work in this area? *(Skill 2.1)*

    A. Krashen
    B. Fishman
    C. Hymes
    D. Pinker

17. Interlanguage strategies are best described as: *(Skill 2.1)*

    A. Being able to transfer between oral and written discourse
    B. Being bilingual or multilingual (reading, writing, listening and speaking in at least 2 languages)
    C. Being a common process in second language learning
    D. Being characterized by poor grammar

18. Chomsky's Language Acquisition Device (LAD) includes all of the following hypotheses except: *(Skill 2.1)*

    A. Language learners form hypotheses based on the language they receive.
    B. Language learners' egocentric speech is actually private speech.
    C. Language learners test out hypotheses in speech and texts.
    D. Language learners construct language.

19. A team of teachers is looking over assessments and comparing notes on two middle-school English students. They are using Krashen's Natural Order hypothesis to try to understand if one of the students has a learning disability. The Natural Order hypothesis can help them to: *(Skill 2.1)*

    A. Monitor and verify that language instruction is following a specific order - if not, ELLs will suffer and may appear to have learning disabilities
    B. Understand how learners follow a predictable pattern as they learn language - if they fall outside the pattern, they can/should be monitored
    C. Identify that there are two basic ways of acquiring language so students who diverge from these ways can be monitored more closely
    D. Maintain orderly, safe environments so that language acquisition can take place for all students

20. An ESOL Kindergarten teacher is worried that one of her students is not meeting the Kindergarten English language reading standards. Which of the following theorists would tell her that she shouldn't really be teaching reading in Kindergarten? *(Skill 2.2)*

    A. BF Skinner
    B. Piaget
    C. Holdaway
    D. Gessell

21. An elementary ESOL teacher is a big believer in the impact that Big Books and shared reading can have on literacy development for English language learners. These ideas are based on the theories of: *(Skill 2.2)*

    A. Holdaway's Foundations of Literacy
    B. Piaget's Cognitive Development Theories
    C. Marie Clay's Emergent Literacy Theory
    D. The Stages Model of Reading Development

22. Schools that use Reading Recovery programs, are based on theories that identify: *(Skill 2.2)*

    A. Family literacy intervention as a key factor in helping struggling ELL readers
    B. The steps that children generally engage in before the acts of 'reading' and 'writing' formally take place
    C. Phases that children go through from learning the letters of the alphabet to being selective about what to read, when and why
    D. The knowledge and skills to be learned and breaks them down into smaller units

23. L1 and L2 learners follow approximately the same order in learning a language. Identify the correct sequence from the options below. *(Skill 2.2)*

    A. Silent period, experimental speech, private speech, lexical chunks, formulaic speech.
    B. Silent period, private speech, lexical chunks, formulaic speech, experimental speech.
    C. Private speech, lexical chunks, speech emergency, formulaic speech, experimental speech.
    D. Private speech, speech emergence, lexical chunks, formulaic speech, experimental speech.

24. Skills such as inferring, classifying, analyzing, synthesizing, and evaluating are key components of: *(Skill 2.3)*

    A. BICS
    B. SPEAKING
    C. CALP
    D. PRAC

25. Read the following excerpt from a middle school ESOL student's mid-year report to answer the question below.

    Andrea's understanding of spoken English is adequate. Although listeners can understand her when she is speaking, she often has to rephrase what she is trying to say first. Andrea uses reading strategies and some supports to assist with reading comprehension, and her writing skills are beginning to develop.

    According to Andrea's proficiency level, what are some instructional supports ESOL teachers can provide to help her move to the next level? *(Skill 2.3)*

    A. Work on expanding use of vocabulary and syntax, including explicit instruction in grade level academic discourse
    B. Work on some basic vocabulary and simple phrases and sentences and foundational literacy skills
    C. Work on extending language strategies for more sophisticated oral and written production (e.g., style, tone, voice, audience)
    D. Work on basic vocabulary and structures for social/academic experiences, strengthen decoding and comprehension, develop key writing skills

26. The affective domain affects the possibility for students to acquire a second language because: *(Skill 2.4)*

    A. Learning a second language may make the learner feel vulnerable and afraid to take risks
    B. This is a false premise. The affective domain does not really affect a student's second language acquisition.
    C. When you are effective in the four integrated skills, you are more likely to achieve second language proficiency.
    D. It promotes facilitative anxiety, which determines our reaction to competition and is positive.

27. Research has shown that one of the factors below significantly improves the bilingualism of English language learners. Which factor is most likely to increase the likelihood of ELL students becoming bilingual? *(Skill 2.4)*

    A. Insisting that ELLs only speak L2 in the school (outside the classroom)
    B. Community appreciation and valuing of the L2.
    C. Providing a block schedule so that ELLs can learn specific skills during different times of the day
    D. Utilizing interlanguage devices between L1 and L2

28. Which of the following is NOT a possible effect of an ESOL teacher using too many strategies that rely on instrumental or extrinsic motivation? *(Skill 2.4)*

    A. Students become afraid of taking risks or deviating from what is expected
    B. Students become too competitive and miss out on collaborative opportunities and learning.
    C. Students move through fluency levels too quickly and end up feeling socially isolated from their peers in academic settings.
    D. Students become too dependent on rewards and instant gratification.

29. An ESOL teacher is working with an English language learner who is almost ready to move into the next English language proficiency level. By working with the student on making inferences, which domain is the teacher working in? *(Skill 2.5)*

    A. Monitor
    B. Cognitive
    C. Affective
    D. Psychomotor

30. A high school English language learner does very well in collaborative and group work and seems to flourish when working with peers or small groups. During independent activities, however, including assessments, the student's output is consistently below the standard.

    Which of the following should be the ESOL teacher's first step in helping the student? *(Skill 2.4)*

    A. Perform a needs assessment to identify the area where the student is struggling.
    B. Contact the parents, as there may be something going on at home that is interfering with the student's ability to concentrate or perform.
    C. Bring in another teacher who teaches the student to observe and see if they can identify what the issue may be.
    D. Talk with the student to see whether an affective issue may be causing the problem.

31. An ESOL teacher encourages students to keep track of their progress in English language learning. Which set of learning strategies does this practice fall into? *(Skill 2.5)*

    A. Metacognitive
    B. Cognitive
    C. Affective
    D. Social

32. Literature that reflects the culture of English Language Learners is a potentially valuable resource because: *(Skill 3.1)*

    A. It is more interesting than regular literature for students.
    B. By having a cultural context that makes sense, students can focus on comprehension.
    C. By showing different backgrounds it promotes equality.
    D. It will have familiar words in it for students whose first language is not English.

33. There are a number of socio-cultural factors that can affect language acquisition. Which of the following could negatively impact an ELL student's progress in learning English? *(Skill 3.1)*

    A. Learning English can bring academic success but it can also causes a 'break' from the family's home culture.
    B. Learning English may make an adolescent student very reluctant to make mistakes in front of her/his peers.
    C. There are clear cultural differences between the student's new environment and where s/he is from.
    D. Students may not have been raised in an environment that fosters a well-developed attention span.

34. According to Schumann, the acculturation of English language learners is dependent on three key factors and affects the rate at which ELLs acquire a second language. Which of the following is not one of Schumann's key acculturation factors? *(Skill 3.2)*

    A. The length of time a student's family stays in the country
    B. The student's and family's belief that the majority culture respects them
    C. The parents' job success (financial and professional) and the student's perception of that success
    D. The perception that they (student and family) feel welcome in the community (school and local)

35. According to Peregoy and Boyle, the important role that culture plays in our lives can affect student participation, learning, and adjustment to a different country/school in several ways. Which of the following concepts does an ESOL teacher need to consider in terms of culture and ELLs in the classroom? *(Skill 3.1)*

    A. Concepts and practices around roles, interpersonal relationships, family, and religion
    B. Concepts and practices around time, physical space, stage and age and discipline
    C. None of the above
    D. All of the above

36. Schumann's model of acculturation asserts that: *(Skill 3.2)*

    A. The degree to which a learner adjusts to or assimilates into the target language group will control the degree to which he acquires the second language.
    B. Motivation can be viewed as either a trait or a state and some cultures have the trait of motivation.
    C. New, nonstandard English words can represent a particular group's identity, or function as a means to solidify social relationships.
    D. What is polite in one culture may not be polite in another.

37. Which of the following ESOL models incorporates the idea that native speakers and English language learners should interact more? *(Skill 3.2)*

    A. Two-way Dual Language Bilingual Education (two languages being learned)
    B. The Silent Way (no pressure to speak keeps ensures learners are comfortable)
    C. Marie Clay's Emergent Literacy (peer tutoring in reading recovery)
    D. Skinner's Behaviorist Model (reward positive interactions between language groups)

38. Culture and cultural differences: *(Skill 3.2)*

    A. Must be addressed by the teacher in the ELL classroom by pointing out cultural differences whenever possible.
    B. Should be the starting point for learning about a new ELL's attitude.
    C. Negatively affects how well ELLs perform in the language classroom.
    D. May affect the way that ELLs understand written and spoken performance tasks.

39. A middle school ELL student does equally well on independent activities and collaborative tasks but when working in small groups with an individual-specific tasks, the student seems to falter and doesn't put forth much effort. What theory is most likely to account for this behavior? *(Skill 3.2)*

    A. The student is intimidated by the students in the groups s/he is placed in for small group work.
    B. The student is cognitively challenged by the specific tasks that the ESOL teacher tends to assign during non-collaborative group work.
    C. The student comes from a culture that values loyalty and cooperation over competition.
    D. The student prefers to work independently so that s/he doesn't have to deal with group members who tend to do all the work or who don't do their fair share of the work.

40. A successful elementary school ESOL teacher leads parent workshops at least once a semester and invites parents to observe and even present lessons on various topics. What is the ESOL teacher's primary goal in involving parents and the wider school community in the classroom? *(Skill 3.4)*

    A. Enabling parents from different cultures to see for themselves rather than depending on their children to tell them what's going on in the classroom
    B. Creating a culturally diverse, inclusive learning environment
    C. Ensuring parental support in case there is a potential conflict with colleagues and/or administrators over cultural issues in the classroom
    D. Creating a classroom environment that is less teacher-directed to appeal to cultures that learn cooperatively

41. Which of the following strategies will best help an ESOL teacher to promote a culturally inclusive learning environment? *(Skill 3.4)*

    A. Use inclusive language and appropriate modes of address
    B. Make classroom time for monthly foods of the world events
    C. Have students create posters that illustrate or represent their countries of origin
    D. Make a point to share travel experiences so that students feel their countries of origin are valued

42. The Natural Approach (1980s) contributed which important language-learning concept to effective ESOL teaching: *(Skill 4.1)*

    A. Physical movement in response to imperatives (works well with vocabulary instruction)
    B. The importance of trusting classroom relationships (teacher-student, student-student)
    C. The value of using realia in the classroom to make learning tasks more relevant and authentic
    D. The idea of comprehensible input to promote more successful language acquisition

43. TPR activities can contribute significantly to students' listening comprehension proficiency because: *(Skill 4.1)*

    A. Students learn to follow simple commands, which they will have to do in the real world.
    B. Students bonding with their classmates, which helps create a positive learning environment.
    C. Students are actively involved in the listening process without being pressured to speak
    D. Students are getting some physical exercise; physically active students are more likely to learn

44. The Natural Approach theory is based on the idea that: *(Skill 4.1)*

    A. Language is learned by imitating and practicing natural sounds
    B. Language learning and skills grow naturally when learners are in an empathetic, supportive environment
    C. Language is learned through natural principles taught through direct instruction
    D. Language is learned subconsciously when interacting for natural, meaningful purposes

45. Which of the following is not a characteristic of differentiated instruction? *(Skill 4.2)*

    A. Flexible groupings of students
    B. Assessment of each student's needs
    C. Self-paced learning
    D. Varied ways of demonstrating learning and proficiency

46. According to Krashen and Terrell's Input Hypothesis, language learners are able to understand: *(Skill 2.1)*

    A. Slightly more than they can produce.
    B. The same as they speak.
    C. Less than they speak.
    D. Lots more than they speak.

47. When an ESOL teacher uses an integrative approach to teach English language skills and a teaching method that includes presentation, practice and production, what ESOL method is s/he using to model her teaching strategies on? *(Skill 4.1)*

    A. Communicative Language Teaching
    B. The Direct Method
    C. Community Language Learning
    D. The Natural Approach

48. ESL, Sheltered Instruction and Dual Language classes are all: *(Skill 4.1)*

    A. Mandated by state and federal law for Title 1 Schools
    B. Main instructional ESOL models used in the United States
    C. Based loosely on the Grammar Translation Method
    D. Standards based teaching models

49. Which of the following mandates the presence of state requirements for learning standards for English language learners? *(Skill 4.2)*

    A. The Bilingual Education Act
    B. Lau v. Nichols
    C. The Every Student Succeeds Act
    D. The Common Core

50. When differentiating standard-based instruction for ELLs, what components of instruction can be differentiated? *(Skill 4.2)*

    A. Student groupings - group by ability as a regular practice to ensure student growth
    B. Assessment (don't grade ELLs as strictly as native-English speakers)
    C. Content, process and product
    D. Standards, outcomes and benchmarks

51. Graves' acronym, SARS describes a method for choosing resources to use with English language learners. The acronym stands for: *(Skill 4.3)*

    A. Select, adapt, reject, supplement
    B. Substitute, augment, revise, sample
    C. Substantiate, acquire, rank, scrutinize
    D. Synchronize, achieve, rearrange, solve

52. Collaboration has been identified as one of the key instructional criteria to support ELLs in the content areas. All of the following statements about collaborative activities are true *except*: (Skill 4.4)

    A. Collaborative activities can involve teachers and students actively working together.
    B. Collaborative activities can also include interacting with people outside the classroom.
    C. Collaborative activities are oral-based activities rather than writing based activities.
    D. Collaborative activities can take place in pairs, small groups, or large groups.

53. Content-based instruction suggests ELLs students need an additional 5-7 years to pick up academic language (CALPS). During this time period, content area teachers should not: (Skill 10.3)

    A. Correct the ELL's oral language mistakes as it might make ELLs feel anxious about speaking.
    B. Speak more slowly, enunciate carefully as it might make ELLs feel singled out.
    C. Demonstrate new concepts using visuals and other materials to increase input as it might privilege visual over auditory learners.
    D. Check frequently for comprehension by asking students to explain what was said to a classmate or back to the teacher as it might make students feel micromanaged.

54. Which of the following is an activity that Communicative Language Teaching (the Communicative Approach) should not involve? (Skill 4.1)

    A. Real communication - students, teachers and others interacting and communicating
    B. Meaningful tasks - activities and tasks relate to real-world situations and matter to students
    C. Instructor interaction with students by way of commands and gestures with students responding physically
    D. Meaningful language - language is applicable to contexts and situations the learner encounters or will encounter (social, academic, workplace, subject-specific, etc.)

55. The shift in the teaching of speaking skills has moved away from a focus on perfect accuracy towards a focus on fluency and communicative effectiveness. This has had an effect on the kinds of activities that ESOL instructors use to help English Language Learners develop their speaking skills. Which of the following approaches was created before this shift occurred? (Skill 4.1)

    A. The Grammar Translation Method
    B. The Cognitive Academic Language Learning Approach (CALLA)
    C. The Natural Approach
    D. Total Physical Response

56. Read the phrases below to answer the question that follows.

    Where were you?
    Text me tomorrow.
    What are you doing tonight?
    What is that?

    The phrases above are examples of:
    (Skills 1.4, 2.5 and 4.3)

    A. CALP
    B. BICS
    C. PRAC
    D. SARS

57. **What is a crucial element of successfully integrating technology in the ESL/ENL classroom?** *(Skill 4.5)*

    A. Developing effective management and instructional strategies
    B. Ensuring all students have access to a device at all times (1:1 program)
    C. Ensuring that all resources are available in the learner's first language
    D. All of the above

58. **In what ways does technology have the potential to enhance English Language learning?** *(Skill 4.5)*

    A. Technology can take the place of the teacher when the teacher is grading papers.
    B. Technology can give students the valuable element of privacy they need to succeed in English Language learning.
    C. Technology can be used to keep students' interests because sometimes the teacher is boring.
    D. Technology can allow students to have more control over their learning.

59. **The following ideas are part of which instructional theory/practice:** *(Skills 4.1 and 10.2)*

    Learners do not learn L2 through singular instruction in the language's rules; they learn from meaningful interaction in the language and although conversational fluency in L2 is a goal, speaking is not sufficient to develop the academic cognitive skills needed.

    A. Content-based Instruction
    B. The Natural Approach
    C. TPR (Total Physical Response)
    D. Sheltered Immersion

60. **In the United States, in schools with large immigrant populations of diverse origin, the most commonly used ESOL model of the models below is:** *(Skills 4.1 and 10.1)*

    A. Submersion model
    B. ESL/ENL/EAL Pullout model
    C. Specially Designed Academic Programs In English
    D. Two-way Dual Immersion model

61. Team planning with colleagues, supporting curriculum reviews, and participating in school events are important ways for ESOL teachers to: *(Skill 5.1)*

    A. Act as advocates for cultural and linguistic diversity
    B. Network for improved job prospects
    C. Show administrators and colleagues that they are committed to the school
    D. Show students that they are not just 'teachers' but also human beings

62. An elementary school ELL student received some very low scores on a series of in-class math assessments but scored much better on the state standardized math test. What is the best explanation for this discrepancy? *(Skill 5.1)*

    A. The student dislikes math class.
    B. The in-class math tests involved a lot of reading.
    C. The teacher dislikes the student and gives their in-class tests a lower score.
    D. The standardized math tests were not timed so the student could take as long as they needed to answer the questions.

63. A new high school principal has announced some major changes to the ways in which ELL students are assessed. She wants multiple raters to interpret the students' results, clear scoring criteria, and multiple assessment measures for every English language learner. The best argument for making these changes is to ensure: *(Skills 5.1 and 5.2)*

    A. Teacher accountability
    B. Consistency among teachers in different subjects
    C. A high quality ranking for the school by improving test scores
    D. The reliability of tests to classify students

64. Formative assessment is an essential part of determining: *(Skill 5.1)*

    A. A student's reading level
    B. Whether a student has a learning disability
    C. Whether a student is in the appropriate learning environment
    D. A student's progress in order to plan and adapt instruction

65. A reliable assessment test for ELLs will have the following three attributes: *(Skills 5.1 and 5.4)*

    A. Validity, reliability, and practicality
    B. Validity, reliability, and flexibility
    C. Practicality, reliability, and privacy
    D. Reliability, validity, and familiarity for students

66. Which of the following is a commonly held belief about effective collaboration that is NOT backed up by research? *(Skill 6.3)*

    A. A need to establish a clear conceptualization of the task
    B. The incorporation of explicit goals for ESL development into curriculum and assessment planning processes
    C. A shared understanding of ESL and mainstream teachers' roles/responsibilities
    D. The inclusion of a variety of similar activities in various content areas

67. Which of the following accommodations may be allowed for ELLs on most state standardized assessments? *(Skills 5.3 and 6.1)*

    A. Giving extra time
    B. Asking proctor to explain certain words or test items
    C. Paraphrasing the prompt
    D. Use of general English-heritage translating dictionaries

68. Advantages of informal assessment techniques include all of the following EXCEPT: *(Skill 5.3)*

    A. Recognizing opportunities for reteaching
    B. Giving feedback to students to improve learning
    C. Recognizing learning disabilities
    D. Adjusting or planning instructional opportunities

69. Which one of the following is NOT a way to establish reliability when placing English language learners with disabilities? *(Skill 5.2)*

    A. Including assessments in the learner's native language
    B. Including multiple assessment measures and multiple raters
    C. Establishing clearly specified scoring criteria
    D. Using the Woodcock-Johnson III Diagnostic Reading Battery

70. Norm-referenced assessments may not provide accurate results when used with ELL students because: *(Skill 5.4)*

    A. The test is not in the student's home/first language.
    B. The student will not understand the test.
    C. The tests are too difficult for ELL students.
    D. The norm group may not be reflective of the ELL student.

71. An ESOL teacher has decided to use an end-of-unit assessment where prompts or tasks are open-ended and have no 'right answer'. Both the process and the final product are going to be assessed. What type of assessment is this? *(Skill 5.1)*

    A. Performance based assessment
    B. Norm referenced assessment
    C. Criterion referenced assessment
    D. Observation based assessment

72. Which of the following assessments is a performance-based assessment? *(Skill 5.1)*

   A. A multiple choice test with optional questions to account for student interests
   B. A student presentation
   C. A formative quiz that checks for understanding
   D. A think-pair-share summarization strategy

73. Which of the following is NOT recommended as a consideration for teams of teachers to look at when analyzing testing procedures to determine whether an ELL has a learning disability? *(Skill 5.2)*

   A. Identify student using observations from peers
   B. Criterion-referenced assessments
   C. Identify student using observations from home
   D. Comparison of student's cultural teaching style (e.g., teacher-centered) with the school's teaching style (e.g., student-centered)

74. Assessment data can be used for ALL BUT ONE of the following actions: *(Skill 5.2)*

   A. Create meaningful, language-rich, and safe environments for English Language Learners that provide them with differentiated language practice and use
   B. Communicate and plan with other teachers in order get to know students' strengths and challenges outside of your classroom
   C. Help in the selection of appropriate learning materials
   D. Deemphasize some curricular outcomes because they are difficult to assess

75. A 7th grade ELL student is struggling in his science and social studies classes. He is doing well in English language arts and math classes. Which of the following factors would have the biggest impact on his poor performance? *(Skill 5.2)*

   A. The student may have been exited early from the ELL program.
   B. There may be parental pressure to earn top grades in all classes and not just the classes that the student enjoys.
   C. There may be a competitive atmosphere in those classes, which makes the student lose confidence.
   D. The student may have an inflated sense of his own abilities in those subjects and is not studying or working hard enough.

76. A high school ESOL teacher hosts a parent meeting after assessment results from standardized tests have gone home. At the meeting several parents are very upset about their children's scores on the tests. Which of the following assessment 'best practices' would help the teacher most at this meeting? *(Skill 5.4)*

   A. Knowing and working towards the achievement of the state and national learning standards that are measured on the test
   B. Aligning goals for learners so that as their English language proficiency develops, so does their content-area learning and output
   C. Knowing how to interpret standardized assessments with respect to ELLs
   D. Communicating regularly with parents about assessment methods and results as well instructional practice

77. To protect students from inequities in the referral process, federal law explicitly allows the option for: *(Skill 6.1)*

   A. Non-discriminatory evaluation procedures
   B. An independent education evaluation
   C. A multidisciplinary team using several pieces of information to formulate a referral
   D. Testing of the child in L1 unless clearly not feasible to do so

78. The Every Student Succeeds Act (ESSA) contains some important points relating to English language learners. Which of the following points is part of the ESSA? *(Skill 6.1)*

   A. Schools must report on the number of ELLs meeting academic standards (even for four years after exiting any English language support programs)
   B. Schools may not exclude any students based on language(s) of origin.
   C. Schools must provide resources for personnel, instructional materials, and space for teaching English language learners.
   D. Schools may not exempt English language learners from any state or federal assessments.

79. Which statement about the Lau vs. Nichols case (1974) is FALSE? *(Skill 6.1)*

   A. The Supreme Court ruling required changes that later became federal law as part of the Equal Opportunities Education Act
   B. The Supreme Court ruling included a requirement that bilingual education programs must produce results that indicate the language barrier is being overcome.
   C. The main argument of the case was that students were not being taught required classes in their native language
   D. It was a class action suit filed on behalf of the Chinese community in San Francisco

80. At the beginning of a new school year, a high school ESOL teacher is approached by a former parent who is very angry. The parent does not understand why his daughter was exited from the ELL program because she is struggling with all of her class subjects, including English Language Arts, one of her strong subjects from the year before. Which of the following statements below is most likely the cause of his upset? *(Skills 6.1, 6.4, 6.5 and 5.2)*

   A. His daughter was probably exited from the ELL program before she was ready.
   B. He doesn't like his daughter's new teachers very much - he obviously feels comfortable with the teacher from last year.
   C. He doesn't know what the school's policies and procedures are for exiting students from ELL programs.
   D. His daughter is probably rebelling - she is at the age when adolescents sometimes lose motivation to study and work hard.

81. Metacognitive strategies in educators can help improve instructional practice and professionalism. Which of the following is an effective metacognitive strategy for teachers? *(Skill 6.2)*

   A. Teachers read performance evaluations carefully, looking for strengths and challenges identified by an evaluator (principal, colleague, etc.).
   B. Teachers read parent and student evaluations looking for specific positive and negative feedback.
   C. Teachers make detailed lesson plans several months in advance to ensure plans match the standard timelines.
   D. Teachers reflect on teaching, making 'just in time' adaptations to instruction.

82. It is most important for ESOL teachers to stay informed on issues, ideas and theories in language learning and the ESOL field so that they can: *(Skill 6.2)*

   A. Be prepared for potential jobs and/or professional opportunities coming up
   B. Be better teachers and connect with others in the school and local community
   C. Be prepared to ensure that lessons will go as planned
   D. Be able to offer advice and suggestions to principals on how to make the ELL program more successful

83. An elementary school ESOL teacher is not able to take any days away from school to attend professional development workshops, but she has set professional growth goals for the year. A colleague gives her some suggestions. Which of the following is NOT likely to lead to improved professional practice: *(Skill 6.2)*

   A. Practice your craft. If you teach English, write. If you teach history, do some research.
   B. Join a professional organization to have access to resources, readings and people that you can learn from.
   C. Use some of your professional development budget to purchase some technology that will benefit some of your ELLs.
   D. Do some action research with colleagues (from your school or another school)

84. What is a key reason for collaboration between ESOL and content-area teachers: *(Skill 6.3)*

   A. Provides consistent expectations for students and monitors student development
   B. Saves teachers valuable time by co-planning
   C. ESOL teacher serves as a model for other teachers
   D. Teachers should know and understand legislation and case law regarding ELLs

85. Teacher Assistance Teams (TATs) should be composed of all of the following EXCEPT the: *(Skill 6.3)*

   A. School administrators
   B. Guidance counselors
   C. Media specialists
   D. Parent(s)

86. Two sixth teachers want to collaborate; one is a content-area teacher and one is an ESOL teacher. The school is supportive of the collaboration but tells them that they cannot co-teach any classes, as there would be too many students in the class, even with two teachers. Which of the following is NOT recommended for the two sixth grade teachers if they can't co-teach? *(Skill 6.3)*

   A. Choosing a common goal for ELL development in the content-area and plan how to assess it
   B. Getting advice on classroom dynamics and understanding specific students
   C. Choosing specific students and having them sit together in both classes so that teachers can monitor and work with them on learning goals
   D. Choosing a project that students can work on in both classes

87. By modeling effective teaching practices and sharing resources both with colleagues and families, the ESOL teacher can help to maximize the learning opportunities available to all students.

    The statement above is based on: *(Skill 6.4)*

    A. Research and evidence-based best practices
    B. Wishful thinking - teachers simply don't have time
    C. ESSA requirements for Title I schools
    D. State mandated in at least 14 states

88. Which of the following assessments is NOT for English language learners? *(Skills 7.2, 9.1, 9.2 and 5.1)*

    A. Woodcock-Muñoz Language Survey
    B. Peabody Picture Vocabulary Test
    C. Summative, graded in-class end of unit assessments
    D. The National Assessment of Educational Progress

89. What practice(s) describe an English language development program in a standards-based environment? *(Skill 5.2)*

    A. Teachers have high standards for their students, knowing that students will do better with high expectations
    B. In schools with standards-based environments, students who do not meet the standards are often exited out
    C. A school's assessment procedures and tools are closely tied with EL standards and content-area standards
    D. Teachers who work in standards-based environments frequently assign letter grades to individual assignments to let students know whether they have met the linguistic, content-skill or content-knowledge standards for the assignment

90. An essential component of an ESOL teacher's job is the facilitation of communication between students, families, and all teachers. Which of the following is an evidence-based method for facilitating this communication? *(Skill 6.5)*

    A. Provide opportunities for stakeholders to come into the school and participate in activities designed to encourage their participation in the schooling of their children
    B. Use students as translators during parent conferences to ensure that parents fully understand their child's learning issues
    C. Make sure that you communicate good news to parents; let report cards and counselors tell them the bad news so that you can maintain a good relationship with them
    D. Let families know that you are sharing with them so they can share with you too. Try to find out as much as you can about the child's family situation so that you can differentiate instruction to maximize student learning.

91. A high school teacher assigns a research project for all students. Some students begin immediately while a few seem confused and unsure what to do. Which of the following steps should the teacher have taken before assigning the project? *(Skill 7.1)*

    A. Differentiated instruction
    B. A needs assessment
    C. Brainstorming with students
    D. Hands-on activities

92. Choosing literature that represents the culture of a number of ELL students from class helps students with literacy because: *(Skill 7.1)*

    A. The books will likely contain some words that ELL students know.
    B. ELL students will feel included in the class.
    C. Prior knowledge will provide context for understanding.
    D. There will likely be a stronger home-school connection from reading multicultural literature.

93. In addition to students' level of English language proficiency, what other factors would a teacher likely take into account in trying to personalize instruction? *(Skill 7.1)*

    A. Level of home/L1 language proficiency
    B. Level of motivation
    C. Student's hobbies and interests outside of school
    D. Student's cultural background

94. An ESOL teacher observes that a student seems to have plateaued in his language development. The student tends to stick to what he knows in oral and written language activities. Sentence structure, for example, is correct but still quite simple. On the other hand, his listening and reading comprehension have continued to improve. To address this imbalance, which strategy below would be most effective? *(Skills 7.1 and 7.2)*

    A. Creative writing activities
    B. Flexible, small group work with clear roles
    C. Open-ended discussion questions
    D. One-on-one conferencing with the student to discuss the issue

95. Student-student engagement in the classroom (as opposed to teacher-student engagement) offers which of the following benefits in language learning? *(Skills 7.2 and 7.3)*

    A. Authentic opportunities for communication
    B. More frequent engagement than teacher-student engagement
    C. Varied types of communication
    D. All of the above

96. **Differentiation and personalization of instruction share many things in common. However, there are some important differences. Which of the following is an important difference?**
    (Skills 7.1, 7.2 and 7.3)

    A. The teacher may adapt or select different teaching materials.
    B. The teacher and student may set specific content-area goals.
    C. The student decides what s/he wants to study and what goals to set.
    D. The teacher may change or adapt instructional methods.

97. **Communicative Language Teaching (CLT) emphasizes a progression from 'presentation' to 'practice' to 'production' when working with ELL students. What does this approach offer students?**
    (Skill 7.2)

    A. This progression scaffolds student learning and language proficiency.
    B. This progression emphasizes fundamental language skills essential to L2 competency.
    C. This progression provides multiple ways of assessing student growth.
    D. This progression puts students at the center of learning.

98. **A holistic approach to language proficiency would involve:** *(Skill 7.2)*

    A. Frequent formative assessment to provide clear feedback to students
    B. Understanding of students' social and emotional needs (in addition to academic)
    C. Cooperative work in classroom to provide authentic communication opportunities
    D. Integration of speaking, listening, writing, and reading

99. **A teacher designs a science project in which students have to conduct an experiment with a partner, research additional information, take notes, and then create a short video presentation about their experimental results. This is an example of Chamot and O'Malley's:**
    (Skills 7.1, 8.5 and 10.2)

    A. CALP
    B. CALLA
    C. BICS
    D. PRAC

100. In social studies class, the teacher has told the students that in the next class meeting they will be discussing the election results and should come prepared to discuss their opinions of the outcome. Which of the following would be the best way for an ESOL teacher to help an intermediate level ELL student participate in an important class discussion? *(Skills 7.2 and 7.3)*

   A. Provide the student with a graphic organizer to take notes during the discussion.
   B. Summarize what other students say during the discussion.
   C. Meet with the student before the discussion to help him/her prepare ideas to share in the discussion.
   D. Provide the student with key election-related vocabulary and a series of model sentences showing ways of expressing ideas.

101. A few days before an upcoming demonstration in science class of a complicated experiment, which of the following would be the most important and practical way in which the science teacher and ESOL teacher could collaborate? *(Skills 7.2, 7.3, 10.1 and 10.2)*

   A. The science teacher could teach the ESOL teacher how to do the experiment so that s/he can review it with ELL students.
   B. They could identify potentially difficult vocabulary and terms for pre-teaching.
   C. They could co-teach the experiment.
   D. The ESOL teacher could observe and take simplified notes on the experiment for ELL students to use in understanding it.

102. Cognitive processing involves using existing knowledge to acquire new knowledge. Which of the following best reflects this from the point of view of an ELL student learning English? *(Skills 7.2 and 2.3)*

   A. Writing a short story about what happened on the weekend
   B. Forming new sentences about ducks after learning the song Old MacDonald
   C. Reflecting on progress and learning
   D. Following the directions for an experiment

103. Which of the following activities likely makes the most linguistic demands of an English language learner? *(Skills 8.1, 9.3, 9.4 and 9.5)*

   A. An oral presentation about his/her home country
   B. Writing an essay about a novel
   C. Researching and taking notes on a historical event
   D. Preparing for a vocabulary test

104. One element of differentiation is the opportunity to demonstrate knowledge and skills in different ways. How is this particularly important in content-area learning for ELL students? *(Skills 10.1 and 10.3)*

   A. They will be more likely to demonstrate learning in a way that is not impacted by language proficiency.
   B. They may not be able to meet the learning standard due to a lack of understanding.
   C. They will have multiple chances to show what they know if they did not 'get it' the first time.
   D. They will be more engaged in the learning process and vested in the outcomes.

105. To determine whether an ELL student has a learning disability, ideally testing and assessment should: *(Skill 7.3)*

   A. Be administered with parental knowledge and consent
   B. Be administered in the student's first language
   C. Be done by the classroom teacher
   D. Be administered more than once

106. In many cases there is no suitable diagnostic test to determine student exceptionalities in the ELL student's first/native language. In this case, what is the best option? *(Skill 7.3)*

   A. Observation, investigation of achievement in different subject areas, consultation with family
   B. Observation, use of existing diagnostic tests, consultation with family
   C. Tentative placement in learning support classes and continued observation of growth
   D. Review of student's past learning records, implementation of differentiated instruction, observation of growth

107. Which of the following language theories about listening is NO LONGER considered valid? *(Skill 8.1)*

   A. Top-down listening processing relies on the listener's bank of prior knowledge and global expectations.
   B. Listening is considered a 'passive' skill.
   C. Bottom-up processing of listening refers to analysis of the language by the listener to find out the intended meaning of the message.
   D. Verbal learning becomes easier when information can be chunked into meaningful patterns.

108. Activating prior knowledge, or schema, is particularly important for English language learners because: *(Skill 8.2)*

   A. It makes learning more meaningful for the students.
   B. It aids in reading and listening comprehension.
   C. It validates cultural knowledge.
   D. All of the above.

109. Which of the following would be the most effective activity to use with Entering or Beginning level ELLs? *(Skill 8.2)*

   A. Asking comprehension questions after completing a listening activity
   B. Frontloading vocabulary
   C. Identify a picture that matches specific passages or parts of passages that the ESOL teacher is playing for the students
   D. Quiz

110. Which one of the scaffolding methods would be most effective in helping ELLs develop listening skills? *(Skill 8.2)*

   A. Front-loading or pre-teaching vocabulary
   B. Asking ELLs to compare/contrast a listening activity with a text passage
   C. Allowing students to listen several times
   D. Creating a word wall

111. Cooperative learning tasks, races and team drawings are examples of:
(Skills 8.2 and 8.3)

   A. Metacognitive tasks
   B. Chomsky's Language Acquisition Device (LAD)
   C. Two-way exchanges of information
   D. Linguistic modifications

112. All of the following can help more advanced ELLs improve listening and speaking proficiency EXCEPT:
(Skills 8.2, 8.3, 8.4 and 8.5)

   A. Memorization of long vocabulary lists
   B. Requiring students to integrate information and evidence from diverse media sources
   C. Emphasizing the authentic use of language (e.g., presentations or debates rather than memorization of language patterns);
   D. Integrating speaking, listening, reading and writing

113. Which of the following are advantages to the instructor's use of students' home language(s) in the English language classroom or in English language instruction? *(Skills 8.4 and 8.5)*

   A. It can reduce anxiety and fear.
   B. It can permit explanation of differences and similarities of home and new languages.
   C. It can reduce time-consuming explanations of abstract concepts.
   D. All of the above.

114. An ELL student who is at the intermediate/developing English language level is speaking in front of the class and telling them about his aunt, who had a big influence on him and his desire to learn. He introduces his aunt by saying, "My Aunt Maria is a profesora." This is an example of: *(Skill 8.1)*

   A. Dialect
   B. Inter-language
   C. Code-switching
   D. Formulaic speech

115. When the teacher is correcting a student's language, the teacher should: *(Skill 8.3)*

   A. Carefully correct all mistakes
   B. Consider the context of the error
   C. Confirm the error by repeating it
   D. Repeat the student's message but correct it

116. Which one of the following is NOT an effective activity used in developing speaking proficiency, especially with beginning and intermediate ELLs? *(Skills 8.3 and 8.5)*

   A. Choral readings
   B. Individual reading (to the whole class)
   C. Structured interviews
   D. Role plays

117. Wait time is a particularly important consideration for teachers of English language learners because: *(Skills 8.3 and 8.5)*

   A. They may need more time to formulate how to express their answers.
   B. They may have anxiety about speaking in front of their peers.
   C. They may take more time to process the question from the teacher.
   D. All of the above.

118. Which of the following is NOT a purpose for a listening assessment? *(Skill 8.1)*

   A. Assessing students' listening strengths and weaknesses at the beginning of a course
   B. Assessing students' mastery of a specific listening skill
   C. Assessing students' progress towards listening standards at the end of a term or important time period
   D. Assessing students listening skills to determine if the student has hearing problems

119. Assessment of speaking skills in English language learners should: *(Skill 8.1)*

   A. Concentrate on the number of errors ELLs make in order to help them become proficient speakers
   B. Focus on the message conveyed by learners in order to evaluate ELLs communicative abilities
   C. Encourage ELLs to memorize what they are going to say in the assessment so that they are not looking down and reading
   D. Concentrate on the student's presentation style; make sure that they are dressed appropriately, standing with proper posture, using effective voice and pitch so that they take the assessment seriously

120. What does the term top down processing mean in terms of language processing? *(Skill 9.3)*

   A. Encouraging students to use prior knowledge to make predictions about meaning
   B. Explicit teaching of tasks by the ESOL teacher
   C. Recognizing main ideas in what is said
   D. Making inferences about possible meanings

121. In a "top down" strategy of literacy development, which one of the following strategies might not help a reader with comprehension? *(Skill 9.3)*

   A. Make guesses about what is going to happen
   B. Look up and record each unfamiliar word
   C. Anticipate the contents of the text
   D. Infer meaning from sentences and paragraphs

122. Activities that help students develop phonological awareness, fluency in word recognition and the ability to sound out words are all key components of instructional strategies designed to: *(Skill 9.3)*

   A. Build cognitive and metacognitive skills
   B. Build semantic and pragmatic skills
   C. Build critical thinking skills
   D. Build literacy skills

123. Which one of the following is NOT an effective instructional literacy practice for elementary ESOL teachers? *(Skill 9.3)*

   A. Providing direct explicit instruction of reading/writing skills based on ongoing student assessment
   B. Devoting less than 50% of the day's instructional time to reading/writing
   C. Assessing student work based on common rubrics
   D. Promoting conversation through purposeful and guided discussions about a book, piece of writing, or topic

124. Activities that focus on increasing fluency in academic reading include all of the following strategies EXCEPT: *(Skill 9.4)*

   A. Modeled reading
   B. Repeated reading of a familiar text
   C. Checking for understanding by asking if there are any questions
   D. Coached reading of appropriate materials

125. To develop reading fluency, ESOL teachers can use all of the following strategies EXCEPT: *(Skills 9.3 and 9.4)*

   A. Choose texts carefully that students are able to read fairly fluently
   B. Read aloud daily to students to model reading fluency
   C. Consistently quiz students after reading fluency activities to ensure success
   D. Have students re-read texts that they have heard before to build fluency

126. Common activities of the "post-reading phase" include: *(Skills 9.3 and 9.4)*

   A. Building background knowledge
   B. Summarizing and organizing information
   C. Asking questions
   D. Annotating text

127. When teaching initial literacy, teachers should focus on all of the following literacy skills EXCEPT: *(Skill 9.1)*

    A. Effect of culture on language learning
    B. Phonemic awareness
    C. Phonics
    D. Comprehension of different types of reading materials

128. Why is an ELL student's ability to read and then successfully paraphrase a text a good indicator of literacy development?
    (Skills 9.3, 9.4 and 9.5)

    A. It demonstrates that the student can recognize main ideas.
    B. It demonstrates that the student is overcoming anxiety about language learning.
    C. This is an important element of BICS.
    D. The student is using appropriate register for an academic setting.

129. Of the following questions, which one would be most effective in helping ELLs learn to infer meaning?
    (Skills 9.3, 9.4 and 9.5)

    A. How can we synthesize what you just said?
    B. What conclusions can you draw?
    C. What is the relationship between...?
    D. What evidence can you find...?

130. Which one of the following skills would probably have the most positive effect on developing literacy skills in ELLs?
    (Skill 9.3, 9.4 and 9.5)

    A. Oral storytelling traditions
    B. Watching documentaries on TV
    C. Visiting art museums
    D. Attending concerts

131. In helping students develop reading strategies for use in analyzing the plot of a novel, which one of the following suggestions is most likely to help build comprehension?
    (Skill 9.4)

    A. Morphemic analysis focusing on prefixes, roots and suffixes
    B. Annotations with arrows showing the relationship between events
    C. The study of cognates
    D. A word wall of commonly used words

132. Encouraging non-graded writing practice can really help English language learners develop writing fluency. Which of the following is NOT a task that encourages students to practice non-graded writing?
    (Skill 9.3)

    A. Writing a dialog in pairs
    B. Rewriting a passage or summary in the ELL's own words
    C. Writing from the perspective of another
    D. Writing a summary of a text to hand in

133. In general, the writing process can be divided into two broad divisions. They are: (Skill 9.5)

   A. Composing; pre-writing
   B. Pre-writing; drafting
   C. Brainstorming; drafting
   D. Composition; revision

134. Which one of the following writing activities is not appropriate for different proficiency levels? (Skills 9.3 and 9.5)

   A. Reading and writing letters to friends, businesses or pen pals
   B. Writing directions for solving a problem
   C. Writing long form book reports
   D. Writing and organizing lists

135. Tests that evaluate an individual compared to others are: (Skill 10.1)

   A. Standardized
   B. Authentic
   C. Norm referenced
   D. Criterion referenced

136. Sheltered content teaching allows teachers to do all of the following except: (Skill 10.2)

   A. Use realia, word lists, gestures, etc.
   B. Reduce language demands
   C. Facilitate learning
   D. Instruct in heritage or home language

137. The Schema Theory of Carrell & Eisterhold suggests that for learning to take place, teachers should: (Skill 10.3)

   A. Integrate content areas with ESOL techniques.
   B. Emphasize all four language skills.
   C. Present comprehensible input in a meaningful context.
   D. Relate new materials to previous knowledge.

138. Content, process and product are the primary areas that can be adapted to support English language learners through: (Skill 10.4)

   A. Parental Communication
   B. Differentiation
   C. Formative assessment
   D. Transfer from L1 to L2

139. ESOL teachers can make academic content accessible for ELL students by implementing which of the following practices? (Skill 10.3)

   A. Pre-teaching vocabulary and concepts
   B. Checking for comprehension during instruction
   C. Teaching the material in multiple ways (e.g. using visual cues, hands-on activities)
   D. Combining all of the above

140. What is a valid conclusion that could be drawn from the claim that vocabulary development is crucial for reading comprehension?
(Skills 10.2 and 10.3)

   A. It is difficult for readers to understand the content unless they know the meaning of most of the words in the text.
   B. It is difficult for students to understand academic, communicative and content-based vocabulary unless they memorize extensive word lists.
   C. It is difficult for learners to master sight word vocabulary without taking frequent spelling tests.
   D. It is difficult for readers to make significant reading progress when they have poor reading comprehension skills.

141. Which of the following is NOT an evidence-based vocabulary development method?
(Skill 10.3)

   A. Working with other teachers at grade level or subject area when designing important vocabulary lessons and/or reading about evidence-based approaches to vocabulary instruction;
   B. Ensuring that reading vocabulary lists emphasize important words and not just decoding;
   C. Working to create some word lists that are common to many subjects, and if not, making word lists available to subject-area teachers to help students practice;
   D. Providing time in class for read-aloud activities where students read their papers aloud, teachers listen to errors, and correct the students as they proceed.

142. Purposeful discourse can be used to design learning activities across the curriculum. Which of the following is not one of the four major kinds of purposeful discourse?
(Skills 10.3 and 10.4)

   A. Shared discourse in which language is used socially to communicate and share meaning in order to accomplish social goals (playing games or planning a short scene),
   B. Fun discourse in which language is used for fun (singing songs and writing riddles)
   C. Thought discourse in which language is used to imagine and create new ideas and experiences (writing poetry or critical thinking)
   D. Practice discourse in which students practice tasks on which they will be assessed.

143. Nonverbal adaptations, elicitation adaptations, and questioning adaptations are examples of what kinds of modifications to help make language more comprehensible for students?
(Skill 10.3)

   A. Modifications in student interaction
   B. Modifications in teacher-talk
   C. Modification in assessment tasks
   D. Modifications in instructional materials

144. When ESOL teachers understand the discourse features of various types of text, they can help English language learners to: *(Skills 10.1 – 10.4)*

   A. Improve reading, writing and vocabulary in the content-areas
   B. Recognize familiar words and figure out words they haven't seen
   C. Understand that different types of dialects or slang are not effective in specific settings
   D. Develop skills that it are most important for them to practice

145. There are many recommended ways of adapting content in Content Based Instruction. Which of the following is NOT a category for adaptation in CBI? *(Skill 10.3)*

   A. Giving directions
   B. Providing contextualization
   C. Assessments
   D. Checking for understanding

146. Paraphrasing, prompts, graphic organizers, guides, syllabi, schedules, learning goals, draft assignments, and practice tests are examples of types of: *(Skill 10.3)*

   A. Scaffolding
   B. Adapting content
   C. The natural approach
   D. Collaborative activities

147. Which of the following are examples of opportunities for students to be creative, solve problems, think critically and collaborate? *(Skill 10.3)*

   A. Working with other students on cloze exercises
   B. Watching an English language movie with subtitles in ELL's home language
   C. Participating in spelling and math bees where students get to physically move around the room and think on their feet
   D. Participating in debates, analyzing media and messages, working through authentic problems

148. An elementary school ESOL teacher takes his students outside in the schoolyard for a short observation walk. As they walk along, they observe different insects, rocks, and playground equipment. The teacher stops and asks the students questions that draw out their critical thinking skills. Which one of the following questions would be least effective in promoting critical-thinking skills? *(Skill 10.4)*

   A. What parts do the ant and the butterfly have in common?
   B. What evidence do you find to support the idea that you can't swing all the way around the pole of the swing set?
   C. How would you classify this type of rock?
   D. What colors are the leaves on that tree?

149. The purpose of frontloading vocabulary is: *(Skills 10.3, 10.4, 9.3 and 9.4)*

   A. Vocabulary development
   B. Increase reading comprehension
   C. Explaining content
   D. Increasing spelling proficiency

150. Sheltered content teaching allows teachers to do all of the following except: *(Skill 10.2)*

    A. Use realia, word lists, gestures, etc.
    B. Reduce language demands
    C. Facilitate learning
    D. Instruct in heritage or home language

ANSWER KEY

1. D	31. A	61. A	91. B	121. B
2. B	32. B	62. B	92. C	122. D
3. B	33. A	63. D	93. A	123. B
4. B	34. C	64. D	94. C	124. C
5. B	35. D	65. A	95. D	125. C
6. A	36. A	66. D	96. B	126. B
7. D	37. A	67. A	97. A	127. A
8. C	38. D	68. C	98. D	128. A
9. B	39. C	69. D	99. B	129. D
10. B	40. B	70. D	100. D	130. A
11. A	41. A	71. A	101. B	131. B
12. C	42. D	72. B	102. B	132. D
13. D	43. C	73. A	103. C	133. D
14. A	44. D	74. D	104. A	134. C
15. C	45. C	75. A	105. B	135. C
16. C	46. A	76. C	106. A	136. D
17. C	47. A	77. B	107. B	137. D
18. B	48. B	78. A	108. D	138. B
19. B	49. C	79. B	109. C	139. D
20. D	50. C	80. C	110. C	140. A
21. A	51. A	81. D	111. C	141. D
22. B	52. C	82. B	112. A	142. D
23. B	53. A	83. C	113. D	143. B
24. C	54. C	84. A	114. C	144. A
25. D	55. A	85. C	115. D	145. C
26. A	56. B	86. C	116. B	146. A
27. B	57. A	87. A	117. D	147. D
28. C	58. D	88. B	118. D	148. D
29. B	59. A	89. C	119. B	149. B
30. D	60. B	90. A	120. A	150. D

TEACHER CERTIFICATION STUDY GUIDE

PRACTICE TEST

1. An ESOL teacher notices that a student is struggling to understand change in register when speaking with peers, with teachers and when approaching people she doesn't know to ask for information. *(Skill 1.6)*

   In which of the following areas should a teacher work with the student?

   A. Phonemic awareness and phonology
   B. Pragmatics and morphology
   C. Semantics and syntax
   D. English language variations

The correct answer is D. English language variations.
English language usage is characterized by the social situation of its users. Speakers often shift their language use to adapt to a particular social situation. This shift, or change in register, can depend on such sociolinguistic variables as: the formality of the situation, the speaker's attitude towards the topic or towards the listeners and the relation of the speaker to others. Teaching ELLs explicitly about English language variations can help with aural comprehension and oral proficiency.

2. In addition to learning and practicing with phonemes, English language learners must also learn to recognize all of the following aspects of phonology, except: *(Skill 1.1)*

   A. How sounds influence communication
   B. How phrases and clauses influence communication
   C. How pitch and stress affect meaning
   D. How graphemes affect pronunciation

The correct answer is B. How phrases and clauses influence communication.
Phrases and clauses do influence communication and affect meaning but they are related to the area of syntax and semantics - not phonology. Pitch and stress, sounds, and graphemes are all aspects of phonology that ELLs must learn to recognize and interpret in order to understand the meaning of specific words and sentences they are listening to or reading.

3. ESOL teachers should have a thorough understanding of pragmatics so that they can help students understand: *(Skill 1.5)*

   A. The effect of contemporary culture on language use
   B. The ways in which context impacts the interpretation of language
   C. Meaning which is "stored" or "inherent", as well as "contextual"
   D. The ways in which roots or bases determine the meaning of words

The correct answer is B. The ways in which context impacts the interpretation of language
Pragmatics is the study of how context impacts the meaning of language. Pragmatic knowledge provides ELLs with a set of expectations to guide English language reception skills. Building contextual understanding by teaching ELLs about pragmatics is a scaffolding strategy that helps ELLs tackle new and unfamiliar content, which can be especially useful when supporting students in content-area learning.

4. If one of your ELL students says, "I to school go," their error is one of: *(Skill 1.3)*

   A. Semantics
   B. Syntax
   C. Pragmatics
   D. Morphology

The correct answer is B. syntax
Syntax involves the order in which words are arranged to create meaning. Different languages use different patterns for sentence structure. In Spanish, for example, it is correct to say, "A la casa fuimos," which in English would literally translate to, "To the house we went." ELLs are more likely to make syntactical errors as a result of L1 and L2 transfer. Explicit instruction in English language syntax can help with this problem.

5. An elementary school ESOL teacher asks a beginning level ELL student where her pencil is. The student answers, "He is in my locker." Which of the following explanations should the teacher assume is the best explanation of why the student used the word *'he'* instead of the word *'it'*? (Skill 1.3)

   A. The student may be confused about what the word 'pencil' means
   B. The student's native language is one that marks objects as well as people by gender.
   C. The student doesn't understand the difference between inanimate and animate objects in general.
   D. The student is overgeneralizing rules for pronoun use as a result of fossilization.

The correct answer is B. The student's native language is one that marks objects as well as people by gender.
Many languages, including Spanish, French and Italian mark inanimate objects by gender. This type of mistake is very common with English language learners whose native languages do this. Although some ELLs do overgeneralize, it is definitely not fossilization when a student is a beginner. To assume that the student doesn't understand the difference between inanimate and animate objects may be assuming too much cognitively.

6. ESOL experts generally posit that phonographemic differences such as 'here' and 'hear' be taught explicitly. What is the best explanation for why this is important for intermediate level English language learners? (Skill 1.1)

   A. Sound-letter relationships in English are not always consistent.
   B. This is actually not true. Teaching about homophones is not encouraged for ESOL teachers anymore.
   C. Teaching figurative language and idiomatic expressions helps English language learners make sense of communicative input.
   D. It provides extra practice in reading words and sentences

The correct answer is A. Sound-letter relationships in English are not always consistent.
Some languages have consistent sound-letter relationships (e.g., Spanish and Turkish), but English does not. ELL students may not recognize the distinction between 'here' and 'hear' and use the *wrong* word with the *right* spelling. Homophones and homonyms are a common source of confusion for English language learners and need to be taught explicitly with engaging learning activities.

7. A principal is observing an elementary school ESOL teacher during a reading lesson. After the observation, the principal suggests that the teacher do some morphemic analysis study with the students. What does the principal mean by 'morphemic analysis'? *(Skill 1.2)*

   A. Studying the order in which words occur in a sentence, e.g., SVO
   B. Studying the way words can have the same spellings but different meanings
   C. Studying the way in which speech sounds form patterns
   D. Studying the smallest unit within a language system to which meaning is attached

The correct answer is D. Studying the smallest unit within a language system to which meaning is attached
The smallest unit within a language system to which meaning is attached is a *morpheme*. The principal is encouraging the teacher to study roots, prefixes and suffixes to help build students' understanding of English vocabulary. The study of the way in which speech sounds form patterns is called *phonology*. The way words can have the same spellings but a different meaning is also related to *phonology*. Studying the order is which words occur in a sentence is related to syntax and semantics. Therefore, Answer D is correct.

8. When ESOL teachers teach English language learners about English morphemic analysis, they are providing students with the tools necessary to: *(Skill 1.2)*

   A. Understand English grammar
   B. Understand English idioms
   C. Understand unfamiliar words
   D. Understand oral and written discourse markers

The correct answer is C. Understand unfamiliar words
Morphemes are the smallest units of a language that have meaning. Though some morphemes (e.g., and) can provide grammatical information in a sentence, they do not provide an understanding of grammar. Similarly they do not give insights into idioms. Morphemic analysis can, however, help in breaking down a word and understanding it. For example, 'disrespectful' contains the morphemes 'dis' and 'ful'. Knowing their meaning can help in understanding the whole word.

TEACHER CERTIFICATION STUDY GUIDE

9. Use the text example below to answer the question that follows.

   "The plane leaves at 6:00 make sure you are at the airport before 4:00!"

   The exclamation above best illustrates which of the following grammatical errors? *(Skill 1.3)*

   A. A misuse of articles
   B. A run-on sentence
   C. A sentence fragment
   D. An inappropriate use of the imperative

The correct answer is B. A run on sentence.
Even though this book does not define a run-on sentence, ESOL teachers should be able to teach English language learners to identify and fix run-on sentences. This study guide specifically mentions the importance of teaching independent and dependent clauses to ELLs. It also discusses articles, sentence-fragments and the imperative explicitly. A run-on sentence is a sentence that contains two independent clauses without a conjunction or appropriate punctuation. Therefore, Answer B is correct.

10. Which of the following variables have an impact on discursive forms? *(Skill 1.4)*

    A. Mood, anxiety, and self-esteem
    B. Language, structure, context and topic
    C. Age, literacy history and aptitude
    D. Phonology, morphology and semantics

The correct answer is B. Language, structure, context and topic.
Both oral and written discourses are influenced by the language of the speaker, the structure of discourse in the learners L1 and L2 languages, the context in which the discourse is taking place and the topic of the discourse. Discourse shapes the way language is transmitted and how we organize our thoughts. For ELL students learning the basics of English, distinguishing between the different forms of discourse is an essential part of becoming proficient in English and of maximizing academic success.

TEACHER CERTIFICATION STUDY GUIDE

11. An ESOL teacher notices a student struggling to make friends. Other students have also complained to the teacher that the student is difficult to work with. The teacher has observed the student working in a small group and knows exactly what the problem is. What oral communication principle would the teacher work on with the student? *(Skill 1.4)*

    A. Taking turns in conversation.
    B. Choice of topic.
    C. Elaboration.
    D. Requesting and giving clarification.

The correct answer is A. Taking turns in conversation.
For discourse to be successful in any language, a set of ingrained social rules and discourse patterns must be followed. The choice of topic is an important element of discourse in English, but not the cause of the student's problem, as the topic when working together is clearly defined. Elaboration and requesting/giving clarification are good oral communication skills to teach ELLs, but if the student is having trouble making friends *and* working with others, it is her/his turn taking that needs work.

12. Empty or perfunctory language is a feature of what type of discourse? *(Skill 1.4)*

    A. Academic discourse
    B. Poetic discourse
    C. Polite discourse
    D. Expressive discourse

The correct answer is C. Polite discourse
"Empty language" or perfunctory speech is language that has little meaning but is important in social exchanges. Frequently English speakers start a conversation by asking, "How are you?" and don't really want to hear anything other than, "Fine," unless they know the person they are speaking to. Learning that questions like, "What's new?" and "How's it going?" are variations on "How are you?" and also don't have to be answered with a detailed narration of how the ELL is doing is an important aspect of learning and practicing polite discourse as a part of BICS. Answer D, may seem correct, but in fact, 'expressive discourse' refers to a type of written discourse focusing on the experience of the narrator.

13. When beginning to use textbooks with English language learners, which of the following discourse characteristics should the ESOL instructor teach? *(Skill 1.4)*

   A. Genre
   B. Passive voice
   C. Pronoun reference
   D. All of the above

The correct answer is D. All of the above
Each genre has a distinct organizational pattern and writing style. Since the features of some genres may be unfamiliar to an ELL student, A is true. The passive voice is common in textbooks, especially science textbooks, so B is true as well. Finally, to whom or what a pronoun refers in academic texts can be obscure and cause problems for ELL students (and many native speakers as well), so C is also true. Thus, D is the correct choice. Textbook language is difficult for most ELLs for many different reasons, and ESOL teachers need to teach learners strategies for understanding the language, tone, structure and genres of the academic texts they will be reading.

14. Complete the following sentence with one of the answers below:

   An understanding of pragmatics helps ELLs with comprehension in social conversation and in reading content-area texts because: *(Skill 1.5)*

   A. Building contextual understanding is a scaffolding strategy that can help ELLs tackle new and unfamiliar content.
   B. Pragmatics helps ELLs recognize repeating patterns and develop decoding skills
   C. Pragmatics helps build productive and receptive vocabulary without depending on translation dictionaries
   D. Developing recognition of native English speaker's use of intonation, connotation and synonyms helps ELLs understand the meanings of words and sentences

The correct answer is A. Building contextual understanding is a scaffolding strategy that can help ELLs tackle new and unfamiliar content.
Whether ELLs are learning how to understand social communication or how to read a science text, teaching pragmatics is a key area in which the ESOL teacher can support English language learners. It will help ELLs understand and produce socially appropriate communication and help them comprehend and read between the lines to get the meaning from texts by understanding the contexts.

15. **The term diglossia:** *(Skill 1.6)*

    A. Refers to the use of language restricted to a limited close circle of speakers
    B. Means speaking
    C. Is defined as the use of separate dialects or use of different language to communicate in different situations or groups
    D. Refers to a method of speaking when speakers do not share similar experiences or background

The correct answer is C. Use of separate dialects or use of different language to communicate in different situations or groups
Answer A refers to Bernstein's restricted code and D to his elaborated code. Answer B is an acronym Hymes devised to explain the abilities of a native speaker. Answer C is a definition of diglossia and the correct choice.

16. **The acronym SPEAKING (setting, participants, ends, act sequence, key, instrumentalities, norms, genre) was used to explain knowledge that native language speakers have about the relationship between language and its social context (also known as communicative competence). Which of the following theorists is known for his work in this area?** *(Skill 2.1)*

    A. Krashen
    B. Fishman
    C. Hymes
    D. Pinker

The correct answer is C. Hymes
A Krashen formulated The Monitor Model, and the Natural Approach, among other theories. B. Fishman was famous for his work on diglossia, while Pinker wrote about language instinct. Hymes wrote about communicative competence and his model of discourse analysis that explained the relationship between society, culture and language. He believed that native speakers' competence to speak their language was not only about their ability to use grammatically correct forms but also to use language appropriately.

17. **Interlanguage strategies are best described as:** *(Skill 2.1)*

    A. Being able to transfer between oral and written discourse
    B. Being bilingual or multilingual (reading, writing, listening and speaking in at least 2 languages)
    C. Being a common process in second language learning
    D. Being characterized by poor grammar

The correct answer is C. Being a common process in second language learning
Interlanguage occurs when the second language learner lacks proficiency in L2 and tries to compensate for his or her lack of fluency in the new language. Three components are overgeneralization, simplification, and L1 interference or language transfer.

18. Chomsky's Language Acquisition Device (LAD) includes all of the following hypotheses except: *(Skill 2.1)*

    A. Language learners form hypotheses based on the language they receive.
    B. Language learners' egocentric speech is actually private speech.
    C. Language learners test out hypotheses in speech and texts.
    D. Language learners construct language.

The correct answer is B. Language learners' egocentric speech is actually private speech.
The essence of Chomsky's theory is that children do not enter the world as a blank slate, but rather have a LAD, which permits the construction of their language regardless of which language it may be. The LAD is innate. Option B is the correct choice as it refers to one of Vygotsky's theories that private speech is the child's way of using words to think about something.

19. A team of teachers is looking over assessments and comparing notes on two middle-school English students. They are using Krashen's Natural Order hypothesis to try to understand if one of the students has a learning disability. The Natural Order hypothesis can help them to: *(Skill 2.1)*

    A. Monitor and verify that language instruction is following a specific order - if not, ELLs will suffer and may appear to have learning disabilities
    B. Understand how learners follow a predictable pattern as they learn language - if they fall outside the pattern, they can/should be monitored
    C. Identify that there are two basic ways of acquiring language so students who diverge from these ways can be monitored more closely
    D. Maintain orderly, safe environments so that language acquisition can take place for all students

The correct answer is B. Understand how learners follow a predictable pattern as they learn language - if they fall outside the pattern, they can/should be monitored
Krashen's Natural Order hypothesis holds that language learners acquire different aspects of language in a typical order. Some grammatical structures, for example, are learned early while others are acquired later in the language learning process. L1 and L2 language acquisition also follow this pattern, so if a student is not learning in this particular order, it's possible that s/he may need additional support and/or assessment to determine whether there is a language acquisition exceptionality.

TEACHER CERTIFICATION STUDY GUIDE

20. An ESOL Kindergarten teacher is worried that one of her students is not meeting the Kindergarten English language reading standards. Which of the following theorists would tell her that she shouldn't really be teaching reading in Kindergarten? *(Skill 2.2)*

    A. BF Skinner
    B. Piaget
    C. Holdaway
    D. Gessell

The correct answer is D. Gessell.
Gessell's Maturationist Theory holds that children are not ready to read until they are 6 years old because they are not mature enough to have developed the reading readiness skills they need. He believes that children will learn to read when they are ready and that teachers should not be pushing them to read before that time.

21. An elementary ESOL teacher is a big believer in the impact that Big Books and shared reading can have on literacy development for English language learners. These ideas are based on the theories of: *(Skill 2.2)*

    A. Holdaway's Foundations of Literacy
    B. Piaget's Cognitive Development Theories
    C. Marie Clay's Emergent Literacy Theory
    D. The Stages Model of Reading Development

The correct answer is A. Holdaway's Foundations of Literacy
Holdaway developed a series of instructional practices based on oral literacy practices in the home, including the 'shared book experience' instructional strategy. He believed that learning to read and write should be a positive experience and that some of the challenges that ELLs faced could be overcome by creating a positive learning environment and by recreating some of the experiences English language learners had with their parents reading and listening in their home language(s).

22. Schools that use Reading Recovery programs, are based on theories that identify: *(Skill 2.2)*

    A. Family literacy intervention as a key factor in helping struggling ELL readers
    B. The steps that children generally engage in before the acts of 'reading' and 'writing' formally take place
    C. Phases that children go through from learning the letters of the alphabet to being selective about what to read, when and why
    D. The knowledge and skills to be learned and breaks them down into smaller units

The correct answer is B. The steps that children generally engage in before the acts of 'reading' and 'writing' formally take place.
Marie Clay's Emergent Literacy theory helped form the basis of many reading recovery programs. If children did not have these steps in place, then teachers would have to use and teach a specific set of instructional strategies to help ELLs learn these pre-literacy foundations.

23. **L1 and L2 learners follow approximately the same order in learning a language. Identify the correct sequence from the options below.** *(Skill 2.2)*

    A. Silent period, experimental speech, private speech, lexical chunks, formulaic speech.
    B. Silent period, private speech, lexical chunks, formulaic speech, experimental speech.
    C. Private speech, lexical chunks, speech emergency, formulaic speech, experimental speech.
    D. Private speech, speech emergence, lexical chunks, formulaic speech, experimental speech.

The correct answer is B. Silent period, private speech, lexical chunks, formulaic speech, experimental speech.
The correct order is B. Understanding that students must go through a predictable, sequential series of stages helps teachers to recognize the ELL's progress and respond effectively. In answer A, experimental speech is a different name for the Advanced proficiency stage, so it wouldn't follow the silent period. In answers C and D lexical chunks and speech emergence are different names for the same stage.

24. **Skills such as inferring, classifying, analyzing, synthesizing, and evaluating are key components of:** *(Skill 2.3)*

    A. BICS
    B. SPEAKING
    C. CALP
    D. PRAC

The correct answer is C. CALP.
CALP stands for Cognitive Academic Language Proficiency, which is a term Cummins used to describe the more challenging skills and language needed for ELLs to succeed in academic settings. BICS stands for Basic Interpersonal Communication System, which is Cummin's other term for basic social language. SPEAKING is the acronym used by Hymes to explain *communicative competence* and PRAC is a set of cognitive strategies ELLs can use to achieve proficiency.

TEACHER CERTIFICATION STUDY GUIDE

25. Read the following excerpt from a middle school ESOL student's mid-year report to answer the question below. *(Skill 2.3)*

   Andrea's understanding of spoken English is adequate. Although listeners can understand her when she is speaking, she often has to rephrase what she is trying to say first. Andrea uses reading strategies and some supports to assist with reading comprehension, and her writing skills are beginning to develop.

   According to Andrea's proficiency level, what are some instructional supports ESOL teachers can provide to help her move to the next level?

   A. Work on expanding use of vocabulary and syntax, including explicit instruction in grade level academic discourse
   B. Work on some basic vocabulary and simple phrases and sentences and foundational literacy skills
   C. Work on extending language strategies for more sophisticated oral and written production (e.g., style, tone, voice, audience)
   D. Work on basic vocabulary and structures for social/academic experiences, strengthen decoding and comprehension, develop key writing skills

The correct answer is D. Work on basic vocabulary and structures for social/academic experiences, strengthen decoding and comprehension, develop key writing skills.
Andrea is at the *developing* level of English language proficiency. That means that she needs support with basic vocabulary and structures so that she can speak without rephrasing. It means that if she works on decoding and reading comprehension, she will be able to read without as many supports or strategies because her reading will become more fluent. Developing important writing skills will help her take her writing to the next level of proficiency.

26. The affective domain affects the possibility for students to acquire a second language because: *(Skill 2.4)*

   A. Learning a second language may make the learner feel vulnerable and afraid to take risks
   B. This is a false premise. The affective domain does not really affect a student's second language acquisition.
   C. When you are effective in the four integrated skills, you are more likely to achieve second language proficiency.
   D. It promotes facilitative anxiety, which determines our reaction to competition and is positive.

The correct answer is A. Learning a second language may make the learner feel vulnerable and afraid to take risks
The affective domain refers to the full range of human feelings and emotions that come into play during second language acquisition. Learning a second language may make the learner vulnerable because they have to leave their comfort zone behind. This discomfort can be especially difficult for adults who are used to feeling competent or in control in their professions, but it also affects children and teens.

TEACHER CERTIFICATION STUDY GUIDE

27. Research has shown that one of the factors below significantly improves the bilingualism of English language learners. Which factor is most likely to increase the likelihood of ELL students becoming bilingual? *(Skill 2.4)*

    A. Insisting that ELLs only speak L2 in the school (outside the classroom)
    B. Community appreciation and valuing of the L2.
    C. Providing a block schedule so that ELLs can learn specific skills during different times of the day
    D. Utilizing interlanguage devices between L1 and L2

The correct answer is B. Community appreciation and valuing of the L2.
Motivation, attitude, comfort level and family/community support are key factors in language learning. When an ELL has community support for second language/cultural learning, studies show that bilingualism is more likely to be achieved.

28. Which of the following is NOT a possible effect of an ESOL teacher using too many strategies that rely on instrumental or extrinsic motivation? *(Skill 2.4)*

    A. Students become afraid of taking risks or deviating from what is expected
    B. Students become too competitive and miss out on collaborative opportunities and learning.
    C. Students move through fluency levels too quickly and end up feeling socially isolated from their peers in academic settings.
    D. Students become too dependent on rewards and instant gratification.

The correct answer is C. Students move through fluency levels too quickly and end up feeling socially isolated from their peers in academic settings.
When ESOL teachers rely too heavily on behavioral (Skinner) techniques that appeal to instrumental or extrinsic motivation, they risk A, B and D in their students. This can impede rather than enhance language and content-area proficiency. Only answer C. does not directly relate to the type of motivation - students can end up in this situation with both types.

NES ESOL

TEACHER CERTIFICATION STUDY GUIDE

29. An ESOL teacher is working with an English language learner who is almost ready to move into the next English language proficiency level. By working with the student on making inferences, which domain is the teacher working in? *(Skill 2.5)*

    A. Monitor
    B. Cognitive
    C. Affective
    D. Psychomotor

The correct answer is B. Cognitive
The cognitive domain is the domain in which the explicit teaching of skills and strategies can help ELLs build content-knowledge, language proficiency and the skills they will need as both language and content become more challenging. Answer D is the domain of motor skills, communication and creating. Answer C is the domain of feelings, attitudes, and values. Answer A is not a domain at all but part of a learning theory by Krashen.

30. A high school English language learner does very well in collaborative and group work and seems to flourish when working with peers or small groups. During independent activities, however, including assessments, the student's output is consistently below the standard. *(Skill 2.4)*

    Which of the following should be the ESOL teacher's first step in helping the student?

    A. Perform a needs assessment to identify the area where the student is struggling.
    B. Contact the parents, as there may be something going on at home that is interfering with the student's ability to concentrate or perform.
    C. Bring in another teacher who teaches the student to observe and see if they can identify what the issue may be.
    D. Talk with the student to see whether an affective issue may be causing the problem.

The correct answer is D. Talk with the student to see whether an affective issue may be causing the problem.
If the student can perform well and meet standards in the group, then it is possible that the affective domain is an issue. Talking with the student can identify whether this is the case before involving parents, additional assessments or bringing in another teacher (which might all contribute to the student becoming more nervous and anxious). If this is the case, the ESOL teacher can work with the student on affective strategies (e.g., LET).

31. **An ESOL teacher encourages students to keep track of their progress in English language learning. Which set of learning strategies does this practice fall into?** *(Skill 2.5)*

    A. Metacognitive
    B. Cognitive
    C. Affective
    D. Social

The correct answer is A. Metacognitive.
This ESOL teacher is instructing ELLs in strategies that help them learn how to learn, or think about how they think. By being aware of their learning strategies, ELLs are more empowered to set their own goals, assess their progress and address their own learning challenges.

32. **Literature that reflects the culture of English Language Learners is a potentially valuable resource because:** *(Skill 3.1)*

    A. It is more interesting than regular literature for students.
    B. By having a cultural context that makes sense, students can focus on comprehension.
    C. By showing different backgrounds it promotes equality.
    D. It will have familiar words in it for students whose first language is not English.

The correct answer is B. By having a cultural context that makes sense, students can focus on comprehension
When a cultural context makes sense to them, students can focus on comprehension. Students who are still building English language proficiency may still struggle with books that deal with unfamiliar contexts. Even though they may understand the vocabulary in a book, meaning may be obscured by unfamiliar references. Even though it is entirely in English, a book that deals with a cultural experience that is familiar may allow students to concentrate on building vocabulary and comprehension skills. There is nothing about multicultural literature that is inherently 'more interesting' or 'equal'.

33. There are a number of socio-cultural factors that can affect language acquisition. Which of the following could negatively impact an ELL student's progress in learning English? *(Skill 3.1)*

   A. Learning English can bring academic success but it can also cause a 'break' from the family's home culture.
   B. Learning English may make an adolescent student very reluctant to make mistakes in front of her/his peers.
   C. There are clear cultural differences between the student's new environment and where s/he is from.
   D. Students may not have been raised in an environment that fosters a well-developed attention span.

The correct answer is A. Learning English can bring academic success but it can also cause a 'break' from the family's home culture.
Answer A is a clear socio-cultural factor that some students experience. Learning English can be seen as a rejection of the culture in which a student was raised. When this occurs, it is most often in environments in which the student's home culture/language are looked down on and not respected. Answer B describe affective factors, unrelated to culture, that can impact a student's language learning. Answer C may be true but does not equate to a negative impact on student progress. Answer D is simply unrelated to culture and family background - it is an individual factor.

34. According to Schumann, the acculturation of English language learners is dependent on three key factors and affects the rate at which ELLs acquire a second language. Which of the following is not one of Schumann's key acculturation factors? *(Skill 3.2)*

   A. The length of time a student's family stays in the country
   B. The student's and family's belief that the majority culture respects them
   C. The parents' job success (financial and professional) and the student's perception of that success
   D. The perception that they (student and family) feel welcome in the community (school and local)

The correct answer is C. The parents' job success (financial and professional) and the student's perception of that success
Economic status is not generally viewed as a factor in acculturation. Instead it is the attitudes of the community that have a large impact on acculturation. Economic and job status are more related to individual factors that have an impact on English language learners.

TEACHER CERTIFICATION STUDY GUIDE

35. According to Peregoy and Boyle, the important role that culture plays in our lives can affect student participation, learning, and adjustment to a different country/school in several ways. Which of the following concepts does an ESOL teacher need to consider in terms of culture and ELLs in the classroom? *(Skill 3.1)*

    A. Concepts and practices around roles, interpersonal relationships, family, and religion
    B. Concepts and practices around time, physical space, stage and age and discipline
    C. None of the above
    D. All of the above

The correct answer is D. All of the above
Peregoy and Boyle (2008) identify some of the many different ways that culture can affect students in their participation, learning, and adjustment to a different society and its schools. ESOL teachers who create culturally safe, inclusive and respectful environments are more likely to promote ELL's language learning and academic achievement.

36. Schumann's model of acculturation asserts that: *(Skill 3.2)*

    A. The degree to which a learner adjusts to or assimilates into the target language group will control the degree to which he acquires the second language.
    B. Motivation can be viewed as either a trait or a state and some cultures have the trait of motivation.
    C. New, nonstandard English words can represent a particular group's identity, or function as a means to solidify social relationships.
    D. What is polite in one culture may not be polite in another.

The correct answer is A. The degree to which a learner adjusts or assimilates into the target language group will control the degree to which he acquires the second language.
According to Schuman, if ELLs and native speakers view each other with mutual respect, and have optimistic attitudes about each other, for example, language acquisition and proficiency are more likely to occur.

TEACHER CERTIFICATION STUDY GUIDE

37. Which of the following ESOL models incorporates the idea that native speakers and English language learners should interact more? *(Skill 3.2)*

   A. Two-way Dual Language Bilingual Education (two languages being learned)
   B. The Silent Way (no pressure to speak keeps ensures learners are comfortable)
   C. Marie Clay's Emergent Literacy (peer tutoring in reading recovery)
   D. Skinner's Behaviorist Model (reward positive interactions between language groups)

The correct answer is A. Two-way Dual Language Bilingual Education (two languages being learned)
If both groups of students are learning each other's languages, then students learning the ELL student's first language can work on projects together with the ELLs. When native speakers get a chance to appreciate the ELL students' language skills in their first language, attitudes change and ELLs have an opportunity to shine.

38. Culture and cultural differences: *(Skill 3.2)*

   A. Must be addressed by the teacher in the ELL classroom by pointing out cultural differences whenever possible.
   B. Should be the starting point for learning about a new ELL's attitude.
   C. Negatively affects how well ELLs perform in the language classroom.
   D. May affect the way that ELLs understand written and spoken performance tasks.

The correct answer is D. May affect the way that ELLs understand written and spoken performance tasks
Culture and cultural differences may affect the way that ELLs understand written and spoken performance tasks. If students already have a strong background in literacy from previous schooling in their home/native language, they may be accustomed to reading/writing texts that communicate ideas in a different way than is customary in English. Answer A, Culture and the skillful ESOL teacher may address cultural differences, but pointing out cultural differences is not necessarily the right way to start. With regard to Answer B, culture should not be the starting point for learning about a student's attitude - as it is important to get to know the student before deciding that culture is the reason for something. Answer C is simply biased.

39. **A middle school ELL student does equally well on independent activities and collaborative tasks but when working in small groups with an individual-specific tasks, the student seems to falter and doesn't put forth much effort. What theory is most likely to account for this behavior?** *(Skill 3.2)*

    A. The student is intimidated by the students in the groups s/he is placed in for small group work.
    B. The student is cognitively challenged by the specific tasks that the ESOL teacher tends to assign during non-collaborative group work.
    C. The student comes from a culture that values loyalty and cooperation over competition.
    D. The student prefers to work independently so that s/he doesn't have to deal with group members who tend to do all the work or who don't do their fair share of the work.

The correct answer is C. The student comes from a culture that values loyalty and cooperation over competition.
Many cultures promote group loyalty and cooperation over competition and the idea of winning. Some students may be reluctant to participate in activities that they perceive could cause their peers to 'lose' or be embarrassed or they may defer to others because of the others' perceived status. Recognizing these potential effects will help ensure that teachers create the best possible learning situations for a diverse student body.

40. **A successful elementary school ESOL teacher leads parent workshops at least once a semester and invites parents to observe and even present lessons on various topics. What is the ESOL teacher's primary goal in involving parents and the wider school community in the classroom?** *(Skill 3.4)*

    A. Enabling parents from different cultures to see for themselves rather than depending on their children to tell them what's going on in the classroom
    B. Creating a culturally diverse, inclusive learning environment
    C. Ensuring parental support in case there is a potential conflict with colleagues and/or administrators over cultural issues in the classroom
    D. Creating a classroom environment that is less teacher-directed to appeal to cultures that learn cooperatively

The correct answer is B. Creating a culturally diverse, inclusive learning environment
Creating a culturally diverse learning environment can include creating a learning community that involves parents and the wider school community. It also provides more support for students to see their parents being valued and helps enhance understanding and communication between parents and teachers.

41. Which of the following strategies will best help an ESOL teacher to promote a culturally inclusive learning environment? *(Skill 3.4)*

    A. Use inclusive language and appropriate modes of address
    B. Make classroom time for monthly foods of the world events
    C. Have students create posters that illustrate or represent their countries of origin
    D. Make a point to share travel experiences so that students feel their countries of origin are valued

The correct answer is A. Use inclusive language and appropriate modes of address
Pronouncing students' names correctly (including asking them which name they prefer to be called), referring to students by name as much as possible, and using language that is not ethnocentric can help promote a culturally inclusive learning environment. This, in turn, helps maximize ELL's opportunities for learning and academic achievement.

42. The Natural Approach (1980s) contributed which important language-learning concept to effective ESOL teaching: *(Skill 4.1)*

    A. Physical movement in response to imperatives (works well with vocabulary instruction)
    B. The importance of trusting classroom relationships (teacher-student, student-student)
    C. The value of using realia in the classroom to make learning tasks more relevant and authentic
    D. The idea of comprehensible input to promote more successful language acquisition

The correct answer is D. The idea of comprehensible input to promote more successful language acquisition
Krashen and Terrell's idea of comprehensible input was that students would be exposed to language that they can understand, even though they don't know all of the vocabulary or understand all of the structures (i+1). Comprehensible input helps ELLs learn naturally rather than consciously, which parallels first language learning and therefore is more likely to be an effective ESOL teaching method.

43. TPR activities can contribute significantly to students' listening comprehension proficiency because: *(Skill 4.1)*

    A. Students learn to follow simple commands, which they will have to do in the real world.
    B. Students bonding with their classmates, which helps create a positive learning environment.
    C. Students are actively involved in the listening process without being pressured to speak
    D. Students are getting some physical exercise; physically active students are more likely to learn

The correct answer is C. Students are actively involved in the listening process without being pressured to speak.
Studies show that incorporation of other activities into listening comprehension can help students retain and use the new language. In addition, many ELLs may understand what they hear but struggle to produce language by speaking or writing. TPR gives students the opportunity to show that they understand without the challenges of producing language. Although answers B and C may be true, they are not as closely correlated to improved listening comprehension proficiency.

44. The Natural Approach theory is based on the idea that: *(Skill 4.1)*

    A. Language is learned by imitating and practicing natural sounds
    B. Language learning and skills grow naturally when learners are in an empathetic, supportive environment
    C. Language is learned through natural principles taught through direct instruction
    D. Language is learned subconsciously when interacting for natural, meaningful purposes

The correct answer is D. Language is learned subconsciously when interacting for natural, meaningful purposes
The underlying assumption of The Natural Approach is that any learner of any age has the ability to receive comprehensible speech input and determine its pattern without someone else having to spell it out for them. Furthermore, speech emerges from motivated language use and not artificial practice.

TEACHER CERTIFICATION STUDY GUIDE

45. Which of the following is not a characteristic of differentiated instruction? *(Skill 4.2)*

    A. Flexible groupings of students
    B. Assessment of each student's needs
    C. Self-paced learning
    D. Varied ways of demonstrating learning and proficiency

The correct answer is C. Self-paced learning
Self-paced learning is not a feature of differentiated instruction. In an individualized program students may choose their own pace for learning or even what they learn, but differentiation as an instructional model does not do this. Differentiation is something that teachers implement. Teachers who differentiate may give students voice and choice and adapt instruction to student needs, but they still follow an established curriculum.

46. According to Krashen and Terrell's Input Hypothesis, language learners are able to understand: *(Skill 2.1)*

    A. Slightly more than they can produce.
    B. The same as they speak.
    C. Less than they speak.
    D. Lots more than they speak.

The correct answer is A. Slightly more than they can produce.
Krashen and Terrell's Input Hypothesis (i + 1) states that instruction should be at a level slightly above the language learner's production level. In this way the learner will have the basis with which to understand but will have to figure out the unknown language in context.

47. When an ESOL teacher uses an integrative approach to teach English language skills and a teaching method that includes presentation, practice and production, what ESOL method is s/he using to model her teaching strategies on? *(Skill 4.1)*

    A. Communicative Language Teaching
    B. The Direct Method
    C. Community Language Learning
    D. The Natural Approach

The correct answer is A. Communicative Language Teaching
Communicative Language Teaching (CLT) emphasizes interaction amongst students and amongst the four skills (reading, writing, listening and speaking) to work on authentic tasks. One of the goals of CLT is to produce anxiety-free learning as much as possible. A criticism of this method is that there should be more of an emphasis on teaching grammar and linguistic structures.

48. ESL, Sheltered Instruction and Dual Language classes are all: *(Skill 4.1)*

    A. Mandated by state and federal law for Title 1 Schools
    B. Main instructional ESOL models used in the United States
    C. Based loosely on the Grammar Translation Method
    D. Standards based teaching models

The correct answer is B. Main instructional ESOL models used in the United States
These models do not determine the methodologies and language acquisition principles used by ESOL teachers; they are more about how to organize student groupings to maximize proficiency and learning. Although individual schools may use standards-based instruction with these models, they are not intertwined.

49. Which of the following mandates the presence of state requirements for learning standards for English language learners? *(Skill 4.2)*

    A. The Bilingual Education Act
    B. Lau v. Nichols
    C. The Every Student Succeeds Act
    D. The Common Core

The correct answer is C. The Every Student Succeeds Act (ESSA).
The ESSA requires that all states have English language proficiency standards aligned with their academic standards. The Bilingual Education Act provided funding for English language instruction but did not mandate state standards. Lau v. Nichols was a court case, and the Common Core is a national set of standards that many states have adopted but they are not required.

50. When differentiating standard-based instruction for ELLs, what components of instruction can be differentiated? *(Skill 4.2)*

    A. Student groupings - group by ability as a regular practice to ensure student growth
    B. Assessment (don't grade ELLs as strictly as native-English speakers)
    C. Content, process and product
    D. Standards, outcomes and benchmarks

The correct answer is C. Content, process and product.
It is important that teachers know what is essential in the curriculum and in the learning standards so that even though certain things are being modified, other things remain intact in a specific order. Disrupting central components of a curriculum can actually damage a student's ability to learn something successfully. In addition, it is essential to remember that every student is learning the same core content but in a different way. Differentiated instruction with standards provides opportunities for all learners to demonstrate understanding and to meet skills and language standards.

51. Graves' acronym, SARS describes a method for choosing resources to use with English language learners. The acronym stands for: *(Skill 4.3)*

    A. Select, adapt, reject, supplement
    B. Substitute, augment, revise, sample
    C. Substantiate, acquire, rank, scrutinize
    D. Synchronize, achieve, rearrange, solve

The correct answer is A. Select, adapt, reject and supplement
With Grave's method and a knowledge of the standards and of the students in the class, the ESOL teacher is in a good position to choose, adapt and design materials and resources that will enable her/his students to learn to their potential.

52. Collaboration has been identified as one of the key instructional criteria to support ELLs in the content areas. All of the following statements about collaborative activities are true *except*: *(Skill 4.4)*

    A. Collaborative activities can involve teachers and students actively working together.
    B. Collaborative activities can also include interacting with people outside the classroom.
    C. Collaborative activities are oral-based activities rather than writing based activities.
    D. Collaborative activities can take place in pairs, small groups, or large groups.

The correct answer is C. Collaborative activities are oral-based activities rather than writing based activities.
Collaborative activities can be of just about any type - written, spoken, recorded, physical, etc. Groupings are flexible and do not have to take place solely within the classroom environment.

TEACHER CERTIFICATION STUDY GUIDE

53. Content-based instruction suggests ELLs students need an additional 5-7 years to pick up academic language (CALPS). During this time period, content area teachers should not: *(Skill 10.3)*

    A. Correct the ELL's oral language mistakes as it might make ELLs feel anxious about speaking.
    B. Speak more slowly, enunciate carefully as it might make ELLs feel singled out.
    C. Demonstrate new concepts using visuals and other materials to increase input as it might privilege visual over auditory learners.
    D. Check frequently for comprehension by asking students to explain what was said to a classmate or back to the teacher as it might make students feel micromanaged.

The correct answer is A. Correct the ELL's oral language mistakes as it might make ELLs feel anxious about speaking
When students are learning English, teaching mini-lessons on common oral language mistakes can help build speaking skills and strategies, but pointing out individual learner's oral mistakes may impede fluency and embarrass the student. Speaking slowly and enunciating, demonstrating new concepts with a variety of materials and checking for comprehension are all evidence-based strategies that help ELLs pick up academic language.

54. Which of the following is an activity that Communicative Language Teaching (the Communicative Approach) should not involve? *(Skill 4.1)*

    A. Real communication - students, teachers and others interacting and communicating
    B. Meaningful tasks - activities and tasks relate to real-world situations and matter to students
    C. Instructor interaction with students by way of commands and gestures with students responding physically
    D. Meaningful language - language is applicable to contexts and situations the learner encounters or will encounter (social, academic, workplace, subject-specific, etc.)

The correct answer is C. Instructor interaction with students by way of commands and gestures with students responding physically.
This is a feature of TPR (Total Physical Response) - a command-driven instructional technique.

TEACHER CERTIFICATION STUDY GUIDE

55. The shift in the teaching of speaking skills has moved away from a focus on perfect accuracy towards a focus on fluency and communicative effectiveness. This has had an effect on the kinds of activities that ESOL instructors use to help English Language Learners develop their speaking skills. Which of the following approaches was created before this shift occurred? *(Skill 4.1)*

    A. The Grammar Translation Method
    B. The Cognitive Academic Language Learning Approach (CALLA)
    C. The Natural Approach
    D. Total Physical Response

The correct answer is A. The Grammar Translation Method.
The Grammar Translation Method was one of the first formal methods of language teaching and involved students memorizing long lists of vocabulary words without any requirement to speak in the L2 language. The other methods all incorporate fluency and communicative competence.

56. Read the phrases below to answer the question that follows. *(Skills 1.4, 2.5 and 4.3)*

    Where were you?
    Text me tomorrow.
    What are you doing tonight?
    What is that?

    The phrases above are examples of:

    A. CALP
    B. BICS
    C. PRAC
    D. SARS

The correct answer is B. BICS
BICS (basic interpersonal communication skills) refers to the ability to communicate with peers, teachers, friends, people in stores, etc. in routine social situations. CALP stands for Cognitive Academic Language Proficiency, PRAC is a set of cognitive strategies and SARS is a way to select and adapt instructional resources.

57. What is a crucial element of successfully integrating technology in the ESL/ENL classroom? *(Skill 4.5)*

    A. Developing effective management and instructional strategies
    B. Ensuring all students have access to a device at all times (1:1 program)
    C. Ensuring that all resources are available in the learner's first language
    D. All of the above

The correct answer is A. Developing effective management and instructional strategies.
When technology use is planned carefully and managed effectively it can increase learning opportunities for ELL students. It is not necessary for all students to have a device; many schools make use of carts or labs in which access is shared. It is not reasonable to expect that all resources will be available in all languages.

58. In what ways does technology have the potential to enhance English Language learning? *(Skill 4.5)*

    A. Technology can take the place of the teacher when the teacher is grading papers.
    B. Technology can give students the valuable element of privacy they need to succeed in English Language learning.
    C. Technology can be used to keep students' interests because sometimes the teacher is boring.
    D. Technology can allow students to have more control over their learning.

The correct answer is D. Technology can allow students to have more control over their learning.
Competent use of technology may allow students to have more control over the direction of their learning by controlling their time, speed of learning, autonomy, choice of topics, or even their own identity (Hoven, 1992).

TEACHER CERTIFICATION STUDY GUIDE

59. **The following ideas are part of which instructional theory/practice:** *(Skills 4.1 and 10.2)*

    Learners do not learn L2 through singular instruction in the language's rules; they learn from meaningful interaction in the language and although conversational fluency in L2 is a goal, speaking is not sufficient to develop the academic cognitive skills needed.

    A. Content-based Instruction
    B. The Natural Approach
    C. TPR (Total Physical Response)
    D. Sheltered Immersion

The correct answer is A. CBI or content-based instruction.
Content-based instruction (CBI) integrates language acquisition and the basic content areas of math, science, social studies, literature, and other subjects with students learning about the content areas using the target language (L2). The Natural approach depends more on natural language acquisition in a classroom setting. TPR is based on physical responses to teacher commands and not really related to content-based learning. Sheltered immersion is a model for bilingual education programs and not an instructional theory.

60. **In the United States, in schools with large immigrant populations of diverse origin, the most commonly used ESOL model of the models below is:** *(Skills 4.1 and 10.1)*

    A. Submersion model
    B. ESL/ENL/EAL Pullout model
    C. Specially Designed Academic Programs In English
    D. Two-way Dual Immersion model

The correct answer is B. ESL/ENL/EAL Pullout model.
Today, the most commonly used model is a pullout ESL model for linguistically diverse immigrants. This model allows specific instruction in English while keeping new students in mainstream classrooms for the rest of the day. ESL pullout teachers do not have to speak the home language of their students and different language backgrounds can be accommodated in the same class. SDAIE or Specially Designed Academic Programs in English is a structured immersion model that is not commonly used. The submersion model does not provide the necessary support that ELLs need and is in disfavor. Two-way Dual Immersion models are used when the immigrant population speaks the same language.

TEACHER CERTIFICATION STUDY GUIDE

61. **Team planning with colleagues, supporting curriculum reviews, and participating in school events are important ways for ESOL teachers to:** *(Skill 5.1)*

    A. Act as advocates for cultural and linguistic diversity
    B. Network for improved job prospects
    C. Show administrators and colleagues that they are committed to the school
    D. Show students that they are not just 'teachers' but also human beings

The correct answer is A. Act as advocates for cultural and linguistic diversity.
The ESOL teacher plays an important role in ensuring that cultural and linguistic diversity are embraced in the school instead of being seen as obstacles that must be overcome. If this can be achieved, ELL students are more likely to have a positive attitude towards learning and will therefore be more likely to succeed. Teachers may find many opportunities to ensure that cultural diversity is valued.

62. **An elementary school ELL student received some very low scores on a series of in-class math assessments but scored much better on the state standardized math test. What is the best explanation for this discrepancy?** *(Skill 5.1)*

    A. The student dislikes math class.
    B. The in-class math tests involved a lot of reading.
    C. The teacher dislikes the student and gives their in-class tests a lower score.
    D. The standardized math tests were not timed so the student could take as long as they needed to answer the questions.

The correct answer is B. The in-class math tests involved a lot of reading.
Tests that require extensive language skills to demonstrate understand put ELL students at a disadvantage. Even criterion-referenced tests, in which students must demonstrate specific skills or knowledge, can be problematic. A criterion-referenced test of students' math skills could provide inaccurate results for ELLs because the language skills needed to understand the questions may make it difficult or impossible for an ELL student with outstanding math skills to solve the test problems.

63. **A new high school principal has announced some major changes to the ways in which ELL students are assessed. She wants multiple raters to interpret the students' results, clear scoring criteria, and multiple assessment measures for every English language learner. The best argument for making these changes is to ensure:** *(Skills 5.1 and 5.2)*

    A. Teacher accountability
    B. Consistency among teachers in different subjects
    C. A high quality ranking for the school by improving test scores
    D. The reliability of tests to classify students

The correct answer is D. The reliability of tests to classify students
Though it is not necessary for ALL of these factors to be in place to ensure reliable tests, these are all important ways that the ESOL teacher can help ensure that ELL students are properly assessed for placement in special services.

TEACHER CERTIFICATION STUDY GUIDE

64. **Formative assessment is an essential part of determining:** *(Skill 5.1)*

    A. A student's reading level
    B. Whether a student has a learning disability
    C. Whether a student is in the appropriate learning environment
    D. A student's progress in order to plan and adapt instruction

The correct answer is D. A student's progress in order to plan and adapt instruction
For A, B, and C, more formal diagnostic assessments are needed for accuracy. Formative assessment is useful for seeing how students are progressing towards learning goals and designing instruction to help them meet them.

65. **A reliable assessment test for ELLs will have the following three attributes:** *(Skills 5.1 and 5.4)*

    A. Validity, reliability, and practicality
    B. Validity, reliability, and flexibility
    C. Practicality, reliability, and privacy
    D. Reliability, validity, and familiarity for students

The correct answer is A. Validity, reliability, and practicality
Valid assessments should measure what they assert to measure (not something else). Reliable assessments should yield similar results if taken a second time. Practical assessments are easy to administer, to assess, and test concepts and content similar to what students have encountered in class.

66. **Which of the following is a commonly held belief about effective collaboration that is NOT backed up by research?** *(Skill 6.3)*

    A. A need to establish a clear conceptualization of the task
    B. The incorporation of explicit goals for ESL development into curriculum and assessment planning processes
    C. A shared understanding of ESL and mainstream teachers' roles/responsibilities
    D. The inclusion of a variety of similar activities in various content areas

The correct answer is D. The inclusion of a variety of similar activities in various content areas
Similar activities are not necessary in diverse subject areas for teachers to collaborate on language and learning goals. Without clearly conceptualized tasks, clearly established goals, and well-delineated teacher roles and responsibilities, collaboration will be less effective and beneficial for integrating content and language area objectives for English Language Learners.

67. Which of the following accommodations may be allowed for ELLs on most state standardized assessments? *(Skills 5.3 and 6.1)*

    A. Giving extra time
    B. Asking proctor to explain certain words or test items
    C. Paraphrasing the prompt
    D. Use of general English-heritage translating dictionaries

The correct answer is A. Giving extra time.
In most schools, ELL students may have times extended on assessments. ESOL instructors should check state guidelines on English language learners and accommodations in the ESSA to verify. Answers B - D are explicitly forbidden as they interfere with the validity of the assessment results.

68. Advantages of informal assessment techniques include all of the following EXCEPT: *(Skill 5.3)*

    A. Recognizing opportunities for reteaching
    B. Giving feedback to students to improve learning
    C. Recognizing learning disabilities
    D. Adjusting or planning instructional opportunities

The correct answer is C. Recognizing learning disabilities
Informal or formative assessments are useful opportunities to give feedback to students on progress towards learning goals. They are also useful for teachers in planning instruction or determining if content needs to be retaught. Though informal assessments may indicate to a teacher the presence of a problem, to determine learning disabilities, more formal, diagnostic assessments are needed.

69. Which one of the following is NOT a way to establish reliability when placing English language learners with disabilities? *(Skill 5.2)*

    A. Including assessments in the learner's native language
    B. Including multiple assessment measures and multiple raters
    C. Establishing clearly specified scoring criteria
    D. Using the Woodcock-Johnson III Diagnostic Reading Battery

The correct answer is D. Using the Woodcock-Johnson III Diagnostic Reading Battery
The Woodcock-Johnson III Diagnostic Reading Battery is widely used in formal reading assessments. While unquestionably reliable, it in itself does not establish reliability for placement of students with special needs. Including assessments in the ELL's native language can help clear up if there is a learning disability or a language issue.

70. Norm-referenced assessments may not provide accurate results when used with ELL students because: *(Skill 5.4)*

    A. The test is not in the student's home/first language.
    B. The student will not understand the test.
    C. The tests are too difficult for ELL students.
    D. The norm group may not be reflective of the ELL student.

The correct answer is D. The norm group may not be reflective of the ELL student.
Norm-referenced tests are designed to measure an individual student's performance compared to an 'average' student. Test designers determine an 'average' student's performance by using the test with students from the target audience for the test. Typical norm-referenced reading comprehension tests in the U.S. are intended for American native speakers of English. An ELL student with a high level of English proficiency may still have difficulty with the test if there are reading passages about specific cultural experiences (like Halloween) or activities (like camping) that are unfamiliar. Even if the test is in the student's home language (Answer A), if it has been translated from English, the unfamiliar references will remain. Students may not understand parts of the test (Answer B), but this does not necessarily make the test inaccurate if it is measuring something like comprehension.

71. An ESOL teacher has decided to use an end-of-unit assessment where prompts or tasks are open-ended and have no 'right answer'. Both the process and the final product are going to be assessed. What type of assessment is this? *(Skill 5.1)*

    A. Performance based assessment
    B. Norm referenced assessment
    C. Criterion referenced assessment
    D. Observation based assessment

The correct answer is A. Performance based assessment.
Performance assessments require students to put knowledge and skills in action to complete a task as they combine different elements of what they have learned to create something original.

TEACHER CERTIFICATION STUDY GUIDE

72. **Which of the following assessments is a performance-based assessment?** *(Skill 5.1)*

    A. A multiple choice test with optional questions to account for student interests
    B. A student presentation
    C. A formative quiz that checks for understanding
    D. A think-pair-share summarization strategy

The correct answer is B. A student presentation.
In performance assessments students process information, use skills, and often have to make critical decisions in order to do the task. In this case, the task is a student presentation. Think-pair-share provides students with a process for sharing information and building understanding, and it is a method of formative assessment (like the formative quiz that checks for understanding). The multiple-choice quiz and formative assessments in this question are not open-ended and are structured in-class assessments rather than 'authentic' - a characteristic of performance-based assessments.

73. **Which of the following is NOT recommended as a consideration for teams of teachers to look at when analyzing testing procedures to determine whether an ELL has a learning disability?** *(Skill 5.2)*

    A. Identify student using observations from peers
    B. Criterion-referenced assessments
    C. Identify student using observations from home
    D. Comparison of student's cultural teaching style (e.g., teacher-centered) with the school's teaching style (e.g., student-centered)

The correct answer is A. Identify student using observations from peers.
Research-based recommendations include using a Teacher Assistance Team (TAT) consisting of regular classroom teachers who meet with the referring teacher to discuss problems, brainstorm possible solutions, and develop an action plan. Part of this plan is to analyze and examine testing procedures. The only factor above that is not recommended is using student observations as a consideration. Students may be biased and may make the ELL feel monitored, watched or judged. They have also not been trained in identifying learning disabilities. Checking in with parents, however, can be very helpful because they have a great deal of information to share about the child's early development (starting to speak, for example) and academic history.

TEACHER CERTIFICATION STUDY GUIDE

74. **Assessment data can be used for ALL BUT ONE of the following actions:** *(Skill 5.2)*

    A. Create meaningful, language-rich, and safe environments for English Language Learners that provide them with differentiated language practice and use
    B. Communicate and plan with other teachers in order get to know students' strengths and challenges outside of your classroom
    C. Help in the selection of appropriate learning materials
    D. Deemphasize some curricular outcomes because they are difficult to assess

The correct answer is D. Deemphasize some curricular outcomes because they are difficult to assess
Some curricular outcomes may be difficult to assess, which an ESOL teacher will find out when going over assessment data. Rather than de-emphasizing those outcomes, ESOL teachers can help ELLs by working with a team of teachers and other school staff to brainstorm, design and trial a different assessment to measure the outcome. Involving a team of teachers can help because another teacher may see a way to assess the outcome.

75. **A 7th grade ELL student is struggling in his science and social studies classes. He is doing well in English language arts and math classes. Which of the following factors would have the biggest impact on his poor performance?** *(Skill 5.2)*

    A. The student may have been exited early from the ELL program.
    B. There may be parental pressure to earn top grades in all classes and not just the classes that the student enjoys.
    C. There may be a competitive atmosphere in those classes, which makes the student lose confidence.
    D. The student may have an inflated sense of his own abilities in those subjects and is not studying or working hard enough.

The correct answer is A. The student may have been exited early from the ELL program
In deciding to exit a student from programs designed to support language development, it is also essential to use proper assessments. A student may be succeeding academically in ELA and math classes even without full English language proficiency. This is not enough to exit a student since the ultimate goal of any ELD program is to ensure that all students have the greatest chance of maximizing their learning potential. An early exit could jeopardize that. Knowing and using your school/district/state's exit protocols is essential.

TEACHER CERTIFICATION STUDY GUIDE

76. A high school ESOL teacher hosts a parent meeting after assessment results from standardized tests have gone home. At the meeting several parents are very upset about their children's scores on the tests. Which of the following assessment 'best practices' would help the teacher most at this meeting? *(Skill 5.4)*

    A. Knowing and working towards the achievement of the state and national learning standards that are measured on the test
    B. Aligning goals for learners so that as their English language proficiency develops, so does their content-area learning and output
    C. Knowing how to interpret standardized assessments with respect to ELLs
    D. Communicating regularly with parents about assessment methods and results as well instructional practice

The correct answer is C. Knowing how to interpret standardized assessments with respect to ELLs.
When ESOL teachers know how to interpret standardized assessments with respect to ELLs, they are more likely to be able to help parents understand the results and/or to be able to direct them to someone who can take the time needed to explain them at a different time. Knowing how to interpret the results may put the parents at ease right away, if, for example, the teacher can explain how a norm-reference test works and/or what a test descriptor means.

77. To protect students from inequities in the referral process, federal law explicitly allows the option for: *(Skill 6.1)*

    A. Non-discriminatory evaluation procedures
    B. An independent education evaluation
    C. A multidisciplinary team using several pieces of information to formulate a referral
    D. Testing of the child in L1 unless clearly not feasible to do so

The correct answer is B. an independent education evaluation
Answers A, C, and D are all mandated by federal law. Answer B is an alternative that may be permitted when the parents feel the school's evaluation was inappropriate, but it is not mandated.

TEACHER CERTIFICATION STUDY GUIDE

78. The Every Student Succeeds Act (ESSA) contains some important points relating to English language learners. Which of the following points is part of the ESSA? *(Skill 6.1)*

    A. Schools must report on the number of ELLs meeting academic standards (even for four years after exiting any English language support programs)
    B. Schools may not exclude any students based on language(s) of origin.
    C. Schools must provide resources for personnel, instructional materials, and space for teaching English language learners.
    D. Schools may not exempt English language learners from any state or federal assessments.

The correct answer is A. Schools must report on the number of ELLs meeting academic standards (even for four years after exiting any English language support programs)
ESSA requires schools to report in great detail on the progress of ELL students as well as assess ELLs within 30 days of enrollment. These requirements were designed to keep schools accountable to ELL learners and their families. Answer B is federally mandated by the civil rights act of 1964 and answer C is a result of Castaneda v. Pickard. Answer D is not true. Schools may exempt ELLs, under very specific circumstances (see the ESSA or the ESSA website for details)

79. Which statement about the Lau vs. Nichols case (1974) is FALSE? *(Skill 6.1)*

    A. The Supreme Court ruling required changes that later became federal law as part of the Equal Opportunities Education Act
    B. The Supreme Court ruling included a requirement that bilingual education programs must produce results that indicate the language barrier is being overcome.
    C. The main argument of the case was that students were not being taught required classes in their native language
    D. It was a class action suit filed on behalf of the Chinese community in San Francisco

The correct answer is B. The Supreme Court ruling included a requirement that bilingual education programs must produce results that indicate the language barrier is being overcome.
The Supreme Court ruling in Answer B was as a result of Castaneda v. Pickard.

TEACHER CERTIFICATION STUDY GUIDE

80. At the beginning of a new school year, a high school ESOL teacher is approached by a former parent who is very angry. The parent does not understand why his daughter was exited from the ELL program because she is struggling with all of her class subjects, including English Language Arts, one of her strong subjects from the year before. Which of the following statements below is most likely the cause of his upset? *(Skills 6.1, 6.4, 6.5 and 5.2)*

   A. His daughter was probably exited from the ELL program before she was ready.
   B. He doesn't like his daughter's new teachers very much - he obviously feels comfortable with the teacher from last year.
   C. He doesn't know what the school's policies and procedures are for exiting students from ELL programs.
   D. His daughter is probably rebelling - she is at the age when adolescents sometimes lose motivation to study and work hard.

The correct answer is C. He doesn't know what the school's policies and procedures are for exiting students from ELL programs.
The ESSA requires that states and schools determine their own policies and procedures for ELLs entering and exiting language programs and that they communicate those policies and procedures to parents. Additionally, states (and schools) are required to notify parents of assessment results. As it is the beginning of a new school year, it's too soon to tell if the student has been exited early.

81. Metacognitive strategies in educators can help improve instructional practice and professionalism. Which of the following is an effective metacognitive strategy for teachers? *(Skill 6.2)*

   A. Teachers read performance evaluations carefully, looking for strengths and challenges identified by an evaluator (principal, colleague, etc.).
   B. Teachers read parent and student evaluations looking for specific positive and negative feedback.
   C. Teachers make detailed lesson plans several months in advance to ensure plans match the standard timelines.
   D. Teachers reflect on teaching, making 'just in time' adaptations to instruction.

The correct answer is D. Teachers reflect on teaching, making 'just in time' adaptations to instruction.
Although A and B may help teachers improve - they are more cognitive than metacognitive. By reading evaluations carefully, teachers are thinking about what someone else said about their teaching, rather than reflecting on what and how they are teaching. Making lesson plans far in advance does not involve reflection and, in fact, can make it difficult to adapt, if needed. Reflecting on teaching while it is happening is a truly metacognitive process and allows for quicker lesson adaptation and effectiveness.

TEACHER CERTIFICATION STUDY GUIDE

82. It is most important for ESOL teachers to stay informed on issues, ideas and theories in language learning and the ESOL field so that they can: *(Skill 6.2)*

    A. Be prepared for potential jobs and/or professional opportunities coming up
    B. Be better teachers and connect with others in the school and local community
    C. Be prepared to ensure that lessons will go as planned
    D. Be able to offer advice and suggestions to principals on how to make the ELL program more successful

The correct answer is B. Be better teachers and connect with others in the school and local community
It is important for ESOL teachers to stay informed about current research-based teaching practice in order to provide the best possible learning opportunities for students. Acting as a teacher model also helps make the school community more conducive to English language learning. Connecting with others, even outside the school, gives teachers a good cohort for learning new things, trying them out and talking about next steps. Answer A may be true but it's not a reason to stay informed - improving student learning should be a prime motivator in staying current with ESOL issues. Answer C - it's impossible to guarantee that lessons will go as planned, and sometimes teachers learn the most when they don't.

83. An elementary school ESOL teacher is not able to take any days away from school to attend professional development workshops, but she has set professional growth goals for the year. A colleague gives her some suggestions. Which of the following is NOT likely to lead to improved professional practice: *(Skill 6.2)*

    A. Practice your craft. If you teach English, write. If you teach history, do some research.
    B. Join a professional organization to have access to resources, readings and people that you can learn from.
    C. Use some of your professional development budget to purchase some technology that will benefit some of your ELLs.
    D. Do some action research with colleagues (from your school or another school)

The correct answer is C. Use some of your professional development budget to purchase some technology that will benefit some of your ELLs.
Although technological purchases may have an impact on student learning, they won't necessarily lead to improved professional practice. Participating in professional organizations, performing action research and practicing your craft can all increase professional growth, which leads to improved professional practice.

84. What is a key reason for collaboration between ESOL and content-area teachers? *(Skill 6.3)*

    A. Provides consistent expectations for students and monitors student development
    B. Saves teachers valuable time by co-planning
    C. ESOL teacher serves as a model for other teachers
    D. Teachers should know and understand legislation and case law regarding ELLs

The correct answer is A. Provides consistent expectations for students and monitors student development.
It is important, particularly when second language learners have multiple teachers, such as in middle or high school, that teachers communicate and collaborate as much as possible. Where there is inconsistency, teachers should work to uncover what it is that is keeping the student from excelling in a particular class. Answers B and C are not key reasons for collaboration as student learning should be the most important factor. Answer D is true but is not a reason for collaboration; it is something the school administrators should be communicating to all teachers.

85. Teacher Assistance Teams (TATs) should be composed of all of the following EXCEPT the: *(Skill 6.3)*

    A. School administrators
    B. Guidance counselors
    C. Media specialists
    D. Parent(s)

The correct answer is C. Media specialists
Answer A, B, and D may all be members of a TAT. Media specialists could be consulted for additional materials that would help in special education cases but would not form part of the normal TAT. Answer C is the correct choice.

86. Two sixth teachers want to collaborate; one is a content-area teacher and one is an ESOL teacher. The school is supportive of the collaboration but tells them that they cannot co-teach any classes, as there would be too many students in the class, even with two teachers. Which of the following is NOT recommended for the two sixth grade teachers if they can't co-teach? *(Skill 6.3)*

    A. Choosing a common goal for ELL development in the content-area and plan how to assess it
    B. Getting advice on classroom dynamics and understanding specific students
    C. Choosing specific students and having them sit together in both classes so that teachers can monitor and work with them on learning goals
    D. Choosing a project that students can work on in both classes

The correct answer is C. Choosing specific students and having them sit together in both classes so that teachers can monitor and work with them on learning goals
A, B, and D are all effective options for teachers who want to collaborate. Answer C is singling students out in both classes, which will likely cause them anxiety and impede their socialization skills with the rest of the students.

87. By modeling effective teaching practices and sharing resources both with colleagues and families, the ESOL teacher can help to maximize the learning opportunities available to all students. *(Skill 6.4)*

    The statement above is based on:

    A. Research and evidence-based best practices
    B. Wishful thinking - teachers simply don't have time
    C. ESSA requirements for Title I schools
    D. State mandated in at least 14 states

The correct answer is A. Research and evidence-based best practices
This is true, especially when communication is difficult because of language barriers. The ESOL teacher can bridge the gap to make a significant impact in bringing all stakeholders together to work towards supporting the academic, linguistic, and social/emotional development of the student.

88. **Which of the following assessments is NOT for English language learners?** *(Skills 7.2, 9.1, 9.2 and 5.1)*

    A. Woodcock-Muñoz Language Survey
    B. Peabody Picture Vocabulary Test
    C. Summative, graded in-class end of unit assessments
    D. The National Assessment of Educational Progress

The correct answer is B. Peabody Picture Vocabulary Test
The Peabody test assesses a student's receptive vocabulary and potential scholastic aptitude but is not intended for students whose first language is not English. Because the images used in the test are representations of 'mainstream' culture, any student not from the dominant/majority cultural group may perform below his/her level because of cultural background - not ability.

89. **What practice(s) describe an English language development program in a standards-based environment?** *(Skill 5.2)*

    A. Teachers have high standards for their students, knowing that students will do better with high expectations
    B. In schools with standards-based environments, students who do not meet the standards are often exited out
    C. A school's assessment procedures and tools are closely tied with EL standards and content-area standards
    D. Teachers who work in standards-based environments frequently assign letter grades to individual assignments to let students know whether they have met the linguistic, content-skill or content-knowledge standards for the assignment

The correct answer is C. A school's assessment procedures and tools are closely tied with EL standards and content-area standards
Standards-based, ongoing assessment helps determine whether students are making adequate progress towards grade-level standards. This information is generally the primary basis of reporting achievement in standards-based schools.

90. An essential component of an ESOL teacher's job is the facilitation of communication between students, families, and all teachers. Which of the following is an evidence-based method for facilitating this communication? *(Skill 6.5)*

    A. Provide opportunities for stakeholders to come into the school and participate in activities designed to encourage their participation in the schooling of their children
    B. Use students as translators during parent conferences to ensure that parents fully understand their child's learning issues
    C. Make sure that you communicate good news to parents; let report cards and counselors tell them the bad news so that you can maintain a good relationship with them
    D. Let families know that you are sharing with them so they can share with you too. Try to find out as much as you can about the child's family situation so that you can differentiate instruction to maximize student learning.

The correct answer is A. Provide opportunities for stakeholders to come into the school and participate in activities designed to encourage their participation in the schooling of their children.
The other answers are not supported by evidence or research and, in fact, can significantly challenge effective and positive communication between students, families and teachers.

91. A high school teacher assigns a research project for all students. Some students begin immediately while a few seem confused and unsure what to do. Which of the following steps should the teacher have taken before assigning the project? *(Skill 7.1)*

    A. Differentiated instruction
    B. A needs assessment
    C. Brainstorming with students
    D. Hands-on activities

The correct answer is B. A needs assessment
The teacher and students would have benefitted from doing a needs assessment to determine whether or not students had experience and skills necessary to do a research project. This is a key first step in differentiating instruction (Answer A). Students would likely benefit from brainstorming of some kind before starting to actually do the project, but again, determining what the needs of all students are is a key first step.

92. **Choosing literature that represents the culture of a number of ELL students from class helps students with literacy because:** *(Skill 7.1)*

    A. The books will likely contain some words that ELL students know.
    B. ELL students will feel included in the class.
    C. Prior knowledge will provide context for understanding.
    D. There will likely be a stronger home-school connection from reading multicultural literature.

The correct answer is C. Prior knowledge will provide context for understanding.
Though B and D are possible effects of choosing books that represent the culture of ELL students, these are not directly tied to literacy. These are sociocultural factors that may have academic benefits. Many books representing other cultures are entirely in English, so A is not correct. Choosing books with a familiar setting gives the students a familiar context to understand what they are reading about. This allows students to focus on comprehension, vocabulary development, etc. instead of having to simultaneously learn about an unfamiliar context.

93. **In addition to students' level of English language proficiency, what other factors would a teacher likely take into account in trying to personalize instruction?** *(Skill 7.1)*

    A. Level of home/L1 language proficiency
    B. Level of motivation
    C. Student's hobbies and interests outside of school
    D. Student's cultural background

The correct answer is A. Level of home/L1 language proficiency
In personalizing instruction to meet the needs of students, the level of L1 proficiency is very important. For example, a student who can read and write in her/his L1 would likely need very different teaching strategies to build English literacy than a student with little or no literacy skills in L1. The latter student would likely need instruction in basic phoneme/grapheme awareness. Though C and D are relevant factors in a student's learning, they would not likely affect instruction as most teachers must follow a set curriculum. Motivation might affect interactions with the student but not be a cause for differentiation.

94. An ESOL teacher observes that a student seems to have plateaued in his language development. The student tends to stick to what he knows in oral and written language activities. Sentence structure, for example, is correct but still quite simple. On the other hand, his listening and reading comprehension have continued to improve. To address this imbalance, which strategy below would be most effective? *(Skills 7.1 and 7.2)*

    A. Creative writing activities
    B. Flexible, small group work with clear roles
    C. Open-ended discussion questions
    D. One-on-one conferencing with the student to discuss the issue

The correct answer is C. Open-ended discussion questions
Open-ended discussion questions require spontaneous speaking with no 'right' answer. An answer can easily lead to another question. This would require the student (who is not a beginner) to use language in unexpected ways 'on the fly', likely causing some experimentation with language structure. Creative writing, though an outlet for creative expression, still allows for planning and editing. The student from this scenario would likely stick to the patterns he knows because they are 'right'. Group work with clear roles would similarly allow the student to stick to the language structures he knows. Talking to the student about your observation (formative feedback) is a good idea, but unless the student makes a conscious decision to change behavior, this is unlikely to work.

95. Student-student engagement in the classroom (as opposed to teacher-student engagement) offers which of the following benefits in language learning? *(Skills 7.2 and 7.3)*

    A. Authentic opportunities for communication
    B. More frequent engagement than teacher-student engagement
    C. Varied types of communication
    D. All of the above

The correct answer is D. All of the above
Teacher-student engagement (in the form of conversation, questions/responses, feedback, assessment commentary, etc.) is essential to learning, but because of the ratio of teachers to students, student-student engagement is also essential. Students will communicate about work projects, problem solving, readings, etc. and also engage in social communication. This frequent, unpredictable, varied and 'real' communication can push learning forward.

TEACHER CERTIFICATION STUDY GUIDE

96. Differentiation and personalization of instruction share many things in common. However, there are some important differences. Which of the following is an important difference? *(Skills 7.1, 7.2 and 7.3)*

    A. The teacher may adapt or select different teaching materials.
    B. The teacher and student may set specific content-area goals.
    C. The student decides what s/he wants to study and what goals to set.
    D. The teacher may change or adapt instructional methods.

The correct answer is B. The teacher and student may set specific content-area goals.
A and D are features of both personalized and differentiated instruction. C is not a characteristic of either approach. B is the correct answer. In differentiation, the goals for each student remain the same (and are based on grade level standards). When personalizing, however, a teacher might set goals that are unique to each student.

97. Communicative Language Teaching (CLT) emphasizes a progression from 'presentation' to 'practice' to 'production' when working with ELL students. What does this approach offer students? *(Skill 7.2)*

    A. This progression scaffolds student learning and language proficiency.
    B. This progression emphasizes fundamental language skills essential to L2 competency.
    C. This progression provides multiple ways of assessing student growth.
    D. This progression puts students at the center of learning.

The correct answer is A. This progression scaffolds student learning and language proficiency.
Presentation involves teacher directed instruction of skills or content. Practice refers to independent and/or guided practice in which students often have the opportunity to work in small groups with teacher support. Finally, production refers to independent application of skills and knowledge, often to complete a performance task designed to specifically assess the content and skills taught. This progression allows students to build skills while moving towards independence.

98. **A holistic approach to language proficiency would involve:** *(Skill 7.2)*

    A. Frequent formative assessment to provide clear feedback to students
    B. Understanding of students' social and emotional needs (in addition to academic)
    C. Cooperative work in classroom to provide authentic communication opportunities
    D. Integration of speaking, listening, writing, and reading

The correct answer is D. Integration of speaking, listening, writing, and reading
Though answers A, B, and C are beneficial for language development, D, the integration of speaking, listening, reading, and writing, reflects the idea of a holistic approach to language proficiency.

99. **A teacher designs a science project in which students have to conduct an experiment with a partner, research additional information, take notes, and then create a short video presentation about their experimental results. This is an example of Chamot and O'Malley's:**
(Skills 7.1, 8.5 and 10.2)

    A. CALP
    B. CALLA
    C. BICS
    D. PRAC

The correct answer is B. CALLA (Cognitive Academic Language Learning Approach)
Chamot and O'Malley sought to show that content learning (in this case, science) could be integrated with language learning. In this case, the student is using speaking and listening (for the experiment), reading (for research), writing (for notes and preparation of the video presentation), and speaking (for the video itself). A is Cognitive Academic Language Proficiency and describes proficiency using language in an academic context. C is Basic Interpersonal Communication Skills. D is Practicing, Receiving and sending messages, Analyzing and reasoning, and Creating structure for input/output.

100. In social studies class, the teacher has told the students that in the next class meeting they will be discussing the election results and should come prepared to discuss their opinions of the outcome. Which of the following would be the best way for an ESOL teacher to help an intermediate level ELL student participate in an important class discussion? *(Skills 7.2 and 7.3)*

   A. Provide the student with a graphic organizer to take notes during the discussion.
   B. Summarize what other students say during the discussion.
   C. Meet with the student before the discussion to help him/her prepare ideas to share in the discussion.
   D. Provide the student with key election-related vocabulary and a series of model sentences showing ways of expressing ideas.

The correct answer is D. Provide the student with key election-related vocabulary and a series of model sentences showing ways of expressing ideas.
Answer A is useful in helping the student keep track of and make sense of what other students say, but it may not help with participation. B is not practical and may make the student feel self-conscious. C does not allow the student to take ownership for forming his/her opinions and also puts the student in the position of having to explain his/her opinions to the teacher (which is potentially intimidating). D allows the student to work independently (with scaffolding) to both learn about the election and formulate ways to express ideas.

101. A few days before an upcoming demonstration in science class of a complicated experiment, which of the following would be the most important and practical way in which the science teacher and ESOL teacher could collaborate? *(Skills 7.2, 7.3, 10.1 and 10.2)*

   A. The science teacher could teach the ESOL teacher how to do the experiment so that s/he can review it with ELL students.
   B. They could identify potentially difficult vocabulary and terms for pre-teaching.
   C. They could co-teach the experiment.
   D. The ESOL teacher could observe and take simplified notes on the experiment for ELL students to use in understanding it.

The correct answer is B. They could identify potentially difficult vocabulary and terms for pre-teaching.
In this scenario, this is the most effective and practical way of collaboration. The ESOL teacher could help ELL students be prepared with prior knowledge and contextual understanding. Though co-teaching is an appealing option, it is likely not feasible given scheduling. Ensuring that the ESOL teacher could be present is probably complicated. Similarly A and D would require a great deal of time that both teachers likely do not have.

102. Cognitive processing involves using existing knowledge to acquire new knowledge. Which of the following best reflects this from the point of view of an ELL student learning English? *(Skills 7.2 and 2.3)*

   A. Writing a short story about what happened on the weekend
   B. Forming new sentences about ducks after learning the song Old MacDonald
   C. Reflecting on progress and learning
   D. Following the directions for an experiment

The correct answer is B. Forming new sentences about ducks after learning the song Old MacDonald
Though this may seem like a very simple example, in this case a student has learned the names of animals from a children's song and is now forming new sentences about them. This demonstrates the student's ability to use existing knowledge to begin to acquire new knowledge.

103. Which of the following activities likely makes the most linguistic demands of an English language learner? *(Skills 8.1, 9.3, 9.4 and 9.5)*

   A. An oral presentation about his/her home country
   B. Writing an essay about a novel
   C. Researching and taking notes on a historical event
   D. Preparing for a vocabulary test

The correct answer is C. Researching and taking notes on a historical event
Research and note taking require a student to read (in most cases) unfamiliar texts. In the case of a historical event, the texts would likely be context reduced and assume a fair amount of background knowledge. While reading, the student would need to identify relevant information, synthesize it into useful 'chunks', and then summarize it.

104. One element of differentiation is the opportunity to demonstrate knowledge and skills in different ways. How is this particularly important in content-area learning for ELL students? *(Skills 10.1 and 10.3)*

   A. They will be more likely to demonstrate learning in a way that is not impacted by language proficiency.
   B. They may not be able to meet the learning standard due to a lack of understanding.
   C. They will have multiple chances to show what they know if they did not 'get it' the first time.
   D. They will be more engaged in the learning process and vested in the outcomes.

The correct answer is A. They will be more likely to demonstrate learning in a way that is not impacted by language proficiency.
If everyone were required to write an essay or do an oral presentation, many ELL students would be at an immediate disadvantage in demonstrating their understanding and skills. Allowing for other opportunities may give ELL students the chance to show what they know without being hampered by language skills.

TEACHER CERTIFICATION STUDY GUIDE

105. To determine whether an ELL student has a learning disability, ideally testing and assessment should: *(Skill 7.3)*

    A. Be administered with parental knowledge and consent
    B. Be administered in the student's first language
    C. Be done by the classroom teacher
    D. Be administered more than once

The correct answer is B. Be administered in the student's first language
All assessments of learning disabilities must be done with parental consent. This is not optional, so A is not correct. Most schools have designated personnel to administer such diagnostic tests, so C is not correct. D is not correct because the test should not need to be administered more than once. B is correct because, whenever possible, such tests should be in the L1 to ensure validity and reliability. Translation of tests from English to the student's L1 is not a good idea.

106. In many cases there is no suitable diagnostic test to determine student exceptionalities in the ELL student's first/native language. In this case, what is the best option? *(Skill 7.3)*

    A. Observation, investigation of achievement in different subject areas, consultation with family
    B. Observation, use of existing diagnostic tests, consultation with family
    C. Tentative placement in learning support classes and continued observation of growth
    D. Review of student's past learning records, implementation of differentiated instruction, observation of growth

The correct answer is A. Observation, investigation of achievement in different subject areas, consultation with family
When reliable testing instruments are not available, observation of the student in different situations, consultation with all teachers to investigate patterns/differences in achievement, and consultation with family are essential steps. Families may identify past difficulties in learning to speak/read in L1 (or early mastery of reading). For answer B, using existing diagnostic tests is not a good option because of issues of validity/reliability. For answer C, tentative placements are not a good idea (and usually not allowed). Option D is often not enough when dealing with student exceptionalities.

TEACHER CERTIFICATION STUDY GUIDE

107. **Which of the following language theories about listening is NO LONGER considered valid?** *(Skill 8.1)*

    A. Top-down listening processing relies on the listener's bank of prior knowledge and global expectations.
    B. Listening is considered a 'passive' skill.
    C. Bottom-up processing of listening refers to analysis of the language by the listener to find out the intended meaning of the message.
    D. Verbal learning becomes easier when information can be chunked into meaningful patterns.

The correct answer is B. Listening is considered a 'passive' skill.
Listening is not considered a passive skill anymore but a dynamic process that makes a lot of demands on language learners.

108. **Activating prior knowledge, or schema, is particularly important for English language learners because:** *(Skill 8.2)*

    A. It makes learning more meaningful for the students.
    B. It aids in reading and listening comprehension.
    C. It validates cultural knowledge.
    D. All of the above.

The correct answer is D. All of the above.
Activating prior knowledge (schema) connects to students' previous experiences and potentially cultural background(s). Therefore, it can make learning more meaningful while also valuing the students' culture. Additionally, the context provided by prior knowledge aids in comprehension.

109. **Which of the following would be the most effective activity to use with Entering or Beginning level ELLs?** *(Skill 8.2)*

    A. Asking comprehension questions after completing a listening activity
    B. Frontloading vocabulary
    C. Identify a picture that matches specific passages or parts of passages that the ESOL teacher is playing for the students
    D. Quiz

The correct answer is C. Identify a picture that matches specific passages or parts of passages that ESOL teacher is playing for the students.
Answer A is ineffective because students will frequently "tune out" of listening activities because they don't understand and listening is hard work. Answer B may be effective for helping the ELL to understand what he/she is going to hear but may also confuse a beginning English language learner. Answer D is the least effective option because it may raise anxiety levels and block learning. Answer C is the best choice because students will be listening to the entire passage and actively engaging with the passage.

NES ESOL

TEACHER CERTIFICATION STUDY GUIDE

110. **Which one of the scaffolding methods would be most effective in helping ELLs develop listening skills?** *(Skill 8.2)*

    A. Front-loading or pre-teaching vocabulary
    B. Asking ELLs to compare/contrast a listening activity with a text passage
    C. Allowing students to listen several times
    D. Creating a word wall

The correct answer is C. Allowing students to listen several times
While all of the answers are effective scaffolding techniques, until understanding is achieved, learning does not occur. The best option would be C, allowing ELL students to listen several times.

111. **Cooperative learning tasks, races and team drawings are examples of:** *(Skills 8.2 and 8.3)*

    A. Metacognitive tasks
    B. Chomsky's Language Acquisition Device (LAD)
    C. Two-way exchanges of information
    D. Linguistic modifications

The correct answer is C. Two-way exchanges of information.
Ellis concluded that two-way exchanges of information show more benefits for ELLs partly because they require more negotiation of meaning. When learning cooperatively, participating in TPR races, or team drawing, students are focusing on comprehension and on producing the language in some form - whether by drawing, physical movement or communicating with other students. Answer B. Chomsky's LAD refers to children not entering the world as a blank slate. Answer A refers to task where students think about how they learn and how they think.

112. **All of the following can help more advanced ELLs improve listening and speaking proficiency EXCEPT:** *(Skills 8.2, 8.3, 8.4 and 8.5)*

    A. Memorization of long vocabulary lists
    B. Requiring students to integrate information and evidence from diverse media sources
    C. Emphasizing the authentic use of language (e.g., presentations or debates rather than memorization of language patterns);
    D. Integrating speaking, listening, reading and writing

The correct answer is A. Memorization of long vocabulary lists
Answers B, C, and D are examples of materials and strategies that support English language learners' achievement of listening and speaking standards. Answer A, encouraging students to memorize long vocabulary lists is not effective. Although vocabulary building is an important aspect of listening and speaking English language development, long vocabulary lists will be too difficult to learn and retain.

113. Which of the following are advantages to the instructor's use of students' home language(s) in the English language classroom or in English language instruction? *(Skills 8.4 and 8.5)*

    A. It can reduce anxiety and fear.
    B. It can permit explanation of differences and similarities of home and new languages.
    C. It can reduce time-consuming explanations of abstract concepts.
    D. All of the above.

The correct answer is D. All of the above.
There are quite a few benefits to using the home language to scaffold instruction. A caveat is that ESOL teachers need to be judicious in their use of the home language(s) because one danger of this method is that some students may become so dependent on instruction in their first language that they will hesitate to use their knowledge of the second language.

114. An ELL student who is at the intermediate/developing English language level is speaking in front of the class and telling them about his aunt, who had a big influence on him and his desire to learn. He introduces his aunt by saying, "My Aunt Maria is a profesora." This is an example of: *(Skill 8.1)*

    A. Dialect
    B. Inter-language
    C. Code-switching
    D. Formulaic speech

The correct answer is C. Code-switching
Dialect is any form or variety of a spoken language peculiar to a region, community, social group, etc. Inter-language is the language spoken by ELLs that is between their L1 and L2. Formulaic speech refers to speech that is ritualistic in nature and perhaps used for social politeness rather than information. Code-switching refers to the mixing of L1 and L2 or to switching back and forth between them during communication.

TEACHER CERTIFICATION STUDY GUIDE

115. **When the teacher is correcting a student's language, the teacher should:** *(Skill 8.3)*

    A. Carefully correct all mistakes
    B. Consider the context of the error
    C. Confirm the error by repeating it
    D. Repeat the student's message but correct it

The correct answer is D. Repeat the student's message but correct it
To carefully correct all mistakes a student makes would raise the affective filter and probably cause the student to hesitate before speaking. Considering the context of the error gives the teacher insight into the student's learning, but isn't a method of correction. To confirm the error by repeating it would suggest to the student that his or her utterance was correct and is not good practice. The best option is D, which corrects the error, but in a way that shows the student the correct form without embarrassing him or her.

116. **Which one of the following is NOT an effective activity used in developing speaking proficiency, especially with beginning and intermediate ELLs?** *(Skills 8.3 and 8.5)*

    A. Choral readings
    B. Individual reading (to the whole class)
    C. Structured interviews
    D. Role plays

The correct answer is B. Individual reading (to the whole class).
Answers A, C, and D are all effective strategies for developing speaking skills. According to the findings of the National Literacy Panel on Language-Minority Children and Youth, ELL students may be very self-consciousness about making mistakes in front of their peers and/or about having an 'accent'. If pressured to read aloud in front of the entire class, this can actually have a negative impact on their reading fluency and speaking performance tasks. Answer A is the correct choice.

117. **Wait time is a particularly important consideration for teachers of English language learners because:** *(Skills 8.3 and 8.5)*

    A. They may need more time to formulate how to express their answers.
    B. They may have anxiety about speaking in front of their peers.
    C. They may take more time to process the question from the teacher.
    D. All of the above.

The correct answer is D. All of the above.
English language learners may experience all these factors when the teacher asks questions in class. This is another reason that teachers can/should consider alternative ways to let students answer some questions (on slips of paper, backchannel chats, at the end of class, etc.).

TEACHER CERTIFICATION STUDY GUIDE

118. Which of the following is NOT a purpose for a listening assessment?
     (Skill 8.1)

    A. Assessing students' listening strengths and weaknesses at the beginning of a course
    B. Assessing students' mastery of a specific listening skill
    C. Assessing students' progress towards listening standards at the end of a term or important time period
    D. Assessing students listening skills to determine if the student has hearing problems

The correct answer is D. Assessing students listening skills to determine if the student has hearing problems.
A hearing test is not the same thing as a listening assessment. If an ESOL teacher has concerns about an ELL's hearing, they should refer the student to someone who can test their hearing. In terms of answers A - C, they are all valid purposes for listening assessments and the first step in choosing a listening assessment is to have a clear purpose in mind.

119. Assessment of speaking skills in English language learners should:
     (Skill 8.1)

    A. Concentrate on the number of errors ELLs make in order to help them become proficient speakers
    B. Focus on the message conveyed by learners in order to evaluate ELLs communicative abilities
    C. Encourage ELLs to memorize what they are going to say in the assessment so that they are not looking down and reading
    D. Concentrate on the student's presentation style; make sure that they are dressed appropriately, standing with proper posture, using effective voice and pitch so that they take the assessment seriously

The correct answer is B. Focus on the message conveyed by learners in order to evaluate ELLs communicative abilities
Assessment methods that focus on the message conveyed by the learners are more accurate in evaluating oral proficiency. Teachers can still work with students on areas of growth in terms of speaking errors, but the errors should not be the focus of assessment results.

120. What does the term top down processing mean in terms of language processing? *(Skill 9.3)*

   A. Encouraging students to use prior knowledge to make predictions about meaning
   B. Explicit teaching of tasks by the ESOL teacher
   C. Recognizing main ideas in what is said
   D. Making inferences about possible meanings

The correct answer is A. Encouraging students to use prior knowledge to make predictions about meaning.
Top down processing can help ELLs prepare for listening situations that they may encounter in real life. When learners encounter vocabulary they don't know, ESOL teachers can teach them the strategies to use their prior knowledge to build meaning and understanding.

121. In a "top down" strategy of literacy development, which one of the following strategies might not help a reader with comprehension? *(Skill 9.3)*

   A. Make guesses about what is going to happen
   B. Look up and record each unfamiliar word
   C. Anticipate the contents of the text
   D. Infer meaning from sentences and paragraphs

The correct answer is B. Look up and record each unfamiliar word
Options A, C, and D are all elements of a "top down" processing strategy and are desirable reading strategies. Only Option B might not help an English language learner build reading comprehension skills. Looking up and recording definitions of each word while reading can impede fluency and decontextualize the text.

122. Activities that help students develop phonological awareness, fluency in word recognition and the ability to sound out words are all key components of instructional strategies designed to: *(Skill 9.3)*

   A. Build cognitive and metacognitive skills
   B. Build semantic and pragmatic skills
   C. Build critical thinking skills
   D. Build literacy skills

The correct answer is D. Build literacy skills
Answers A, B, and C are all skills that help students academically but they are not specifically focused on literacy development. The correct answer is D.

TEACHER CERTIFICATION STUDY GUIDE

123. Which one of the following is NOT an effective instructional literacy practice for elementary ESOL teachers? *(Skill 9.3)*

    A. Providing direct explicit instruction of reading/writing skills based on ongoing student assessment
    B. Devoting less than 50% of the day's instructional time to reading/writing
    C. Assessing student work based on common rubrics
    D. Promoting conversation through purposeful and guided discussions about a book, piece of writing, or topic

The correct answer is B. Devoting less than 50% of the day's instructional time to reading/writing
Only Answer B is an ineffective strategy. Recommendations are that ESOL teachers devote at least 50% of instructional time to reading and writing a daily basis. Studies have shown that even when teachers have a 90 minute reading block scheduled, for example, often only 10 - 15 minutes of that time is devoted to students actually reading. Successful ESOL and ELA teachers work hard to ensure that their students spend half the day (or half of the instructional time) in reading and writing activities.

124. Activities that focus on increasing fluency in academic reading include all of the following strategies EXCEPT: *(Skill 9.4)*

    A. Modeled reading
    B. Repeated reading of a familiar text
    C. Checking for understanding by asking if there are any questions
    D. Coached reading of appropriate materials

The correct answer is C. Checking for understanding by asking if there are any questions
Answers A, B, and D are appropriate for developing fluency. Answer C would probably not improve the reading of academic texts or literature. It is not an effective way to check for understanding for two reasons. First, students may not feel comfortable asking questions in front of the class. In addition, waiting until the end of class to gauge understanding is not going to give the ESOL teacher timely feedback needed to adapt instruction, particularly if students don't remember their questions because they had to wait.

125. To develop reading fluency, ESOL teachers can use all of the following strategies EXCEPT: *(Skills 9.3 and 9.4)*

    A. Choose texts carefully that students are able to read fairly fluently
    B. Read aloud daily to students to model reading fluency
    C. Consistently quiz students after reading fluency activities to ensure success
    D. Have students re-read texts that they have heard before to build fluency

The correct answer is C. Consistently quiz students after reading fluency activities to ensure success
Reading instruction should include explicit instruction in A, B, and D to develop fluency. Answer C will not develop fluency development and may even inhibit it as students become nervous about performing.

126. Common activities of the "post-reading phase" include: *(Skills 9.3 and 9.4)*

   A. Building background knowledge
   B. Summarizing and organizing information
   C. Asking questions
   D. Annotating text

The correct answer is B. Summarizing and organizing information
Peregoy and Boyle described different reading phases. During the post-reading phase, a common strategy is to summarize and organize information gleaned from the text. This helps to build deeper understanding and to retain information. Annotation and questions are common during reading, and building background knowledge is a feature of the pre-reading phase.

127. When teaching initial literacy, teachers should focus on all of the following literacy skills EXCEPT: *(Skill 9.1)*

   A. Effect of culture on language learning
   B. Phonemic awareness
   C. Phonics
   D. Comprehension of different types of reading materials

The correct answer is A. Effect of culture on language learning
Answers B, C, and D are all important literacy skills. Answer A is not a literacy skill, but rather a factor in language learning. Factors such as culture and the characteristics of the heritage language may affect transfer of language skills to L2. Answer A is the correct choice.

128. Why is an ELL student's ability to read and then successfully paraphrase a text a good indicator of literacy development? *(Skills 9.3, 9.4 and 9.5)*

   A. It demonstrates that the student can recognize main ideas.
   B. It demonstrates that the student is overcoming anxiety about language learning.
   C. This is an important element of BICS.
   D. The student is using appropriate register for an academic setting.

The correct answer is A. It demonstrates that the student can recognize main ideas.
As students develop literacy skills, the ability to recognize central ideas from a text is an important skill. It has applicability to research, writing, and discussion/debate. Paraphrasing, or restating an idea in one's own words, requires recognition of what is important and synthesis to successfully convey meaning.

129. Of the following questions, which one would be most effective in helping ELLs learn to infer meaning? *(Skills 9.3, 9.4 and 9.5)*

   A. How can we synthesize what you just said?
   B. What conclusions can you draw?
   C. What is the relationship between…?
   D. What evidence can you find…?

The correct answer is D. What evidence can you find…?
Answer A is a paraphrasing technique. Both Answers B and C refer to drawing conclusions. Only Answer D asks the student to support meaning, which is inferred.

130. Which one of the following skills would probably have the most positive effect on developing literacy skills in ELLs? *(Skill 9.3, 9.4 and 9.5)*

   A. Oral storytelling traditions
   B. Watching documentaries on TV
   C. Visiting art museums
   D. Attending concerts

The correct answer is A. Oral storytelling traditions
While all of the above could positively affect literacy development, the most probable would be Answer A. Oral storytelling encourages developing readers to follow a storyline, look for the climax or main idea, and compare the written word to prior knowledge.

131. In helping students develop reading strategies for use in analyzing the plot of a novel, which one of the following suggestions is most likely to help build comprehension? *(Skill 9.4)*

   A. Morphemic analysis focusing on prefixes, roots and suffixes
   B. Annotations with arrows showing the relationship between events
   C. The study of cognates
   D. A word wall of commonly used words

The correct answer is B. Annotations with arrows showing the relationship between events
Though strategies A, B, and D can help students build vocabulary and, by extension, reading comprehension, only B (annotations showing the relationships between events) would have a direct impact on understanding the plot of a novel. Teachers may model this strategy for students as a way of keeping track of the plot development with novels and stories, especially as students begin to work with more complex texts.

132. Encouraging non-graded writing practice can really help English language learners develop writing fluency. Which of the following is NOT a task that encourages students to practice non-graded writing? *(Skill 9.3)*

   A. Writing a dialog in pairs
   B. Rewriting a passage or summary in the ELL's own words
   C. Writing from the perspective of another
   D. Writing a summary of a text to hand in

The correct answer is D. Writing a summary of a text to hand in
Answers A, B, and C are ways students can practice writing without a teacher's evaluation. They encourage students in meaningful activities that they can do collaboratively and/or independently in response to comprehensible and meaningful input. They are also activities that can be written and reflected upon and learned from by the students themselves. Answer D, writing a summary to be handed in, suggests evaluation, however informal. Students will not be as likely to be engaged in 'practicing' writing to develop writing fluency if they know they are going to hand in their work. They will be more concerned about how the ESOL teacher or content-area teacher is going to judge their summary and/or writing.

133. In general, the writing process can be divided into two broad divisions. They are: *(Skill 9.5)*

   A. Composing; pre-writing
   B. Pre-writing; drafting
   C. Brainstorming; drafting
   D. Composition; revision

The correct answer is D. Composition; revision
Only Answer D considers the revision process, which is an integral part of the writing process, and thus, the correct choice.

134. Which one of the following writing activities is not appropriate for different proficiency levels? *(Skills 9.3 and 9.5)*

   A. Reading and writing letters to friends, businesses or pen pals
   B. Writing directions for solving a problem
   C. Writing long form book reports
   D. Writing and organizing lists

The correct answer is C. Writing long form book reports
ELLs should work on purposeful, authentic writing activities. Answer A, B, and D are authentic tasks. Answer C is not. It is an artificial construct for the purposes of schooling.

135. Tests that evaluate an individual as compared to others are: *(Skill 10.1)*

A. Standardized
B. Authentic
C. Norm referenced
D. Criterion referenced

The correct answer is C. Norm referenced
Answer D may be discarded as criterion referenced tests evaluate an individual's knowledge of specific content. Answer A might be true, but standardized tests also include criterion-referenced exams. Answer B concerns tests being relevant to a student's life, not necessarily comparing the student to others. Only Answer C is specifically designed to compare one individual with others.

136. Sheltered content teaching allows teachers to do all of the following except: *(Skill 10.2)*

A. Use realia, word lists, gestures, etc.
B. Reduce language demands
C. Facilitate learning
D. Instruct in heritage or home language

The correct answer is D. Instruct in heritage or home language
Answers A, B, and C are all part of the set of Sheltered Content Teaching strategies. Answer D is not an element of this strategy.

137. The Schema Theory of Carrell & Eisterhold suggests that for learning to take place, teachers should: *(Skill 10.3)*

A. Integrate content areas with ESOL techniques.
B. Emphasize all four language skills.
C. Present comprehensible input in a meaningful context.
D. Relate new materials to previous knowledge.

The correct answer is D. Relate new materials to previous knowledge.
The schema theory of Carrell & Eisterhold suggests that students learn best when they can relate new learning to previous knowledge. When activated, schema allows students to evaluate the new materials in light of previous knowledge. If the arguments made are convincing to the learner, he or she accepts them and integrates the new knowledge into his or her data bank. Otherwise, if the new materials are unconvincing, the learner rejects the new knowledge.

138. Content, process and product are the primary areas that can be adapted to support English language learners through: *(Skill 10.4)*

A. Parental Communication
B. Differentiation
C. Formative assessment
D. Transfer from L1 to L2

The correct answer is B. Differentiation.
Differentiated instruction generally falls in three categories - content, process, and product. Teachers may differentiate in any/all of these areas in meeting the needs of students.

139. ESOL teachers can make academic content accessible for ELL students by implementing which of the following practices? *(Skill 10.3)*

A. Pre-teaching vocabulary and concepts
B. Checking for comprehension during instruction
C. Teaching the material in multiple ways (e.g. using visual cues, hands-on activities)
D. Combining all of the above

The correct answer is D. Combining all of the above.
Teachers should demonstrate knowledge of techniques that create a positive learning environment for all students, which means that content needs to be accessible to students with different learning styles and language needs.

140. What is a valid conclusion that could be drawn from the claim that vocabulary development is crucial for reading comprehension? *(Skills 10.2 and 10.3)*

A. It is difficult for readers to understand the content unless they know the meaning of most of the words in the text.
B. It is difficult for students to understand academic, communicative and content-based vocabulary unless they memorize extensive word lists.
C. It is difficult for learners to master sight word vocabulary without taking frequent spelling tests.
D. It is difficult for readers to make significant reading progress when they have poor reading comprehension skills.

The correct answer is A. It is difficult for readers to understand the content unless they know the meaning of most of the words in the text.
Vocabulary development is particularly important for beginner ELL students, both to support comprehension and to avoid frustration. Even in more advanced literacy proficiencies, research shows that focused, meaningful and consistent vocabulary development helps English language learners build literacy, academic and content area skills. Answers B and C are both techniques that effective ESOL teachers do not use frequently anymore. Long word lists are hard to remember in the long term and a focus on spelling can distract from vocabulary learning. Answer D is true but not really a natural conclusion from the question's claim.

141. Which of the following is NOT an evidence-based vocabulary development method? *(Skill 10.3)*

   A. Working with other teachers at grade level or subject area when designing important vocabulary lessons and/or reading about evidence-based approaches to vocabulary instruction;
   B. Ensuring that reading vocabulary lists emphasize important words and not just decoding;
   C. Working to create some word lists that are common to many subjects, and if not, making word lists available to subject-area teachers to help students practice;
   D. Providing time in class for read-aloud activities where students read their papers aloud, teachers listen to errors, and correct the students as they proceed.

The correct answer is D. Providing time in class for read-aloud activities where students read their papers aloud, teachers listen to errors, and correct the students as they proceed.
When Read-aloud techniques are used, the purpose is to help students correct grammatical errors in their own writing. They are not part of a set of recommended strategies for fostering vocabulary development.

142. Purposeful discourse can be used to design learning activities across the curriculum. Which of the following is not one of the four major kinds of purposeful discourse? *(Skills 10.3 and 10.4)*

   A. Shared discourse in which language is used socially to communicate and share meaning in order to accomplish social goals (playing games or planning a short scene),
   B. Fun discourse in which language is used for fun (singing songs and writing riddles)
   C. Thought discourse in which language is used to imagine and create new ideas and experiences (writing poetry or critical thinking)
   D. Practice discourse in which students practice tasks on which they will be assessed.

The correct answer is D. Practice discourse in which students practice tasks on which they will be assessed.
If students are just practicing for a test, they are not participating in purposeful discourse. The missing discourse from this list is Fact discourse in which language is used to acquire new information and concepts.

143. Nonverbal adaptations, elicitation adaptations, and questioning adaptations are examples of what kinds of modifications to help make language more comprehensible for students? *(Skill 10.3)*

   A. Modifications in student interaction
   B. Modifications in teacher-talk
   C. Modification in assessment tasks
   D. Modifications in instructional materials

The correct answer is B. Modifications in teacher-talk.
Enright (1991) put forward the above teacher talk modifications that could help make language accessible to the students. With a combination of these teacher-adaptations and learning activities, teachers can help English language learners increase foundational content, knowledge and skills.

144. When ESOL teachers understand the discourse features of various types of text, they can help English language learners to: *(Skills 10.1 – 10.4)*

   A. Improve reading, writing and vocabulary in the content-areas
   B. Recognize familiar words and figure out words they haven't seen
   C. Understand that different types of dialects or slang are not effective in specific settings
   D. Develop skills that it are most important for them to practice

The correct answer is A. Improve reading, writing and vocabulary in the content-areas.
When ESOL teachers understand discipline specific and interdisciplinary discourse features of different text types, they can provide students with contexts, scaffolds and background knowledge in reading, writing and vocabulary tasks in content-area classes.

145. There are many recommended ways of adapting content in Content Based Instruction. Which of the following is NOT a category for adaptation in CBI? *(Skill 10.3)*

   A. Giving directions
   B. Providing contextualization
   C. Assessments
   D. Checking for understanding

The correct answer is C. Assessments
Objective 10 (in this book) outlines CBI adaptations in the areas of giving directions, providing contextualization, and checking for understanding. While teachers may offer a range of assessments to give ELL students options that suit their language ability, CBI does not include the adaptation/changing of assessments as strategy for making content more accessible. With CBI, ESOL and content-area teachers make adaptations for students.

146. Paraphrasing, prompts, graphic organizers, guides, syllabi, schedules, learning goals, draft assignments, and practice tests are examples of types of: *(Skill 10.3)*

   A. Scaffolding
   B. Adapting content
   C. The natural approach
   D. Collaborative activities

The correct answer is: A. Scaffolding
Scaffolds can be verbal, instructional and metacognitive. They help students access language and content that is just beyond their comfort level, which helps them develop more independence, more content area knowledge, more subject-specific skills and more language proficiency.

147. Which of the following are examples of opportunities for students to be creative, solve problems, think critically and collaborate? *(Sill 10.3)*

   A. Working with other students on cloze exercises
   B. Watching an English language movie with subtitles in ELL's home language
   C. Participating in spelling and math bees where students get to physically move around the room and think on their feet
   D. Participating in debates, analyzing media and messages, working through authentic problems

The correct answer is D. Participating in debates, analyzing media and messages, working through authentic problems.
Creating structured opportunities with clear goals, methods and assessments for English language learners to develop skills of problem-solving, critical thinking, and collaboration can enhance progress in literacy, knowledge and language production.

148. An elementary school ESOL teacher takes his students outside in the schoolyard for a short observation walk. As they walk along, they observe different insects, rocks, and playground equipment. The teacher stops and asks the students questions that draw out their critical thinking skills. Which one of the following questions would be least effective in promoting critical-thinking skills? *(Skill 10.4)*

   A. What parts do the ant and the butterfly have in common?
   B. What evidence do you find to support the idea that you can't swing all the way around the pole of the swing set?
   C. How would you classify this type of rock?
   D. What colors are the leaves on that tree?

The correct answer is D. What colors are the leaves on that tree?
Questions that support critical-thinking skills are A, B, and C. Answer D asks about color. A critical-thinking skill about colors could be, "Based on what you know, why are these leaves a different color than the leaves on that tree?"

149. The purpose of frontloading vocabulary is: *(Skills 10.3, 10.4, 9.3 and 9.4)*

    A. Vocabulary development
    B. Increase reading comprehension
    C. Explaining content
    D. Increasing spelling proficiency

The correct answer is B. Increase reading comprehension
All of the answers are interrelated and valuable instructional goals. Nevertheless, the main goal is B, increasing reading comprehension.

150. Sheltered content teaching allows teachers to do all of the following except: *(Skill 10.2)*

    A. Use realia, word lists, gestures, etc.
    B. Reduce language demands
    C. Facilitate learning
    D. Instruct in heritage or home language

The correct answer is D. Instruct in heritage or home language
Answers A, B, and C are all part of the set of Sheltered Content Teaching strategies. Answer D is not an element of this strategy.

www.ingramcontent.com/pod-product-compliance
Lightning Source LLC
Chambersburg PA
CBHW080730230426
43665CB00020B/2682